THE STAR

OF THE

MAGI

THE MYSTERY THAT HERALDED THE COMING OF CHRIST

By

Courtney Roberts

NEW PAGE BOOKS
A division of The Career Press, Inc.
Franklin Lakes, NJ

Copyright © 2007 by Courtney Roberts

THE STAR OF THE MAGI
EDITED BY KARA REYNOLDS
TYPESET BY EILEEN DOW MUNSON
Cover design by
Printed in the U.S.A. by Book-mart Press

To order this title, please call toll-free 1-800-CAREER-1 (NJ and Canada: 201-848-0310) to order using VISA or MasterCard, or for further information on books from Career Press.

The Career Press, Inc., 3 Tice Road, PO Box 687,
Franklin Lakes, NJ 07417
www.careerpress.com
www.newpagebooks.com

Library of Congress Cataloging-in-Publication Data
Roberts, Courtney, 1957-
    The Star of the Magi : the mystery that heralded the coming of Christ / By Courtney Roberts.
       p. cm.
    Includes bibliographical references and index.
    ISBN-13: 978-1-56414-962-6
    ISBN-10: 1-56414-962-5
     1. Star of Bethlehem. 2. Jesus Christ—Nativity. Magi. I. Title.

BT315.3.R625 2007
232.92'3—dc22

2007027818

To
Roz Park
of Magdalen Villa

May your faith always be rewarded.

Acknowledgments

Writing can be very lonely work, so I am truly grateful for the patience and persistence of the friends who have supported and indulged me throughout this project. Although I can only offer words of acknowledgement here, I hope that whenever you need help or encouragement in fulfilling your own dreams, you won't hesitate to ask; or better yet, you won't even have to, but will find in me a very willing friend indeed.

I want to thank my agent, Gary Heidt, who is a genius, and Michael Pye, the acquisitions editor for New Page, both of whom believed enough in this book to make it happen. A big thank-you goes to my editors, Kara Reynolds and Kirsten Dalley, who have patiently persisted to the end. Every editor I have worked with has helped me to be a better writer. Some of them have even helped me to be a better person; but then there is Nan Geary, who, along with Tem Tarriktar and all the kind folks at *The Mountain Astrologer*, do all of that and so much more.

I especially want to acknowledge Garry Phillipson, James Brockbank, Dorian Gieseler Greenbaum, and Robert Schmidt, for their invaluable assistance and collegial support in coming to terms with the Greek of the Gospel of Matthew. Of course, I am so very grateful to Michael Conrad for his help with the drawings and diagrams, and for his comments on the text. Thanks to Peter Marko as well, for reading and commenting on the work in progress. As always, thanks to Liam McGinley, of Farron McBride, the very spirit of Glencolmcille, for his continued support and friendship, and for reading and commenting on the work in progress.

I'm sure no one was more surprised at reading the dedication of this book than Roz Park herself. She has been not only a faithful and generous friend, through good times and bad, but was right there from the very start, back in our grueling post-graduate days in Bath, listening closely and encouraging me all along. I will always be eternally grateful for my brother, Conrad Roberts, the spiritual genius of the family, who has been such a source of healing and inspiration, both in my life and in my daughter's.

I must thank the giants of this converging field, my own heroes in astronomy, astrology, history, and religious studies, who have long inspired and informed my own efforts. Such a list can never be complete, but it would certainly include names such as Edward S. Kennedy, J.D. North, Franz Cumont, Percy Seymour, Abraham-Hyacinthe Anquetil du Perron, Mary Boyce, Hipparchus, al-Biruni, Masha'allah, et al. At the same time, I am also very grateful for some of my lesser-known sources, such as Jona Lendering and his wonderful Livius site (which can take you anywhere), Dr. Michael McGee of Frome, and Dr. Lloyd Barre.

A book can't help but take on a sense of the place in which it was written, where the environment and the atmosphere season both the language and the tone. I have been so fortunate in that regard. This began in the springtime in Somerset, and there is no gentler place on earth. The sturdy accents of country boys like Martin, beloved tapster of the healing waters in the Pump Room at Bath, or Derrick, who healed up the holes in our pokey old house on Sydney Buildings, must surely have penetrated this work in its early days. Likewise, the kindness of dear old Sheila Mundle, who is actually a McGregor from Edinburgh, though you would never know it.

From there, the book traveled to the seaside, composing itself in long hours spent gazing across the ever-changing tides of the bay at Machaire Clogher, Bunbeg, in Gweedore, County Donegal. No matter how far I roam, we'll never truly part. Writing in English by day, and studying Irish by night—or for that matter, every time I went to the shop—drew me deep into the mysteries of language. Learning to start sentences all over again with ancient verbs goes a long way towards freeing one from the painful prison of subjectivity. For that, and a thousand other kindnesses, I have to thank my Irish teacher at the Crannog, Michail O'Dohmnaill.

But then, we're so spoiled for inspiration in Donegal. From the old English chapel in Dunlewey, at the foot of Mt. Errigal and the doorway to the Poisoned Glen, to the graciousness and neighborly good manners I so tried to learn from the likes of Mairead Ni Mhaonaigh, or Rosemary and Manus at Pobail le Cheile, to the antics of Oisin, Oscar, and Foxy, three Donegal hounds who faithfully accompanied me on my adventures along the shore every evening at sundown, there's no stinting the flow. And the music—such music. It's all in here.

Moving on to the other side of the world, this book further came to be at the foot of the mountains of Gangwando, South Korea, where the two rivers meet in Youngwol; maybe one of the most normal places ever. The friendliness and generosity of the Korean people is a constant source of delight. Having suffered more starvation than even the Irish, they are forever giving you food, now that they have it. On my many hikes up the mountain path, past the cairns and barrows of the old religion, kind souls always insisted on sharing whatever they had with me, even if I wasn't entirely sure what it was. It was on such adventures that I came to the mysteries of the cult of the boy-king Dan Jong, innocent and martyr, and befriended the spirit of the wandering poet, Kim Sat Gat, whose timeless humor and goodwill needed no translation.

I did try to learn their language, with its Confucian syntax and class structure, but although I could handle the Hangul, the rest of it escapes me. Still, it's in here somewhere, seasoning this book throughout, along with a lot of noodles, kimchi, tofu, green tea, red-hot chili sauce and *kim*— that shimmering, emerald-green seaweed paper. For their lessons in emptiness and interminable bowing, I want to thank the monks and masters of the Zen Chogye order; particularly that rare combination of kindness and steel they call Master Lee, the *san mudo* instructor at Gulgusa. Long may the fighting monks of Gyeongju defend the southern coast.

At the end of the day, the teacher is the one in the classroom who is learning the most, and my greatest thanks go to every one of my many students who taught me in Youngwol and at Hwagyesa, in the mountains north of Seoul. I wonder if any of them will ever realize how much English I learned by teaching them, or what an exquisite contribution they made to this book of mine.

At long last, this book came to its final stages on the green banks of the Neversink River, part of the great watershed that drains the Catskills. Here, it has been caught up in that ceaseless rush of the sparkling "Champagne of Waters" that flows down to New York, which may be the greatest city in the world, but it's always thirsty for more. In collecting and pulling together all the various streams into one, buoyed by the warmth and hospitality of my wonderful Jewish and Russian neighbors, I realize that the one place this book hasn't been is Persia. That will change soon enough, but in the meantime, I must acknowledge the one person who inspired me most, and who I most wanted to write about: Koresh—the one we call Cyrus the Great. In a world at such a loss for leadership, his light still shines through. So in closing, I must thank and acknowledge all the good people of Iran and Iraq, who, like so many of us in the West, are sick of war, and are doing all they can to bring peace to our world, and to build a future together.

Contents

Introduction

The Star of the Magi remains one of the most popular, and puzzling, mysteries of the Bible. Its inclusion, at the very beginning of the very First Gospel, raises any number of good questions. For instance, why would the authors (and editors) of the Christian Gospels choose Zoroastrian Magi and astrology to herald the coming of Jesus Christ? Did the Magi have some special significance then that we have since lost? After all, the New Testament narrative opens with them. So who were they, and did their astrological beliefs really lead them to Jesus?

Once we understand who the Magi were, how their astrology informed their beliefs, and how much those beliefs influenced their Jewish neighbors, some strikingly obvious conclusions emerge. This work highlights their surprisingly widespread influence, shedding new light on the rise of monotheism and messianic expectations in the Middle East, and the Christian West.

Many other solutions to this mystery have been proposed. Modern astronomers have taken on the Star, and the last several decades have witnessed the appearance of a heavenly host of books, papers, and planetarium shows proposing just about everything from comets, supernovas, chance sightings of Uranus, and any number of planetary conjunctions, eclipses, and occultations. Their methods usually involve examining a list of likely astronomical events to see if anything fits the meager descriptions in the book of Matthew. Once a particular event has been chosen, creative explanations are then offered as to why it must have been meaningful to the Jews. No real consensus has ever arisen from this line of inquiry, for there are too many phenomena to choose from, and it's too easy to back-engineer a religious rationalization from any of them—which is what these researchers must do, without a solid background in astrology and religious studies.

More recently, the astronomer Michael Molnar received a lot of attention (and rightly so) for his 1999 book, *The Star of Bethlehem: The Legacy of the Magi*. Molnar concludes that an occultation of Jupiter by the moon in the sign Aries was the most likely candidate for the Star of Bethlehem, and he touts a date of April 17, 6 BCE, for the birth of Jesus Christ. He even produces a birth chart for Jesus, with the sun, moon, Jupiter, and Saturn all in the fiery, aggressive sign of Aries; the Lamb of God as the Ram of God.

In arriving at his conclusions, Molnar is one of the first astronomers to attempt to factor in the principles of ancient astrology. In fact, as Professor Bradley E. Schaefer of the University of Texas says in his review of Molnar's work in *Sky & Telescope*, "...the old astronomical views are guaranteed to be irrelevant...the new astrological paradigm forces the realization that astrology was an important force in historical times so that the disregard of the topic by most historians is blatant chauvinism."[1]

I certainly applaud Molnar for moving in the right direction, and trying to grasp the astrology of the Star as it was perceived in its day. Unfortunately, Molnar was not very particular about *which* ancient astrology he used. His research, as is much of Western scholarship, is firmly entrenched in the classical and Hellenistic camp. For instance, he draws his astrological references from the work of Western astrologers such as Claudius Ptolemy, a second century CE Alexandrian, and Firmicus Maternus, who practiced in Rome in the fourth century CE.

Meanwhile, the Gospel of Matthew makes it clear that the astrologers in question were Magi. They were Persians, not Romans or second century Alexandrians. The Persian Magi were great astrologers. Of that there is no doubt, but to assume that Persian Magi in the first century BCE were practicing the same kind of Hellenistic astrology as Ptolemy or Firmicus Maternus is a big leap in the wrong direction.

The Persians had their own distinct school of astrology, a fact that has been largely ignored, not only in Molnar's work, but throughout most of the research on the Star.[2] This would be entirely in keeping with the Western, classical worldview, which rarely acknowledges the far-reaching scientific and religious contributions of the Persians—the traditional enemies of our heroes, the Greeks and Romans.

On the other hand, Judeans living at the time of Christ were very much aware of the contributions of their Persian neighbors. Greece and Rome had not been kind to the Jews, whereas the nearby Parthian Persians and their Magi had long been their friends and allies against these brutal, foreign invaders. As Norman Cohn puts it, in *Cosmos, Chaos, and the World to Come*: "For some two centuries, Judea formed part of the vast Achaemenian [Persian] Empire...Achaemenian rule was relatively benign, and was recognized by the Jews to be so: whereas there is plenty of Jewish propaganda against Babylonian and Seleucid [Hellenistic] and Roman rule, there is not a single Jewish text, biblical or rabbinic, directed against Persian rule."[3]

The Islamic scholar Said Amir Arjomand drives the point home in his article "Messianism, Millenialism and Revolution," in describing the early days of Jewish messianism: "...Persian notions spread widely in the Hellenistic era and gave rise to a particular oracular form of resistance to Hellenistic domination that was absorbed into intertestamental apocalypticism."[4]

To put it more simply, Judeans were inspired in their endless uprisings against their Greek and Roman overlords by the Persian religion and its astrology. Further, in distinct contrast to the Hellenistic and classical astrology described in Molnar's work, Persian astrology was replete with apocalyptic prophecies and messianic promises. Their astrology thoroughly permeated their religion, and vice versa.

The Astrology of the Magi

The Magi's religion included long-standing and highly developed astrological traditions about a coming world savior; a messiah, who would be born of a virgin. In fact, the Magi were ultimately expecting three world saviors, throughout a period of several thousand years, and they would all be born of virgins at the appropriate astrological intervals. The coming of the third savior would precipitate the apocalypse, the ultimate battle between the forces of good and evil at the end of the world.

These ancient Persian beliefs had tremendous bearing on the development of Jewish messianic expectations, both politically and spiritually. These same Zoroastrian traditions persisted into early Christianity, particularly Syrian and Nestorian Christianity, in which a number of sources still attest to the traditional belief that Zoroaster prophesied the coming of Christ, his star, and the virgin birth.

The Islamic Version

The astrology of the Magi experienced an enthusiastic revival in the work of the Islamic astronomers of the Golden Age of Baghdad (eighth to ninth century BCE). There, the upstart Abbasid caliphs, eager to legitimate their new dynasty, gladly adopted the Persian astrology of the Magi to their own ends, proclaiming themselves the rightful heirs to the imperial majesty of ancient Persia.

The famous eighth century court astrologer Masha'allah produced some of the most influential work of this period, obviously drawn from the Persian traditions of the Magi. In his work, and that of his successors, we find preserved the peculiar Persian passion for the millenniums, and the role of major planetary conjunctions in the rise of great prophets, new religions, and new world orders, albeit reworked to fit the new Islamic revelation.

In the recycled Magism of Masha'allah, major conjunctions of Jupiter and Saturn signal the dawn of new world ages, and heralded the birth of Christ and the rise of Christianity, as well as the birth of Mohammed and the rise of Islam. The same combination of Saturn-Jupiter conjunctions and millenniums confirmed the Muslim caliphs on their throne and held the hope for the future in the coming of the Mahdi, the promised deliverer at the end of the world.

This is the astrology of the Magi, and it's a far cry from anything the Greeks or Romans were doing. Magian astrology provided the chronological underpinning for their entire messianic and apocalyptic worldview. This is what the author of Matthew has been trying to tell us for 2,000 years.

The Star of History

"The historical perspective, which sees Judaism as fulfilling its mission and then making way for the gospel and the Church, has an impressive inner consistency and spiritual allure; the only problem with it is the real history of Judaism."[5]

All history is historiography. It's all an exercise in the writing of history—it is never the thing itself. This is as true of my work as that of all my sources. We are all just chasing ghosts; we never really catch them. It happens every time. Those dim vapors that haunt our dreams slip right through our fingers and race away across a forgotten, foreign landscape, littered with ruins, where, laughing, they mock us from just beyond the next ridge. Just when we think we've finally got it right, some obscure source arises unbidden with the dead-obvious answers to all the questions we forgot to ask, and we're right back to square one, face to face with our own presumption and ignorance.

It's at that point that you realize, if you're lucky, that history, and everything else for that matter, is a magic mirror. You never truly see it as it is, you see it as you are. If you're lucky.

This is even truer in religious studies. As Jack Spong has said so well, and in so many different ways, "We arrogantly suggest we can speak of what God actually is, when all we can do is describe our experience of God."[6] But we also arrogantly suggest that we can speak of what ancient Judaism was, or what Zoroaster or the Persians actually believed and when, but all we can do is describe our very selective experience of it. We are all bringing something different to it, and looking to take something different away.

Try as we might to break free from this prison of subjectivity, our passionate scrutiny of a subject so dear to our hearts transforms it, in time, into an idol shaped by our own hands into our own image. Perhaps it is better to admit these limitations up front, before arrogantly taking exception to another's perceptions. So rather than deny the process, I choose to exult in it, and try to remain ever mindful of the fact that the only thing that justifies the readers' indulgence in my antics is that I am also revealing something important about them.

History is always with us. It is a living force that drives the present moment, whether we choose to acknowledge it or not. The past is past—we can't go back and change it, but what we believe about the past has everything to do with what we believe about the present, and how we build for the future. The sad fact is that even today, underneath all our secularism, humanism, and unbridled consumerism, we still retain, at our core, a medieval, biblical myth of a history that never was, and this vision of the past dims all our future hopes.

Even with all the recent advances in biblical scholarship, this myth remains so engrained, so tacit within our public discourse, so implicit within our foreign policy, that we rarely either question or acknowledge it. It simply is. We may be virtual and wireless in our working lives, but when it comes to the "Holy Land," we are as medieval as the crusaders. If this were not so, the Palestinians would have their own country, and both

America and Israel would enjoy peaceful, prosperous relations with the Muslim countries of the Middle East. Instead, our Western, Judeo-Christian myth, with its chosen people and its holy land, has condemned us to perpetual enmity, and we are forced to live in fear of people who are actually a lot more afraid of us. And well they should be.

Nothing wrecks the present like fighting the ghosts of a past that never was. Until we can transform the way we think about the past, we will go on battling these same ghosts until the end of the world, all the while creating a future nobody wants to live in. As James O'Dea put it: "The transformation of our world requires a new story.... It must be a story in which our desire to settle differences is more exciting than the willingness to die for the rightness of our cause."[7]

If we can take a fresh look, and kick over the traces, another story begins to arise from the ashes of the ancient world; a more inclusive story, starring a God who is infinitely more equitable and just. The centralized, mono-linear narratives we hold so dear, wherein all of history is leading up to us, were carved out of our own narrow nationalism and pride. Once we start to separate the evidence from the myth, unfettering our past from the historical "emplotments" of orthodoxy, we begin to liberate our future as well. As it turns out, no people were more chosen than any other. Some of our history's heavy-hitters were surprisingly overrated, and new stars emerge from the most unlikely shadows. No land was more holy than the next, but everyone, everywhere, has always had a part to play in our growing awareness of the truth about ourselves. That's ultimately more inspiring than anything we were ever led to believe before, and in this story, the Star of Bethlehem is no longer such a mystery, but starts to make perfect sense.

So, in trying to tell that story, I want to offer my humble thanks to everyone whose work has helped to form my own, especially those with whom I most passionately, and respectfully, disagree. They are legion. If we are looking at the same thing, but see it differently, perhaps we are all bringing something different to it, and hoping to take something different away. If, for example, I appear to push the Persians or astrology too far front and center, please consider that they have both been so utterly marginalized that it might be necessary to go to the other extreme, just to restore some balance. At any rate, I hope you will be as patient with my attempts to rewrite history in my own image as I have tried to be with yours, and that in keeping the process civil, we may all benefit over time.

Having said that, I invite you in, to look at the way I see it, and I promise one thing: that if you do, you will never see the world in the same way again.

As Kim Paffenroth insightfully noted, in an article that should be required reading for anyone venturing an opinion on the Star, "...how one frames the question, 'What was the Star of Bethlehem?' and how one answers it, reveals a great deal more about the person making the inquiry than about the Star itself."[8]

A question such as "What was the Star of Bethlehem?" has produced centuries of debate and very little consensus. I hope the questions I'm raising generate different kinds of answers; answers that ultimately expand our entire understanding of how messianism and the three great monotheisms evolved. As we turn in despair from the endless cycles of war and conquest that have brought us to this current crisis, perhaps this Star can guide us toward a more inclusive and genuine appreciation of the common religious heritage we all share.

Chapter 1

Matthew: The Gospel to the Hebrews

The introduction of the Magi and their Star in the overture to the "First Gospel," with all its astrological implications, has raised so many awkward questions for orthodox Christianity that one has to wonder how it ever made the canonical cut in the first place. In fact, the priority of its position within the Christian canon, in the opening chapters of the very first book, is an indication of how significant the Persian Magi and their astrology were among those to whom this Gospel was first addressed.

The only thing preceding the story of the Star in this opening book of the New Testament is a genealogy for Christ. This genealogy raises some rather awkward questions itself. In traditional Old Testament style, the author of Matthew, whoever it truly was, traces the male ancestors of "Jesus Christ, son of David, the son of Abraham," through his stepfather Joseph back to the patriarch Judah, the fourth son, and royal heir of Jacob/Israel. In tracing this long descent, the author makes some glaring historical omissions; for instance, leaving out several of the kings of Judah listed in Chronicles.[1]

"Matthew" seems to prefer the mysteries of number instead. For instance, the generations are neatly ordered into three groups of 14, making Jesus the first of the seventh group of seven. And yet, even though Matthew claims there are 14 generations from the Babylonian Captivity to the birth of Christ, he only lists 13! He then declares that the Holy Spirit, not Joseph, was the father of Jesus, obviating any need for such an extensive family tree. Plus, the genealogy given for Jesus in Matthew is substantially different from the genealogy in the Gospel of Luke (3:23–38).

Discrepancies of this kind continue to fuel the longstanding arguments about whether this "first" gospel was originally written in the Aramaic language (spoken by Jesus and his disciples) or in the Greek preferred by later translators. Even though the consensus opinion has long been that Matthew composed his gospel in Greek, according to "Aramaic Primacy" proponent Christopher Lancaster, the previous nagging contradictions resulted from a fundamental mistranslation of the original Aramaic version of Matthew's gospel into Greek; specifically, the last generation listed in verse 16: "...and Jacob the father of Joseph the husband of Mary, of whom Jesus was born, who is called Christ" (Revised Standard Version, or RSV).

Lancaster credits Paul Younan with the revelation that the Aramaic term *gowra*, with which Matthew designates Joseph, was mistranslated into Greek as "the husband of Mary." *Gowra* can mean "husband," but it can also mean "man" or "father."[2] If Matthew actually meant the "man" or "father" of Mary, the numbers suddenly add up and the genealogy makes much more sense. After all, as Matthew makes it clear in verse 18 that Joseph, Mary's husband, was not the father of Jesus, why would he bother to trace the lineage through him?

When Matthew later introduces Joseph, the husband of Mary (verse 19), he does not identify him as the *gowra,* but instead, uses a different, more common, Semitic word for husband. This might also explain why the author of Luke gives a contradictory genealogy in his gospel. "Luke" did trace the lineage through Joseph, Mary's husband, but with the following caveat: "Jesus...being [as was supposed] the son of Joseph, which was the son of Heli...." (3:23, RSV).

In either language, the serious problem of the historical omissions remains unresolved. However, at this point, we have not even reached the end of the first chapter of the first gospel, and we are already hung up on a number of thorny issues.

The Intended Audience

Still, by tracing a direct descent from David and the royal tribe of Judah, Matthew is asserting a bold claim of authority for Christ among the Judeans. It is widely acknowledged that the author of the Gospel of Matthew was writing specifically for a Jewish audience. According to E. Jacquier in his article on Matthew's Gospel, "There are more allusions to the Old Testament in this Gospel than in the others; it was clearly written for

Jewish Christians, the purpose being to prove that Jesus was the Messiah foretold in the Old Testament."[3]

Matthew's intention to write to and for the Jews is underscored by the testimony of early Christian writers such as St. Irenæus (*Adversus Haereses*, 3.1.1–2) who said that Matthew published among the Hebrews a Gospel in their own language (meaning Aramaic, as opposed to Greek or Latin). Eusebius, in his *Historia Ecclesiastica* (VI xxv, 3, 4), quotes Origen, for the tradition that the First Gospel, Matthew's Gospel, was composed in Hebrew (Aramaic) and published for the converts from Judaism.[4]

Further, this First Gospel assumes a familiarity with Jewish customs and concerns. The debate about the law is a central theme, as is the observance of the Sabbath. Also, the book consistently references events in the life of Christ to Old Testament prophecies and sources in order to present Jesus as the fulfillment of the law, the prophets, and all the promises made to Israel long ago.[5]

To get to the heart of Matthew, we must continually remind ourselves whom its author was writing for, because Matthew's intended audience had very different concerns than our own, and a very different worldview. It might be helpful to think of this Gospel as an advertisement; a propaganda piece intended to spark and confirm conversion to Christianity, in this case, among a specific demographic: first/second century Judeans in the regions of Palestine and Syria.[6] The words and images Matthew employs were carefully chosen for their effect upon this audience. So why does Matthew immediately introduce the Magi to make his case?

This claim of descent from the royal house of David would certainly have been meaningful to this audience. By playing upon such themes, Matthew composed a timely appeal to Judean pride at a point of unparalleled national crisis. Rome had been imposing its own ideas about the divine right of kings on the stiff-necked Judeans for more than 100 years, but the throne of David, even humbled and empty, still wielded sufficient nationalist cachet to incite zealous Jews to reckless, patriotic abandon. Finally, in 69–70 CE, exasperated after suppressing yet another pathetic rebellion in this remote and tiresome province, Rome decided to solve the Jewish problem once and for all.

As the author/s placed the finishing touches on the Gospel of Matthew (approximately 80 CE), Jerusalem and its temple lay in ruins, and the

Judeans were, once again, a people without a home, scattered to the four winds. For some, the destruction of Jerusalem was the apocalypse they had been praying for. Just as Jesus reputedly said (Matthew 23–24), not one stone was left upon another, and many of his own generation lived to see it all come to pass. For the survivors, both Christians and Jews, it was a time of great confusion and hurried reorganization along renewed ideological lines.

Many sought refuge in the north, in Galilee and Syria, and there, struggled to define themselves and their place in this traumatic turning of the ages. In addressing these people, Matthew's Gospel to the Hebrews portrays Christians as the real Jews, as the fulfillment of the law and the prophets, in direct contrast to the complete and utter destruction wrought upon those who rejected Christ. Matthew's Gospel blatantly proclaims Jesus Christ the rightful heir to the throne of Judah. In fact, that is the question Matthew puts into the mouths of the visiting Magi in the chapter immediately following: "Where is he that is born King of the Jews?" (Matthew 2:2).

David, Jerusalem, and the United Kingdom

The Judean national identity centered upon the divine rights of King David, the founding father of the Judean nation and its monarchy. Judeans traditionally believed that their god, Yahweh, chose David, and his city, Jerusalem, especially for this unique destiny, and that Jerusalem was the only place where Yahweh could be worshipped properly. According to the Bible, Yahweh promised David that his royal line would rule from Jerusalem forever (II Samuel 7:12–16). Many among Matthew's audience believed this, despite the fact that a king of David's line had not ruled in Jerusalem since the Babylonian captivity (approximately 586 BCE), just as many continue to believe it today.

But who was David? Aside from all the myths and legends that have accrued, how did this grandiose, theo-political scheme arise in the first place? Christianity and Judaism both teach that it was all revealed directly from God through the prophets and recorded in the Bible, but more recent findings reveal a widening gap between the legend and the evidence. We may need to reconsider everything we ever thought we knew about King David and his glorious reign.[7]

According to the Bible, David, the youngest son of Jesse, was just a lowly shepherd boy from Bethlehem when Yahweh chose him (through the prophet Samuel) to lead his people. In the first book of Samuel, after he slew Goliath and put the fear of the Lord into the Philistines, David went on to succeed the first Israeli king, Saul, and forged a united kingdom between the northern tribes of Israel and the southern men of Judah.

Israel had only just recently taken to the idea of having a king, but the threat posed by the Philistines, the infamous "Sea Peoples," moving inland from the coast and sweeping all before them, made the tribes of Israel cry out to God for a king to lead them in battle, like the other nations. Against Samuel's better judgment, Saul, and his sad destiny, were both anointed for the cause. Saul went seriously astray in the eyes of God, and after his untimely death, the Bible says: "Then came all the tribes of Israel to David to Hebron, and spoke, saying: 'Behold, we are your bone and your flesh. In times past, when Saul was king over us, it was you that did lead out and bring in Israel; and the Lord said to you: You shall feed my people Israel, and you shall be prince over Israel.' So all the elders of Israel came to the king to Hebron; and King David made a covenant with them in Hebron before the Lord; and they anointed David king over Israel...." (II Samuel 5:1–3, RSV.)

In the run-up to building this united kingdom, King David and his armies also seized the Jebusite stronghold of Jerusalem, an act that continues to reverberate throughout modern history. Jerusalem had never been part of Israel, or Judah, before.

The northern tribes of Israel already had their own sacred cult sites and power centers; the ancient shrines of their fathers: Beth-el, Shiloh, Shechem, Mt. Gerizim, and so on, where hoary judges and seers, such as the unforgettable Samuel, had governed from time immemorial. David and his emerging Judean hierarchy had been living as bandits up to this point, and were more in need of a suitable place to settle down. So it was that David proclaimed Jerusalem the capital and spiritual center of his new, united kingdom (II Samuel, ch. 6). In a move revealing his ancestral Bedouin ways, David installed Yahweh's traveling "ark of the covenant" there in triumph. For the first time, this mobile war god had a permanent home.

In the biblical account, there was a brief political union (lasting 70 years) between Judah and Israel under the Judean kings David and Solomon (approx. 930–1005 BCE). The Bible portrays a glorious united kingdom under a heroic and divinely sanctioned Judean leadership, with borders stretching from Syria to the Red Sea, and east unto the great rivers of Mesopotamia. King Solomon, in particular, was renowned not only as the wisest of rulers, but as an inspired builder, with a fabulous temple and splendid palaces to his credit.

It all fell apart with the death of Solomon, when the northern Israeli tribes revolted and set up their own kingdom and their own idolatrous worship. According to the Bible, this was their great sin, and they could do nothing right after that. The very existence of the northern kingdom was an offense to God, and to his divinely established order in Jerusalem, under the divinely established rule of the tribe of Judah.

The Lion of Judah

Judah, the founding father of David's tribe, was the chosen son of Jacob/ Israel, at least according to chapter 49 of the book of Genesis. There, in Father Jacob's dramatic deathbed scene, the dying Israel blesses his 12 sons, establishing his inheritance on Earth before departing to his reward.

Jacob quickly passes over his first three sons: Rueben, the firstborn, he pronounces "unstable as water, thou shall not excel." He then gives Simeon and Levi short shrift as "instruments of cruelty," but Jacob exults when he comes to Judah, the fourth of the sons of Leah, proclaiming:

> 8: Judah, your brothers shall praise you; your hand shall be on the neck of your enemies; your father's sons shall bow down before you.
>
> 9: Judah is a lion's whelp; from the prey, my son, you have gone up. He stooped down, he couched as a lion, and as a lioness; who dares rouse him up?
>
> 10: The scepter shall not depart from Judah, nor the ruler's staff from between his feet, until he comes to whom it belongs; and to him shall be the obedience of the peoples. (RSV)

Here is the Lion of Judah in its origin, blessed by the dying Israel himself, and chosen from among the 12 sons as their preordained ruler. Most Judeans of Matthew's time firmly believed in Judah's God-given ascendancy over the tribes of Israel, even though significant pockets of dissent remained, particularly in Samaria.

Our generation, on the other hand, stands at a unique vantage point in history, the beneficiaries of both an information revolution and a revolution in biblical scholarship, which makes it not only possible, but urgently necessary to discern the more genuinely historical elements underlying all this tribal lore. So while reminding ourselves that the author of the Gospel of Matthew was writing to an audience who, for the most part, took these claims quite literally, let us at least consider the possibility that this blessing story was a myth, a legend of convenience, cobbled together after the fact.

The tribal alliance between Judah and the children of Israel was troubled and tenuous at best, so the creation of a common male ancestor could have been a later attempt to contrive a sense of national unity where, essentially, there was none. In fact, this famous blessing scene actually happens twice: First, in Genesis 48, where Jacob/Israel blesses Joseph and his two sons, Ephraim and Manasseh; then again in Ch. 49, where the 12 sons gather for Jacob's blessing. In the first scene, it is Joseph, and his younger son, Ephraim, who are singled out for special blessings, not Judah. Ephraim was the dominant, ruling tribe of the northern kingdom of Israel, and this version of the blessing scene is possibly earlier, and more "original," than the one in chapter 49.

This double scene betrays something of the dual nature of Judah and Israel, which were originally two separate peoples, with two separate territories and two separate gods, *Yahweh* and *El*.[8] Our version of the Bible was compiled by later Judean editors who substantially modified the early texts to create the impression of an ancient, unified Israel under Judean rule. They never entirely succeeded in their cause, because there is simply too much underlying evidence to the contrary. The Old Testament remains full of incidents and anecdotes, such as the blessing story, that unmask the reality behind the later Judean revisions, at least for those who have an eye to see.

Historically, Judah was a relative latecomer among the tribes of Israel. The earliest mention of Israel (to date) comes from an Egyptian source, the Merneptah Stele (1208–1209 BCE), which describes Israel (*ysrii*) as a rural people inhabiting Canaan. The stele lists them along with, but apparently dwelling outside of, the established city-states of Canaan, Ashkelon, Gezer, and Yanoam.[9] The earliest children of Israel lived in the hill country of eastern Canaan, but shared the same alphabet, language, and material culture with their more urban Canaanite neighbors. In other words, they were Canaanites.[10]

ASSYRIA

MEDITER-
RANEAN
SEA

SIZU

Damascus

Tyre

ARAM-
DAMASCUS

Hazor

PHOE-
NICIANS

Yarmuk R.

ISRAEL

Samaria

Mt. Gerizom

Shechem   Peni-el

Jabbok R.

Shiloh

Bethel

Gezer

Jericho

AMMON

Jerusalem

Askelon

Gaza

Hebron

PHIL-
ISTINES

JUDAH

Beersheba

MOAB

EDOM

Paran

Teman

Mt. Seir

SINAI
PENINSULA

ARABIA

Aqaba

* Location of these sites is highly
controversial, depending on the
source of information.

Map of Judah and Israel.
Image created by Michael G. Conrad.

As the name Isra-El declares, they were devotees of the god El, who was also the head god of the Canaanite pantheon. According to the Bible, the children of Isra-El traced their origins to the decisive struggle between their ancestor Jacob/Israel and his God at Peni-El (Genesis 32:29), and to his vision at Beth-El (the house of El) in Genesis 28.

The Judeans, on the other hand, emerged somewhat later amid the harsher climate of the southern Judean hills, and owed more to the cultural influences of the wandering desert peoples of the Sinai and northern Arabia. Judah had closer tribal ties with the Kenites, the fabled children of Cain; the Edomites, whom the Bible identifies as the children of Esau; and the Moabites, from whom came David's great-grandmother, Ruth; than with the tribes of Israel in the north.[11] Judah and Yahweh's Bedouin roots trailed back and forth across the deserts surrounding Edom, Seir, and Mt. Paran.[12]

The earliest reference (to date) to "Yahweh," the future god of the Judeans, was found on an Egyptian topographical list from the temple of Amon in Soleb (Nubia), dated to the reign of Amenhotep III (1386 BCE). In describing the territory of the Shasu, the Bedouin desert tribes of Seir, there is a reference to "Yahw" of the land of the Shasu.[13]

It was the resistance to the invasions of the "sea peoples," the dreaded Philistines, not some common ancestor, that melded these various southern peoples into a fighting unit, and, ultimately, into alliances with Ephraim and Israel to the north, in approximately the 10–11th centuries BCE. As the Philistine armies pressed inward from the coast, the tribe of Judah coalesced against them, and, as the Bible describes it, from this ongoing warfare, the alliance with Israel was also born.

The book of I Samuel still underscores the fundamental differences between the two when it recounts how Saul, the first king of Israel, when mustering his troops against the Philistines, always numbered the men of the southern tribe of Judah separately from the children of Israel (11:9 and 15:4).

Was there any kind of Judeo-Israeli union or national identity before this time (approx. 1000 BCE)? The orthodox have always assumed that there was, but the evidence is lacking. In fact, as Finkelstein and Silberman admit in *The Bible Unearthed*, "There is good reason to suggest that there were always two distinct highland entities, of which the southern was always the poorer, weaker, more rural, and less influential...."[14]

The biblical accounts of David, Solomon, and their vast kingdom may have been grossly exaggerated. There is simply no evidence that Judea was anything more than a hard-scrabble, hilltop enclave during this period, much as it had been for centuries. The northern kingdom of Israel, though, was a prosperous, highly developed, regional powerhouse— completely the opposite of the way the Bible depicts things. The memories of David and Solomon, and of the Kingdom of Israel, were subjected to the same heavy-handed editorializing of later Judean redactors. The glories of this mythical united kingdom served as a powerful rationale for the territorial ambitions of later Judean monarchs. According to Finklestein and Silberman: "In late monarchic times, [late 7th century BCE], an elaborate theology had been developed in Judah and Jerusalem to validate the connection between the heir of David and the destiny of the entire people of Israel.... These were theological hopes, not accurate historical portraits."[15]

No amount of editing could ever erase the underlying truth. The Bible itself tells us that upon the death of Solomon, the 10 northern tribes of Israel revolted against their southern allies and reasserted their independence, seemingly repudiating any claims of a common ancestor by declaring, in I Kings 12:16: "What portion have we in David? Neither have we inheritance in the son of Jesse: to your tents, O Israel: now see to thine own house, David" (King James Version, or KJV).[16]

The two nations spent the next 200-plus years in bitter political and religious warfare until Israel was destroyed by the Assyrians in 722 BCE, at least according to the Bible. So in the first century CE, the time of Matthew, the northern kingdom of Israel was ancient history, and only Judea remained, the last man standing. This simple fact of survival helped insure the triumph of Judean myth over Israeli history in the public mind, but significant pockets of resistance always remained, particularly in Samaria.

Isaiah's Prophecy

Matthew's genealogy, placing Jesus in the hereditary line of the kings of Judah, while also declaring him the Son of God, would have been quite useful in convincing contemporary Jews of Christ's authority. The author then hastens to anchor the virgin birth to a snippet from the prophet Isaiah, saying in chapter 1, verses 22 and 23: "Now all this was done, that it might be fulfilled which was spoken by the prophet, saying, 'Behold, a virgin [almah] shall be with child, and shall bring forth a son, and they shall call his name Emmanuel, which being interpreted is, God with us" (KJV).

Did Isaiah really prophesy the virgin birth of Jesus Christ? On further analysis, it seems Matthew may have quoted Isaiah entirely out of context. John Dominic Crossan put the prophecy back into its proper setting in his work, *Jesus, A Revolutionary Biography*.[17] The year was 734 BCE, and once again, Israel was at war with Judah.

The prophet Isaiah was trying to persuade Ahaz, king of Judah, then under attack from the combined forces of Syria and Israel, to trust in God rather than appeal to the Assyrian emperor for help. Ahaz refused the offer of divine assistance, and so received a prophecy of doom instead (Isaiah 7:14–25): A young woman shall conceive and bear a son, and before that child knows how to refuse the evil and choose the good—that is, grows to maturity—both the two attacking kingdoms and Ahaz's own kingdom would be destroyed.

In chapter 8, immediately following, Isaiah himself "goes in unto" an *almah*, meaning a veiled, or young woman of marriageable age, called "the prophetess" (8:3). The prophetess conceives, and bears Isaiah a son. Isaiah confirms (8:4) that before this child is old enough to cry "My father and my mother," the promised devastations of these kingdoms would come to pass. Any Jew would readily agree that these verses from their prophet Isaiah do not predict the birth of Jesus from the Virgin Mary. So why does Matthew want to convince his audience that this virgin birth was something the Jews were expecting?

Matthew's Magi

After establishing that Jesus was born in, but apparently not of, the royal house of David, and claiming that Isaiah prophesied the virgin birth, this very first book of the New Testament immediately opts for Zoroastrian astrology. Chapter 2 begins: "Now when Jesus was born in Bethlehem of Judea in the days of Herod the king, behold, there came wise men [Magoi] from the east to Jerusalem. Saying, 'Where is he that is born King of the Jews? For we have seen his star in the east and are come to worship him.'" (KJV).

The protests of later apologists notwithstanding, Matthew's *magoi* certainly appear to be astrologers. Their name and behavior leave little doubt as to what they were about. The author of Matthew specifically calls them *magoi* in the Greek, the plural of *magi*, which means a member of the hereditary priestly caste of the Persian, Zoroastrian religion. The Aramaic version uses the word M'GUSHAI—a magus or Magian.

Magoi does not mean "wise men," as the King James Version has it. The word *magoi* would not have had any particular meaning for the average Christian in 17th century England, just as it carries no specific information for Christians today, other than the popular image of three kings riding camels and bearing gifts.

However, for Matthew's intended audience, the word *magoi* came packed with specific meanings. It was a familiar reference to neighboring Persian Zoroastrian priests.

Most Jews of Matthew's day would have had some idea that Magian scholars were renowned for their learning, and particularly for their skills in dream interpretation and astrology. They would have readily recognized the Persian Magi as longstanding religious and political allies against the Romans. Many Jews of Matthew's time would have also known that the Magi had very definite expectations of a coming world savior, and of a great battle between good and evil at the end of the world; in other words, a messiah and an apocalypse quite similar to their own, all mysteriously encoded and foretold in Magian astrology. This was part of the general culture of the region. Matthew thought this information about Persian Magi and astrology would be of some advantage to his cause, or he wouldn't have included it.

We, however, are so far removed from that time and place that we miss all of the context and information Matthew so succinctly conveyed to his contemporaries in that one word: *Magoi*. We've never met a Magian, and wouldn't know what a Persian astrologer believed. Imagine trying to describe a "Right-wing, conservative Republican" to a second-century Jewish Christian from Antioch. Those words carry immense cultural, political, and even religious significance for us, but they wouldn't mean much to him. So it is with *Magoi*.

Matthew's Math

We can also be fairly certain that the author of Matthew, whoever he was or claims to be, was not there when it happened. This is anything but an eyewitness account. Matthew obviously did not speak to the Magi himself; nor does he give a source for his information. This is a story, and its position and content are calculated to convince a Jewish audience that Jesus Christ was the Son of God and the promised Messiah of Israel.

The story of the Magi was probably a later addition to the collection of material we have come to know as the Gospel of Matthew. This Gospel probably started out simply as the *logia*, or the collected sayings of Jesus. These sayings were compiled by someone who was close to Jesus, and who knew how to read and write. Perhaps this person was the born-again publican who left his taxes and his table to follow Jesus. This character appears throughout the Gospels under the names Matthew and Levi. Although we may never know for sure if this storied taxman actually wrote the book ascribed to him, we do know that Matthew's gospel contains more references to money, and to specific foreign currencies, than any of the other gospels.[18]

The sayings of Jesus in the Gospel of Matthew may be about the closest thing we have to the source, to Jesus himself. Whatever the language or translation, they still ring with an unmistakable authority that has being touching hearts and changing lives for more than 2,000 years now. The narrative story line may have been added later on, possibly in imitation of the Gospel of Mark. These points are all still fiercely debated, so I want to avoid the appearance of certainty about any of it.

The story of the Magi may be the latest part of the book; maybe even as late as 80–90 CE. In other words, it was probably written, or at least edited, well after the destruction of Jerusalem and the temple by the Romans in 70 CE, and well beyond the lifespan, or at least the working life, of any of Jesus' contemporaries. We need to remember this when considering how much confidence to place in Matthew's account.

Many well-intentioned researchers, intent upon positively identifying the Star of Bethlehem, have overly scrutinized these few, slim passages, treating Matthew almost as if he were a modern journalist or reporter. Although I will be gratefully referring to some of their excellent work throughout, particularly in Chapter 6, I do not in any way read this as a factual account.

There's little evidence here that the author of Matthew had any specific knowledge of astronomy or astrology, or that he had any intention of communicating exact information. Matthew wrote as an outsider, a relative stranger to the technicalities of Persian astrology, whose intended audience was similarly lacking in mathematical skills. He does loosely refer to the Star rising in the east (*en te anatole*), but the bulk of his report describes only the observable behavior of the astrologers; for instance, in chapter 2, verse 9: "...they went their way; and lo, the star which they had seen in the East went before them, till it came to rest over the place where the child was."

This fanciful passage is a story—not an example of first-century astrology. Both Hellenistic and Persian astrology were highly technical and had specific terminology for describing planetary motion and position. That kind of language does not appear in the Gospel of Matthew. Further, in chapter 2, verse 7, we read: "Then Herod summoned the wise men secretly and ascertained from them what time the star appeared."

And that's all he says! Why doesn't he give us the Magi's answer to that all-important question, complete with longitude, latitude, and so on? He could have easily spared us 2,000 years of confusion! That is obviously not Matthew's intention, and I am willing to assume that not only did he not understand the math, but it also would have been wasted on his readers.

Others would disagree, and have invested a lot of time in trying to decipher astronomical clues, which in my humble opinion, simply aren't there (please see Chapter 6 where this is all discussed in considerably more depth). Besides, if Matthew completely botched the genealogy, and blew Isaiah's "prophecy" all out of proportion, are we now to trust his astronomy?

Any attempt to treat this story, or indeed any biblical passage, as accurate or descriptive science is probably naïve and misguided at best, and disingenuous at worst. Ancient Judeans didn't do science—we do. As tempting as it is to project our own proclivities onto famous people from the past, in the end, it only prevents us from seeing them as they really were.

I am much more interested in why the author of Matthew turns so quickly to the Magi and astrology to establish his claims for Christ, and why this would be so convincing to his Jewish contemporaries. That has proven to be a much more fruitful line of inquiry, for the Magi and their astrology commanded significant respect among Judeans, especially when it came to the controversial subject of their long-awaited king and messiah.

Chapter 2
Jerusalem's Debt to the Persians

The opinions of the Magi certainly carried some weight with the Jews. Otherwise, why would the author of Matthew devote precious time and space to them at the very beginning of his book? He needed a hook, a strong opening, something that would play upon the Judeans' deepest priorities and immediately grab their attention—but why Persian, Zoroastrian priests and astrology?

Cyrus, the Persian Messiah

What Matthew and his contemporaries knew, and we have since forgotten, is that the Jews owed their return to Jerusalem, and indeed their very existence as a nation, to the Persians. It was not for nothing that the author of the second part of the book of Isaiah referred to Cyrus the Great, the conquering hero and architect of the Persian Empire, as a messiah: "This is what the LORD says to his anointed [meshiach: messiah] to Cyrus, whose right hand I take hold of to subdue nations before him and to strip kings of their armour, to open doors before him so that gates will not be shut"(45:1, New International Version, or NIV).

In the year 586 BCE, Jerusalem was laid waste, its temple defiled and destroyed by the armies of Babylon. Any Jew of rank or substance was either killed or carted off into captivity. There the children of Judah languished by the waters of Babylon, lamenting the loss of everything—their land, their temple, their holy scriptures; everything that defined them as a people, except their hope. It was Cyrus who gave it all back to them.[1]

Cyrus the Great was everything King David was not. He conquered and built the largest empire the world had ever known. When Cyrus took Babylon, he not only repatriated the Jews to Jerusalem (538 BCE), but he also funded their return, providing the resources and the protection necessary to rebuild the city and begin the restoration of the temple—at least, according to the Bible. After his death, when things were not going particularly well in the Jerusalem colony, subsequent emperors Darius and Artaxerxes continued this crucial support through the ensuing centuries.

A later portrait of Cyrus II the Great.
Photo and original image in public domain.

These Persians were not merely being charitable in this effort; their real concern was Egypt. Jerusalem was an important defensive outpost.[2] The Persians could be remarkably tolerant, especially of the native beliefs of the inhabitants of strategic outposts. Besides, the Persians practiced an early form of monotheism themselves.

Meanwhile, the religion of the sixth-century Judean exiles was still developing, having only just barely survived generations of trauma and loss. The destruction of the northern kingdom of Israel (722 BCE) was followed by a century of invasions, leading to the fall of Jerusalem (586 BCE), and then some 50-plus years of exile in Babylon. Upon their return to Jerusalem, the Judean colonists were a people in crisis and transition, and their religion was a far cry from what we recognize as Judaism today.

One God Among Many

The Judean religion had been in turmoil long before the armies of Nebuchadnezzar fell upon Jerusalem. The destruction of the northern kingdom of Israel in 722 BCE had serious consequences for the Judeans, who had long coveted their neighbors' house. Although the Judean scriptures consistently depict Israel as corrupt and deserving of God's punishment, with the demise of the northern kingdom, Judah began a long and complex process of claiming "all things Israel" as its own. In staking this ambitious claim, and co-opting the religious cachet, and the extensive tribal territories of the northern kingdom, the Judeans stood to increase both their status and their borders.[3]

The northern nation of Israel, which claimed 10 tribes and their territories, had always been larger, more prestigious, and more prosperous than tiny Judea. Judea consisted of only two southern tribes: Benjamin and Judah (which had long ago absorbed the tribe of Simeon). These Judeans scratched out a living in a dry and forbidding hilltop environment. Unlike the fertile valleys of northern Israel, where agriculture, urban centers, and a thriving trade in olives and wine had developed, the sparse population of Judah still included many seminomadic herders in constant search of water.

The northern territories were very inviting, indeed, but Judea was in no position to take them; not with the Assyrian giant standing by, but the growing theo-political rationale for a united kingdom ruled by the Davidic dynasty in Jerusalem would not be denied. Part of this assimilation process was the emerging Judean insistence on the priority of the Jerusalem temple and its priesthood, and the centralization of all worship there. This was something the Israelis had never believed.

The biblical books of II Kings (ch. 21–23) and II Chronicles (ch. 33–35) describe these precarious times, when under continual threat of invasion by larger powers such as Egypt, Assyria, and Babylon, the rulers of Jerusalem introduced a series of sweeping religious reforms, intended to boost the power and prestige of their temple cult. The Judean kings Hezekiah (died ca. 687 BCE) and Josiah (died ca. 609 BCE) both dispatched armed missions throughout the northern Israeli territories, specifically to kill priests, destroy cult sites, and stamp out any lingering Israeli practices, so as to redirect all religious attention to Jerusalem. In spite of these ongoing and murderous campaigns, most of their reforms were overturned by their immediate successors (II Chronicles ch. 33; 36:14).

Many see this period as the beginning of what we now recognize as biblical Judaism.[4] In this same time frame, the late eighth and seventh centuries BCE, the priests and scribes in Jerusalem were turning their hands to the task of providing a "national literature." The presumed influx of Israeli refugees from the north meant an influx of Israeli scripture, and the Jerusalem priesthood faced the task of collating two different scriptures from two different nations into one. The result: the puzzling duplication and repetition running throughout the Pentateuch, or the books of Moses.

El and Yahweh

It was in untangling these threads in the 18th century that the famous documentary hypothesis arose, because it was still obvious, even thousands of years later, that these two, El and Yahweh, were not the same. For one thing, the Israeli scriptures called God El, or Elohim, whereas the Judean scriptures called God Yahweh.

In Sunday school we were taught that Yahweh and El were different names for God. But, in fact, they were different gods. The northern tribes of Isra-El had worshipped El (hence the name), a northern, Canaanite deity. El, the god of Isra-El, was originally the king of the Canaanite gods, often represented as a bearded old man on a throne; an image that has retained its currency remarkably well throughout the millennia. Remote but kindly, El presided over a council of lesser deities, who did most of the real work of running the world.[5] This council sometimes included the Judean god, Yahweh.[6]

Yahweh was a war god; a dramatic action hero compared to the sedate El. Yahweh thundered upon the mountains, unfurling his wrath in ferocious storms, and howling winds and rain. His worship arose in the south, from the mountains of Seir and Edom, and he was first invoked in battle by the wandering Bedouin tribes in the Sinai.[7] "The Song of Deborah," one of the oldest pieces of literature in the Old Testament, extols the legendary feats of Yahweh upon the southern mountains in Judges 5:4–5: "LORD [Yahweh] when thou wentest out of Seir, when thou marchest out of the field of Edom, the earth trembled, and the heavens dropped, the clouds also dropped water. The mountains melted from before the LORD, even that Sinai from before the LORD God of Israel" (The Masoretic Text).

In Deuteronomy 33:2, Moses declares with his dying breath, "...The LORD (Yahweh) came from Sinai, and rose up from Seir unto them: he shined forth from the mount Paran, and he came forth with ten thousands of saints: from his right hand went a fiery law for them"(KJV).

Yahweh not only roared upon the mountains like thunder, but as the Lord of Hosts, he flew before his troops in battle in his traveling ark; that is, until King David took the revolutionary step of settling the Bedouin warlord once and for all in the tabernacle in Jerusalem.[8]

In the early Iron Age period of conflict and alliance, when Judah and Israel united to fight the Philistines, we may find the earliest merging of Yahweh with El. A few strategic victories under the war god's banner could have turned Israeli troops into born-again Yahwists, just as a few numbing losses would have weakened their newfound faith.

In the fury of reforms in seventh century Jerusalem, the two became one in an awkward amalgamation that eventually unraveled under 18th century literary criticism. In 1753, the French physician Jean Astruc published a book entitled *Conjectures on the Original Documents That Moses Appeared to Have Used in Composing Genesis*. He speculated that Moses must have composed the book from earlier sources, and that the use of different names for God implied different authors. Astruc identified a "J" author, who consistently called God Yahweh (Jehovah), and an "E" author, who called God El and Elohim. On that basis, Astruc was able to separate out two distinct strands of narrative. German researcher J.G. Eichorn further elaborated on these distinctions in 1787, and thus was modern biblical textual criticism born.[9]

The documentary hypothesis has experienced both wide acceptance and hostile rejection ever since. There will always be lingering questions of authorship, and we may never get it entirely right, but it has proven to be a fruitful methodology, spawning more than two centuries of innovative research. The authors of *The Bible Unearthed*, in presenting the archaeological evidence, describe what amounts to a likely scenario for the origins of the Bible within the religious reforms and territorial ambitions of seventh century Judea, where the desire to meld Israel into Judea was a driving force.[10]

That all would have come to a crashing halt in 586 BCE, with the destruction of Jerusalem, but the Judean dream of ruling over Israel obviously survived the Exile, and was enthusiastically rejoined by the leaders of the post-exilic Jerusalem colony.

The "Victory" of Yahwism

In light of all that, it would be a real stretch to categorize the exiles that Cyrus sent home from Babylon as strict "monotheists." As Mark S. Smith puts it, "Israel's monotheism...emerged only halfway through

Israel's history. It was heir and reaction to a long tradition of Israelite polytheism."[11]

"Tribal henotheists"[12] is the preferred terminology, for although the Judean Yahwists were supposed to be committed to the worship of one god—their ancient tribal god, Yahweh—they certainly recognized the existence of other gods. The familiar gods of their neighbors (Moloch, Tammuz, Ashera, and Baal, Yahweh's chief rival as a militant storm god) appear throughout the Old Testament, and reformers such as Hezekiah and Josiah were not cold in their graves before their successors went right back to worshipping these other gods and restoring their shrines.

The goal of the reforming Judean Yahwists who originally compiled the books of the Bible was the centralized worship in Jerusalem of Yahweh as a "national" god, one who specialized in protecting Judea. Considering its rather precarious position, well within the grasp of ravenous empires such as Assyria and Egypt, Judea needed a lot of protection.

Yahweh's strong suit was victory, but he could not be expected to be faithful to a people who were not faithful to him. Israel's fault, according to the Judean Bible, lay in forsaking Yahweh and his temple in Jerusalem, and everyone knew what happened to them. In this reformed Judean "Yahwism," religious dabbling was not only a threat to the power of the temple, but it was also an open invitation to foreign enemies; tantamount to treason. The historical narrative in the Old Testament repeatedly hammers home this point.

Faith in this tribal/national god was tested for centuries, as Yahweh routinely tired of the Judeans' apostasy and mustered foreign armies to wreak his revenge. Jerusalem was occupied by all the dominant military powers of the day: Egyptians, Assyrians, Babylonians, Persians, Greeks, and Romans, one after another, they all lorded it over Judea, some more brutally than others.

Naturally, this provoked some soul-searching among Yahweh's faithful, and in certain quarters, inspired truly universal sentiments. In others, it sparked a particularly narcissistic and ethnocentric theology. For many Judean Yahwists, their jealous war god only allowed these empires to exist so that he could use their armies to punish Judea for her faithlessness.

Persian Religion Meets Judaism

The only rulers who ever did any good for the Jews, at least in their opinion, were the Persians, who led them out of slavery into the Promised

Land and restored the worship of Yahweh in his temple. The Judean religion did not appear to pose any real problem for the Persians, but then, they believed in one high god too: the supreme, good god, Ahura Mazda (Lord Wisdom). Unlike Yahweh, Ahura Mazda was neither a tribal god nor a war god, but a universal deity who ruled over everything good, right, and true.

Although the Persian Mazda-worshippers had their own monotheistic inclinations, they were also uniquely dualistic. They believed in an opposing principle, a god of evil—Angra Mainyu, or Ahriman, who has come over into Judeo-Christianity as the devil. Ultimately, the good god Ahura Mazda would triumph over Angra Mainyu and vanquish his evil forces forever in a great battle at the end of the world, but for the time being, all creation hung within the ongoing conflict between the two.[13] It was important to know which side you were on, and the Jews seemed to be on the right side, especially when the Persians considered Egypt.

From that perspective, the tribal henotheism of the Judeans presented more of an opportunity than a threat. More to the point, Persian monotheism had a profound and lasting influence on the development of Judaism. During the Second Temple period, Yahweh underwent an impressive theological metamorphosis. In official documents, the former Bedouin warlord was increasingly referred to as the "God of Heaven," appropriating this more universal title and its attributes from Ahura Mazda. Under the Persian auspices, Yahweh grew increasingly almighty, omniscient, and omnipresent, developing into a local expression "of the high god of the empire, Ahura Mazda."[14]

The Persians and the Bible

The Bible itself records that the Judeans lost their scriptures and law in the destruction of Jerusalem (586 BCE). It wasn't until an emissary of the Persian court, Nehemiah, the cupbearer to the emperor Artaxerxes, arrived in Jerusalem (circa 445–433 BCE) to provide crucial financial and military support to the failing colony, that the Second-Temple Judeans received the "Law of Moses." Chapter 8 of the book of Nehemiah describes how Ezra, the ready scribe, who had also been dispatched, generously funded and protected by the Persian court (Ezra, Ch. 7), convened the colonists of Jerusalem in order to proclaim the law and the scriptures. It was all surprisingly new to them.

We have such confidence in the Bible in these fundamentalist times that we forget that considerable controversy raged over the authenticity of the sacred books of the Jews, extending well into the early Christian era. The English researcher E.A. Wallis Budge addressed some of these lingering questions when he refers to the author of the Syriac work *The Cave of Treasures* (dated somewhere between the fourth and sixth century CE) as being "...convinced that all the ancient tables of genealogies which the Jews had possessed were destroyed by fire by the captain of Nebuchadnezzar's army immediately after the capture of Jerusalem by the Babylonians. The Jews promptly constructed new tables of genealogies, which both Christians and Arabs regarded as fictitious. The Arabs were as deeply interested in the matter as the Christians, for they were descended from Abraham, and the genealogy of the descendents of Hagar and Ishmael was of the greatest importance in their sight...."[15]

At this point, the material cut from the Bible is a lot more revealing than what stayed in. In the apocryphal Book of Adam (chapter iv, verse 10), we find the story of the priest Simeon, who, as the library and manuscripts of the Temple burned at the hands of the Babylonians, begged the commander for the ruins. Simeon gathered up the ashes of the books, and hid them in a pot within a vault. He filled a holy censer with coals and incense, and lit it, placing it over the spot where the ashes were hidden. That fire burned until Ezra arrived, almost 150 years later.[16]

The Cave of Treasures sheds more light on some of the popular traditions regarding the retrieval of the Jewish scriptures, in the chapter entitled "The Five Hundred Years from the Second Year of Cyrus to the Birth of Christ": "Now when the people had gone up [to Jerusalem] they had no Books of the Prophets. And Ezra the scribe went down into that pit [wherein Simeon had cast the Books], and he found a censer full of fire, and the perfume of the incense which rose up from it. And thrice he took some of the dust of those Books, and cast it into his mouth, and straightaway God made to abide in him the spirit of prophecy, and he renewed all the Books of the Prophets."[17]

Jewish tradition judiciously sidesteps the whole question, and maintains that Ezra miraculously restored the books from memory; quite a feat, at that. We do have in our possession a later description of the actual process, in the apocryphal second book of Esdras, chapter 14, verses 1–48. In verses 21 and 22, Ezra complains to God: "For your law was destroyed in the fire, and so no one can know about the deeds you have done or intend to do. If I have won your favour, fill me with your holy spirit, so that I may write down the whole story of the world from the very beginning, everything that is contained in your law; then men will have the chance to find the right path, and, if they choose, gain life in the last days... (The New English Bible).

God pledges his help, and directs Ezra to gather five scribes and retreat with them into the wilderness for 40 days. Once they are settled, God again contacts Ezra and commands him to drink:

> 39. So I opened my mouth, and was handed a cup full of what seemed like water, except that its colour was the colour of fire.
>
> 40. I took it and drank, and as soon as I had done so my mind began to pour forth a flood of understanding, and wisdom grew greater and greater within me, for I retained my memory unimpaired.
>
> 41. I opened my mouth to speak, and I continued to speak unceasingly.
>
> 42. The Most High gave understanding to the five men, who took turns at writing down what was said, using characters which they had not known before. They remained at work through the forty days, writing all day, and taking food only at night.
>
> 43. But as for me, I spoke all through the day; even at night I was not silent.
>
> 44. In the forty days, ninety-four books were written (The New English Bible)

And thus were the lost scriptures restored, at least according to this version. By the way, this second book of Esdras is included in the canon of the Russian Orthodox and the Ethiopian Churches, and was extensively quoted by the early Church Fathers, so it isn't even entirely apocryphal.[18]

These accounts are quite revealing, because the canonical books of Ezra and Nehemiah make it plain that the Judean colonists had no scriptures, but do not really say where or how Ezra got them, other than that he brought them from Babylon. They also give no indication of why the Jerusalem colony would have been content to carry on for nearly 100 years without them.

The Redactor

Literary criticism and the ever-evolving documentary hypothesis have revealed the Old Testament to be a complex tapestry, in which very ancient strands were artfully woven among the new.[19] Even if the Babylonian armies did burn all the scriptures in Jerusalem, there is older literature in the Old Testament that must have survived or been reconstructed somewhere, even if only from memory. The communities of exiled Jews and Israelis scattered throughout Mesopotamia may have contributed something to the process. At the same time, there is plenty of newer material in the Old Testament too, much of it a lot newer than it purports to be, which has passed through the hands of nameless editors through the years, each with his own agenda.

So although there is still confusion about exactly how these books came to be, the work gives every appearance of having undergone a serious editing, or redaction process in the years following the return from Babylon. Someone, often believed to be Ezra, worked these texts over thoroughly.

Julius Wellhausen, in 1886, was one of the first to introduce "R," the redactor, into the documentary hypothesis. "E," for editor, was already taken. "R," the redactor, is one of the most influential scribe(s) ever to take up the pen. At this crucial point in Jewish history, when the returning exiles were struggling to rebuild their nation and their religion, this/these scribe(s), whether we call him/them R, or Ezra, assembled what could be found of the ancient texts of Israel and Judah and put them together, in response to the demands of the times. These demands included the express commands of the Persians and their Magi.

The Persian Temple

The books of Ezra and Nehemiah (and their apocryphal counterparts), although certainly entertaining, are not the best sources for information on this period. According to Lester Grabbe, their historicity has been called into question on any number of points.[20] Judea's law and scriptures were canonized and promulgated during the Persian period, but much of that process, and the extensive editing and redaction it entailed, was initiated during the reign of Persian Emperor Darius the Great (522–486 BCE). The scribes involved remain anonymous. Ezra came later, maybe 50 years later, and even though the Bible says that the Persian court dispatched

Ezra from Babylon and gave him the authority to establish the law and practice of religion in the Jerusalem colony, he would have been a relative latecomer in an ongoing process.[21]

The biblical character of Ezra, no doubt originally based on a historical person, evolved over time into a highly contrived but convenient literary device. As L. Grabbe points out, "The final work of Hebrew Ezra—Nehemiah is likely to have been completed after the coming of Alexander..."; in other words, after approximately 336 BCE, and after the fall of the Persian Empire.

The real redactorsremain anonymous, and their motivations have been lost to us, but Ezra emerges, chosen by God as were the prophets of old, to lead the whole post-exilic redaction process. He is presented as a conservative priest, divinely inspired and dedicated to restoring Israel to the ways of its ancestors, when there is no hiding the fact that he was working directly for the Persian government. Ezra was actually setting up something quite new and different in Jerusalem. The fictionalized accounts of Ezra's inspired redactions preserve the myth of a revealed religion, and effectively edit out the entire historical and sociological process.

From the very beginning, the Persian colony of Judea, now known as Yehud, had an important role to play in Persia's overall goals for the Empire. The control of the temple and religion, and the consequent control of public opinion and resources, were essential to the success of Persia's plans. The governors that Persia sent to rule in Yehud were not religious conservatives trying to restore the ways of their ancestors, as Ezra and Nehemiah are portrayed in the Bible. They were men with proven loyalty to the Empire and its goals, or they were out of a job.

The Empire's plans for Judea began to fully materialize during the reign of Darius the Great. The first step was the rebuilding of the New Jerusalem temple, destined for a role in Persia's preparations for a massive invasion of Egypt. Cyrus had originally encouraged the temple project, but it took an order from Darius to really get the construction going. The Second Temple was completed and dedicated in 516/515 BCE.

As Jon L. Berquist puts it, in *Judaism in Persia's Shadow*, the delayed completion of the temple was not, as it has often been represented, the result of religious arguments among the Judeans: "The immediate motivation for the temple construction, then, is threat of force. This links the temple construction more closely to Persian imperial policies than to Yehudite internal debates. As a center for Persian administration, the temple would assure tranquility and supplies for the Persian army as it passed nearby on the way to Egypt.... At the same time, the temple was a symbol of Yehudite and Persian unity, and of Persian favor toward Yehud."[22]

The Second Temple was much more than a religious center. It was the Persian administrative center for Yehud; the headquarters for both the high priest and the governor. Most importantly, it was the tax depot. The official religion practiced there under Persian supervision was designed to support Persian policies, and to keep the revenues flowing.

Darius and the Scriptures

Darius the Great was a man of administrative genius. Among his many accomplishments during his long reign (522–486 BCE), he reorganized the sprawling empire Cyrus had gained into a manageable system of *satrapies*,

Darius the Great on his throne.
Photo is in public domain.

and codified the local laws of the regions under his command, gaining a lasting reputation as "The Lawgiver." Joseph Blenkinsopp, in his commentary on Ezra-Nehemiah, says that in Yehud, "...Persian policy contributed to the redaction of the laws which were to attain their final formulation in the Pentateuch."

Darius's legal policies had lasting influence in Yehud, coinciding with the appearance of a religious canon—a set group of scriptures representing the official religious tradition of the Jerusalem temple. The Judean religion increasingly relied upon these official scriptures, not only to define itself, but to interpret both the past and the present in their light, discouraging further revelations. From this point on, the Judeans became a "people of the book." Again, Berquist is convinced that "The shifts to temple and canon as centers of the Yahwistic religion set the basis for later Jewish and Christian faith in many respects.... Darius's reign as Persian emperor created a reorganization of community life in Jerusalem that greatly affected the development of the religion of Yahweh, and thus this little-known period of history functions as one of the greatest watersheds in the development of both Judaism and Christianity."[23]

The redactors, working under the Persian administration, continued to rewrite the myth of an Israel ruled by Judea that had begun before the Exile, but their editing was also driven by the long-term goals of the emperor and his Magi, who always had the upper hand.

The Persian objectives may have been relatively simple: a loyal, stable colony that would supply, man, and otherwise support the Persian occupation of Egypt and the Mediterranean coast. If that were the case, then the official laws, reforms, and scriptures would have worked toward increasing affinity between Judea and Persia. They would probably encourage compliance and loyalty, without being so obviously rewritten as to arouse resentment among the elders. But what if the Persian objectives were more complex? What if they deliberately sought to transform the Judean religion in their own image?

Either way, the Jerusalem colony had its own problems that would have certainly affected the editing process. The first obstacle facing this new Exodus was that most Jews had no intention of leaving the relative comforts of Babylon to make the dangerous trek to Yehud. The official scriptures needed to be truly inspirational for this to work. In other words, the Jews never needed Moses more.

The ongoing quest for corroborating evidence of the biblical accounts of the Exodus and the conquest of Canaan, after nearly a century of highly charged and controversial research, has produced quite the opposite: an urgent need to revise everything we thought we knew about the origins of Israel, and the roots of our own Judeo-Christian heritage. But in the early days of Persian Yehud, these stories of a divinely inspired lawgiver defeating an Egyptian enemy and leading the people into the Promised Land were more than timely and had a calculated impact. Ditto for David, Solomon, and the glories of the united kingdom.

Of course I am not proposing that Ezra, "R," or anyone else created the entire Exodus saga *ex nihilo*, or that these fabulous kings of Judah did not exist. Surely they did, but probably not as we remember them. Conversely, as James Trotter points out in his book *Reading Hosea in Achaemenid Yehud*, Judean literature from the Persian period, for instance

Ezra 1–2, or Deutero-Isaiah (Isaiah 40–55), consistently presents the return from Babylon as a second exodus or as a new conquest of the land. Joseph Blenkinsopp refers to the presence throughout the post-exilic literature of "...many allusions to the early traditions which form a kind of deep structure to the history of this new beginning."[24] The "redactors" and their Persian overlords were skilled historiographers, retelling the old stories to suit the present, and reshaping the present to suit the past.

The next problem facing the returning exiles was that there were already people living in the Judean territories who, as is so often the case, were not particularly keen to be colonized by "foreign interests."

The People of the Land

The book of Ezra describes how the "people of the land" immediately approached the returning Babylonian exiles to offer their help in rebuilding the temple, saying, "...Let us build with you: for we seek your God, as ye do; and we do sacrifice unto him..." (4:2). Ironically, the exiles rudely rejected their offer, responding: "Ye have nothing to do with us to build a house unto our God: but we ourselves together will build unto the Lord God of Israel, as king Cyrus the king of Persia hath commanded us"(4:3, KJV).

The exiles didn't want any interference from the locals, and insisted on doing things the Persian way; but why? Was the religion returned so radically different from the one that went into exile? And who were "the people of the land"? II Kings 25:12 says that after burning Jerusalem and carrying away the captives, "...the captain of the guard left of the poor of the land to be vinedressers and husbandman." These people, the ones who managed to escape, were generally of the lower classes, or rural farmers. Naturally, they viewed the return of the new ruling class from Babylon with great interest. Still, according to the Bible, they were the worst enemies of the post-exilic colony.

Whatever Happened to Israel?

There was also a sizable population of native Israelis, especially on Judea's northern borders. Lest we forget, Israel was destroyed and sent into exile too, in a series of expulsions that culminated in 722 BCE. The Assyrians even deported and resettled some of the Israeli people (the famous lost tribes of Israel) into parts of Media, the home of the Magi.[25]

The Assyrians made several attempts to colonize the Israeli territories with foreigners, many of whom converted to the worship of the God of Israel (II Kings 17), but many Israelis escaped deportation and managed to stay in the land.

The Bible presents the Judean point of view in II Kings 17:18, which says that Yahweh was angry with Israel and removed all of the people of Israel from the land, and "there was none left but the tribe of Judah only." That is simply not true. These biblical texts come down to us with a deliberate bias, reflecting the ideology of both the seventh-century Judean reformers and the Persian-backed ruling class of Second-Temple Judea. In fact, there were still plenty of the children of Israel in the land, but under the Persian auspices, the name Israel was co-opted even further, until it eventually came to signify only those who had returned from exile in Babylon.

Further, we find repeated references in the post-exilic literature to the empty land, with the underlying assumption that the territories of Judah were completely depopulated and lay desolate until the exiles returned. The archaeological evidence reveals that this was not the case at all.[26] James Trotter concludes, "These texts clearly reflect an ideology of the producing community that emphasized the legitimacy of the exiled community to the exclusion of anyone who had remained in the land."[27]

Berquist puts it even more forcefully, in commenting on the suppression of divergent views by the Persian-backed Jerusalem elite and their ongoing condemnation of the native population: "This form of priestly and political immigrant religion became the only allowed official religion within Yehud, and these groups combined to capture the rights to the older traditions. Soon all religious traditions of ancient monarchic Israel, at least those extant, bore the stamp of a strongly Jerusalemite bias. This bias may have existed before, during the closing years of the monarchy, but in Darius's reign that became official and quite possibly became the published official view...."[28]

But all the while, Israel was intent on surviving destruction and exile too, just as the Judeans were. However, unlike the Judeans, the Israelis didn't have the backing, or the meddling, of a major world empire in this enterprise. In time, the children of Israel did stage a significant comeback in the land of their fathers, and continued their age-old worship at the holiest sites of the northern kingdom.[29]

They remain there today, and still retain their own version of the Torah, which they claim is purer than the post-exilic, Judean version. They still claim to be the descendants of the Israelites from the northern kingdom who stayed behind and never sojourned in Babylon or Assyria. They never accepted the religious reforms of the Jerusalem colony.

Recent DNA testing has confirmed that these people are the descendants of the priests of ancient Israel, at least on the male side. The test results imply that they may have been telling the truth all along. They are the children of Israel.[30] Oddly enough, these are the people the Judeans hated the most—the dreaded Samaritans.

It was the Judeans who declared the 10 tribes of Israel officially "lost." They branded the Samaritans as impostors, mongrel idolaters worthy of nothing but bitter contempt. Ironically, because the reconstituted Judean religion centered exclusively upon the temple cult and priesthood at Jerusalem, their claim to be the spiritual heirs of ancient Israel just doesn't ring true. The Jewish Temple at Jerusalem did not even exist in the time of Jacob/Israel. According to the Bible, Jerusalem only became a Judean city after King David took it from the Jebusites. Jacob/Israel, who would have lived centuries before David, never worshipped at Jerusalem, and neither did Abraham.

Remember the Samaritan woman who met Jesus at the well? (The Gospel of John, ch. 4.) She reminded Christ that her people worshipped at the shrines of their fathers, at Jacob's well, and at the holy mountain where Joshua assembled the tribes. This was Mt. Gerizim, just outside the capital city of Samaria/Nablus, and the children of Israel still worship there today. The Samaritans had no interest in the temple cult in Jerusalem, which they saw as a later Judean and Persian innovation.

So at least in that sense, things were much the same after the exile as they had been before: Judah and Israel were two different nations with two different religions, and they remained bitter enemies. The Holy Bible is a Judean document, and tells the story from the Judean perspective. Therefore, it has nothing good to say about the Samaritans, and claims they are all just descendants of the foreign colonists settled by the Assyrians who worshipped strange gods. The Samaritan scriptures tell a different story, a story that has been borne out in the DNA evidence. Unfortunately, the Judean version, as recorded in the Bible, has dominated throughout Western Judeo-Christian society.

It turns out the "lost tribes of Israel" weren't so hard to find after all, and no one tried harder to make them disappear again than the Judeans themselves! To quote Alan Ereira, "It has been said that if you want evidence that miracles really happen, look at the survival of the Jews. Well, even more startling is the survival of the Samaritans, the smallest nation in the world."[31] The Samaritans are the last lingering remnant of the so-called lost tribes, and, against all odds, they have tried to keep the ways of ancient Israel in the land of their fathers.

Which is more than can be said for the temple cult at Jerusalem. There is no mistaking the Persian, Zoroastrian influence on the Second Temple Judaism that followed. Yahweh, the tribal war god, grew increasingly almighty, omniscient, and omnipresent, in imitation of Ahura Mazda. Meanwhile, the Judean cosmos was torn in two between God and the Devil, and angels and demons descended through the gap, fighting for their masters on either side. Diverse factions of scribes and scholars squabbled and separated; for instance, the Pharisees (the Farsis?), who, as were the Magi, were obsessed with ritual purity—hand-washings, potscrubbings, and such—had an ongoing argument about the resurrection of the dead with the Sadducees (Zadokites), the conservative priests, who rejected the afterlife and tried to keep a lid on the Persian reforms.

As time went on, the Persian apocalypse gained feverish hold, for surely, foreign invaders such as the Greeks were allies of the Devil. How long would Yahweh be mocked? But things only got worse under the Romans, and by the end of the first century BCE, many Jews were convinced that the time was ripe for a messiah, maybe another Cyrus, or one of the promised sons of Zoroaster, to arise and reclaim the throne of David. There is little to no precedent for these beliefs in the religion of ancient Israel.

Chapter 3
The Magi in History

Who Were the Magi?

The Magi were an ancient order of priests and scholars; wise men, if you will, who originated among the tribes of Media.[1] The region the Magi knew as Media is now northwestern Iran, bordering the southern shores of the Caspian Sea, approximately halfway between Baghdad and Tehran.

By the late seventh century BCE, the Medes and their Magi were on the rise. Successfully allied with their Chaldean neighbors to the south, they overthrew the reigning regional powerhouse, the mighty Assyrian empire, sparking serious social and political changes throughout Mesopotamia. No sooner had the Medes expanded into Assyria's former territories, than they themselves were conquered by the neighboring Persian armies of Cyrus the Great and absorbed into his growing fold.

The crowning glory of this marriage between the tribes of the Medes and the Persians was the first universal world empire of antiquity: the Medo-Persian Empire, or more simply, the Persian Empire. At its height, the Medo-Persian Empire stretched from western India to the Danube, and included the North African territories of Libya and Egypt. Cyrus the Great, the original conqueror and architect of the Empire (d. 530 BCE), was a product of the same mixed marriage: his mother, Mandane, was the daughter of the Median king, Astyages; his father, Cambyses, was of the Persian royal house.

The Medes, and particularly the *Magoi*, were forever after associated with the Persians; socially, politically, and religiously. As the map on page 52 shows, they had never been all that far apart in the first place.

The Persian Empire at its height, during the reign of Darius the Great, successor to Cyrus the Great. Judea, and its capital, Jerusalem, were ruled by the Persians and their Magi for more than 200 years. Image in public domain.

The *Magoi* served as the hereditary priesthood for the Persians, much as they had originally done among the Medes, and it is in the role of Persian priests that the Magi usually appear throughout history.

Many ancient societies had their own hereditary caste of priests, scholars, and holy men; particularly the Indo-European and Aryan peoples. In the third century CE, Diogenes Laertes, in his *Lives of the Philosophers*, wrote: "Some say that the study of philosophy originated with the barbarians. In that among the Persians there existed the Magi, and among the Babylonians or Assyrians, the Chaldaei, among the Indians the Gymnosophistae, and among the Celts and Gauls men who were called Druids...."[2]

The Magi's function, as a priestly tribe or caste, was the guardianship of religion and its rites and rituals, education, and the pursuit of higher learning. They also advised kings and generals from their storehouse of wisdom, as did the Celtic Druids or the Brahmans of India. This was a common arrangement throughout the ancient world, and it still echoes beneath the surface of Western society today.

The earliest Magi probably operated within a hereditary and closed caste system. Relying extensively on oral tradition, passed from teacher to student, from generation to generation, they didn't publish their doings for outsiders—which is why primary sources and firsthand, insider accounts are in very short supply (barring anything that might surface unexpectedly from the desert in the future). Further compounding the problem, there were at least two separate attempts to wipe out the Magi and erase their history and teachings, during Alexander's conquest of Persia in the fourth century BCE, and to a lesser extent, during the Muslim conquest of Persia in the seventh century CE.

Fortunately, later Zoroastrian texts have survived that contain detailed descriptions of their priestly functions, but much of what we know about the earliest Magi comes from secondhand, outsider information. We need to make our way cautiously through this contradictory and often gossipy reporting. The human imagination revels in fantasies of secret, mystical brotherhoods, with magical powers and inbred initiatory rites; and the Magi certainly fit that bill. Nevertheless, they were real people, who lived for a long time, spread over a wide area of influence, and interacted meaningfully with their neighbors. Even if we are short on primary sources, the footprints and fingerprints of the Magi are everywhere, throughout the entire corpus of ancient religion, philosophy, and science.

Herodotus and the Magi

One of our most plentiful sources for information on the Magi is Herodotus (b. 486 BCE), the Greek "Father of History." Herodotus identifies the Magi as one of the original tribes of the Medes (Book 1.101), using the same Greek word as Matthew: *Magoi*. His seminal work, *The Histories*, was written specifically to explore the underlying causes of the traumatic Greco-Persian wars (approx. 500–448 BCE) so the Persians and their Magi figure prominently throughout.

The Medo-Persian Empire of Cyrus the Great and his capable successor, Darius, spread so rapidly that by the end of the sixth century BCE, serious border disputes arose with the Greeks in the west. Hostilities escalated over several decades into all-out war between the Persian Empire and the emerging Hellenistic city-states. Persian occupation brought powerful Eastern influences into every aspect of the emerging Greek culture, while at the same time, the consuming conflict with the Persians solidified the nascent Greek nationalism. The Hellenistic identity was forged in prolonged opposition to Persia, at historic battles such as Marathon and Thermopylae, and unfortunately, an anti-Persian bias has slanted "the classics" ever since. Of course, the irony here is that in defining themselves against them, the Greeks ultimately became more similar to the Persians than anyone was willing to admit.

Herodotus claimed to have traveled deep into the Persian Empire in search of his information, as far east as Babylon and Susa, and to have consulted with the leading scholars there. Herodotus was Greek himself, and writing mainly for an Athenian audience, so we might anticipate a certain amount of bias, even if he was trying to be even-handed. Apparently, some found him a bit *too* even-handed, and taunted him with the epithet *philobarbaros*, or "barbarian lover."[3] Nevertheless, in describing Persian customs, Herodotus comes across as an outsider, but at least he serves as a good starting point.

Herodotus refers so often to the *Magoi* in describing the Persians, because as official priests of the Persian religion, they were unavoidable. For instance, Herodotus reports that the Persians could not offer a religious sacrifice without the presence of a Magus (Book 1.132). Herodotus ventures into the historical origins of the mighty Persian Empire, and as he tells it, the Magi with their divinatory skills were there every step of the way, even intervening with their magic in the birth of Cyrus the Great. Herodotus relates the following story about Astyages, the grandfather of Cyrus, and the king of the powerful Median empire:

> (1) Astyages had a daughter, whom he called Mandane: he dreamed that she urinated so much that she filled his city and flooded all of Asia. He communicated this vision to those of the Magi who interpreted dreams, and when he heard what they told him he was terrified; (2) and presently, when Mandane was of marriageable age, he feared the vision too much to give her to any Mede worthy to marry into his family, but married her to a Persian called Cambyses, a man whom he knew to be wellborn and of a quiet temper: for Astyages held Cambyses to be much lower than a Mede of middle rank.[4]

Cyrus the Great sprang from this union. On his way to overrunning the ancient world, he opposed and overthrew his grandfather Astyages, uniting the Medes and Persians under his rule. This is what the Magi foresaw in the colorful imagery of the king's dream. In this story, we see the Magi in their traditional role, advising the Medean king and interpreting royal dreams. The Magi continued to do the same for the Persian emperors, but naturally, they brought a certain amount of Median political gamesmanship into the new alliance.

There were important initial differences in the alliance between the *Magoi* and the Persians, and Herodotus sheds some light on these in the following story. Distressed by the Magi's prophecies, King Astyages commanded his general, Harpagus, to destroy his daughter's son at birth. This, Harpagus could not bring himself to do, and as so often happens in these stories, the baby was taken in and raised by a shepherd family in the country. Some years later, troubling news reached the king's court of a country lad with such natural nobility that his playmates had already crowned him king. They brought the boy to court and Astyages knew right away he had been duped. Again, he consulted the Magi:

> The Magi answered, "If the boy survives, and has ruled as a king without any craft or contrivance, in that case we bid thee cheer up, and feel no more alarm on his account. He will not reign a second time. For we have found even oracles sometimes fulfilled in an unimportant way; and dreams, still oftener, have wondrously mean accomplishments."
>
> "It is what I myself most inciine to think," Astyages rejoined; "the boy having been already king, the dream is out, and I have nothing more to fear from him. Nevertheless, take good heed and counsel me the best you can for the safety of my house and your own interests."
>
> "Truly," said the Magi in reply, "it very much concerns our interests that thy kingdom be firmly established; for if it went to this boy it would pass into foreign hands, since he is a Persian: and then we Medes should lose our freedom, and be quite despised by the Persians, as being foreigners. But so long as thou, our fellow-countryman, art on the throne, all manner of honours are ours, and we are even not without some share in the government. Much reason therefore have we to forecast well for thee and for thy sovereignty. If then we saw any cause for present fear, be sure we would not keep it back from thee. But truly we are persuaded that the dream has had its accomplishment in this harmless way; and so our own fears being at rest, we recommend thee to banish thine. As for the boy, our advice is that thou send him away to Persia, to his father and mother."[5]

This is the stuff of legends, but in these portents surrounding the birth of the great king, the story underscores the fact that the marriage between the Magi and Persians was not without its tensions. This was particularly true during the difficult period following the sudden death of Cyrus the Great in battle in 530 BCE. His heir, Cambyses, the eldest son, succeeded him, but he was away much of the time, fighting in Egypt and Syria. In March of 522 BCE, Cambyses received news that a revolt had broken out back home, and that his younger brother, Smerdis (a.k.a. Bardiya) had seized the throne. This came as a real shock to Cambyses, who thought he had already taken the necessary measures to kill off his little brother, to forestall just such an eventuality; at least, according to Herodotus's *Histories* (3.30.1).

The truth is that Cambyses was a bit mad. Herodotus offers the opinion that he was too fond of his wine, or perhaps suffered from the "sacred disease." Whatever the diagnosis, Cambyses definitely had his demons. The father was a hard act to follow, and the son always suffered in comparison. As Cyrus had earned the respect of his subjects for his tolerance and nobility, Cambyses was notoriously capricious and cruel. Perhaps the inheritance of such a vast and fractious empire doomed the son to failure from the start.

Whatever the reasons, it seems that everyone preferred Smerdis, so there was no great outcry over the coup, especially when the new court immediately issued a three-year suspension of taxes and military obligations—sufficient to silence most dissent. According to the Darius inscription at Behistun, no one knew Smerdis was dead, or at the very least, they believed the reports of his death to have been greatly exaggerated. How that was possible is anyone's guess. The problem was, the man on the throne was not Smerdis, but a Magian named Gaumata, who only looked similar to Smerdis/Bardiya. Or did he? Gaumata's brother, the Magian Patizeithes, who was Cambyses's palace steward, was the reputed mastermind behind the plot.[6]

The problem was further compounded by the sudden death of Cambyses, the real king. As he came rushing back from Syria to reclaim his kingdom, he accidentally stabbed himself with his own sword while getting on his horse.[7] With history like this, who needs fiction? Cambyses died, leaving no heir and no descendant of Cyrus to oppose the Magian impostor on the throne. Enter Darius, son of Hystapes, who, with a select corps of Persian nobles, stormed the Median palace of the false Magians and killed them.

Darius was eventually crowned emperor. Although not a direct heir of Cyrus, he was a royal relation. He certainly proved himself worthy of the throne, however he came by it, and earned the lasting title of Darius the Great by restoring and consolidating the fractured empire. His version of the Magian coup agrees with Herodotus on most points, but Darius, unlike Herodotus, was not satisfied with merely

The larger-than-life figure of Darius the Great crushes the Magian Gaumata, who lies forever bound under the king's right foot, at Behistun. Image in public domain.

writing a book. Instead, he inscribed his story high on a sheer rock cliff at Behistun (ancient *Bagastana*, which translates roughly as "the place of the gods"). Towering nearly 100 meters above the ground, over the main road connecting the ancient capital cities of Babylonia and Media, to this day, you can still see Darius crushing Gaumata, the false Magian, beneath his feet, while Ahura Mazda, the good god of Persian Zoroastrianism, soars overhead. In three columns of text, in the Persian, Babylonian, and Elamite languages, Darius the Great declares that Ahura Mazda chose him to drive the Magian from the throne.

Meanwhile, Cyrus's empire was shattering, as the recently conquered tribes and nations seized the moment to revolt and reclaim their sovereignty. As Darius tells it at Behistun, Ahura Mazda led him in quashing all rebellion, and saved the empire. We can still see the vanquished foes of Darius, the rebel leaders, with their hands tied behind their backs, lined up and awaiting the same grisly fate as the Magian.

So there were serious differences between the Magians and the Persians in the early days of the empire, but there were certain constants as well: the *Magoi* had a taste for power and stayed close to the king, serving as advisors and diviners, and were intimately involved in the administrative life of the court. The rift between the Persian court and the Magi must have healed quickly, because by the time of the reign of the Persian emperor Xerxes (480 BCE), son of Darius the Great, the Magi were back in business. As the Greco-Persian Wars progressed, the Magi were actively involved in the royal train in all of their traditional roles.

In Book 7.19, Herodotus describes how Xerxes struggled in his deliberations about whether to go to war with the Greeks. He had three visions in the night, in which he dreamt he was crowned with an olive wreath, and the shoots of that olive tree covered the whole Earth. The Magi convinced him he should attack, for he was destined to have dominion over all the Earth. So the Magi were still readily interpreting dreams for the Persian Emperor.

In Book 7.37, just as Xerxes had set forth to march his armies to Abydos, he witnessed a spectacular solar eclipse. Naturally, he was concerned and immediately called for the Magi to inquire what this would portend. The Magi reassured him that the darkness of the sun did not bode well for the Greeks, but that the moon, which covered the sun, would protect the Persians. Xerxes then proceeded on his way with confidence. Here we see the Emperor consulting the Magi for their expertise in astrology and astronomy. Herodotus does not mention whether the Magi gave any warning of the impending eclipse.

When Xerxes had marched his army as far as the plain of Illium, he stopped and offered a sacrifice of 1,000 heifers to the goddess Athene, after which the Magi poured out libations in honour of the heroes of Troy.[8] So the Magi were still officiating at royal rituals and sacrifices. Further on, when the Persian armies arrived at the banks of the river Strymon, the Magi sacrificed white horses, looking for good omens.

Finally, in 7.191, a sudden storm arose at sea, causing tremendous damage to the massive Persian fleet. Herodotus reports that the Athenians had been encouraged by an oracle to turn to Boreas, their god of the winds, for protection. After extended prayers and sacrifices, Boreas responded and blew up a storm with enough force to sink 400 Persian vessels. The storm continued for three days, and the Magi were hard at work in a battle of duelling sacrifices, offering victims and chanting incantations to appease the winds. Further offerings were made to Thetis and the Nereids, which caused the storm to cease on the fourth day, or, as Herodotus puts it, maybe it died down on its own.

One thing becomes clear in these passages: Herodotus tends to describe the religious practices of the Magi in much the same way that he describes the oracles and sacrifices of the Greeks. That is only natural, because that was religion, as Herodotus knew it. How similar their practices and beliefs really were is another matter altogether. Herodotus was an outsider, not an initiate. He can only describe the observable behavior of the Magi using his own familiar terms. He can't take us inside their schools, or inside their heads.

Xerxes eventually led his forces into Athens, and burned it to the ground (480 BCE). Fortunately, most of the population had evacuated, so the loss of life was minimal, but the Athenians never forgot the outrage. It took them nearly 150 years to get even. When Alexander the Great conquered Persia in 331 BCE and occupied the capital city, Persepolis, it was payback time. The burning of Athens, and the burning of Persepolis in retaliation, are two of the main reasons why there is still so much mystery surrounding the Persians and their Magi today. The Greeks wanted to make them disappear forever.

The historian Diodorus Siculus (first century BCE), describes the legendary scene of the burning of Persepolis, the capital of the mighty Persian Empire, in his *Bibliotheca Historia*. After an extended evening of revelry, when the feasting and drinking were "far advanced," a fit of drunken madness descended upon Alexander and the Macedonians. They were inspired by a "courtesan" named Thais to "set fire to the palaces"...and permit "women's hands in a minute to extinguish the famed accomplishments of the Persians" and "to take vengeance for the destruction of the Greek temples."[9]

The revelers formed "a victory procession in honor of Dionysus," with Thais the courtesan leading the midnight conga line. Torches and musicians were gathered, and "to the sound of voices and flutes and pipes," Thais was "the first, after the king, to hurl her blazing torch into the palace. As the others all did the same, immediately the entire palace area was consumed, so great was the conflagration." Diodorus adds, "It was most remarkable that the impious act of Xerxes, king of the Persians, against the acropolis at Athens should have been repaid in kind after many years by one woman, a citizen of the land which had suffered it, and in sport."

The same story appears in the work of the Greek author Arrian of Nicomedia. He gives a more restrained account, in which Alexander has a reasonable, Hellenistic discussion with his friends, and they all agree to burn the palace in revenge for the sack of Athens.[10] Whichever version you prefer, the fact remains that by the time the Greeks burned Persepolis, they had already been there long enough to seize anything of value for themselves.

This raises a vexing issue: After the death of Alexander, the Greeks experienced a historic cultural renaissance, in the flowering of Greek philosophy, math, and science from which our Western civilization claims descent. Alexander's city, Alexandria, emerged as the new capital of learning, and its libraries were famous storehouses for the accumulated wisdom of the ancient world. So how did all of this accumulated wisdom wind up in Alexandria?

Many Greeks prided themselves on having invented philosophy and science, in contrast to their barbarian neighbors. As Diogenes Laertius put it in his *Lives and Opinions of Eminent Philosophers*, many "ignorantly impute to the barbarians the merits of the Greeks, from whom not only all philosophy, but even the whole human race in reality originated."[11] The author of the *Epinomis*, who may or may not have been Plato, was a bit more generous, stating that "...whatever Greeks acquire from foreigners is finally turned by them into something nobler."[12]

It was no secret that the earliest Greek mathematicians and scientists (Thales, Pythagoras, Democritus, Eudoxus, Anaximander, et al.) did not learn their math in Greece. They had to go much further east for their education, travelling to Egypt and Babylon to acquire learning, and yet hardly anyone remembers the names of their "barbarian" teachers.

According to Van der Waerden, "we have to abandon the traditional belief that the oldest Greek mathematicians discovered geometry entirely by themselves and that they owed hardly anything to older cultures, a belief which was tenable only as long as nothing was known about Babylonian mathematics."[13] Now we know that the earliest "scientific methods" arose from the meticulous record-keeping of Mesopotamia, where people such as the Assyrians and Babylonians observed the heavens for thousands of years, rigorously recording their observations. These invaluable records were the matrix of mathematics and astronomy, and the Greeks had nothing of their kind.

It has only been quite recently, with the discovery and translation of the earlier Mesopotamian texts, that "Greek" astronomy, astrology, and mathematics have been rightfully traced back to their Babylonian roots, and the Mesopotamians given proper credit for these historic achievements. And yet, although Aristotle and Euclid remain rightly famous, how many ancient Babylonian mathematicians can you name?

The Helleno-centric version of the origin of philosophy and science prevailed in the West, particularly in the 19th century, when the rise of

European nationalism resulted in increasingly Eurocentric versions of history. A different opinion has always prevailed in the East. There, it was widely believed that Alexander seized the accumulated wisdom of the Persian Empire before he burned Persepolis, and sent it back home. For centuries, Western scholars scoffed at the Persians' claim of losing their ancient literature, but as it turns out, the Greeks, although great borrowers, were not always careful about referencing their sources.

We do know that once in Babylon, Alexander and his men seized the astronomical records of the Chaldeans, containing many hundreds of years' worth of priceless observations. In the centuries before Alexander's arrival, the Chaldeans and their Magian supervisors had used these records to devise a mathematically based and increasingly "scientific" astronomy. Now, it was a prize of war.

As it turns out, Alexander's chronicler, Callisthenes of Olynthus, was put in charge of translating the observations. Once accomplished, the material was dispatched to the philosopher Aristotle, who was not only the former teacher of Alexander, but also the uncle of Callisthenes. So even though Western scholars have long dismissed the Persians' claims that the Greeks stole their books from them, maybe there is some genuine history behind these accusations.

It should come as no surprise that Alexander was not remembered as particularly "great" throughout Persia; he was more commonly referred to as "Alexander the Accursed." A later Zoroastrian text, the *Greater Bundahisn,* in bemoaning the fall of Persia to the Greeks, mentions neither the "courtesan" nor the conga line, but describes how the emperor Alexander: "...destroyed all the families of rulers, magi, and public men of Iranshahr [Persia], extinguished an immense number of sacred fires, seized the commentary (zand) and Revelation of Mazda-worship, and sent it to Arum, burned the Avesta, and divided Iranshahr among ninety petty rulers."[14]

The Magi in the Hellenistic World
East vs. West

The burning of Persepolis marked yet another turning point in world history. The fall of the Achaemenids, followed soon after by the untimely death of Alexander himself, meant the sudden refracturing of the ancient world, as Alexander's generals fell to fighting among themselves. The vast, imperial mosaic the Persians had so painstakingly crafted shattered back into a thousand warring pieces; an inauspicious beginning for the Hellenistic Age.

Although the eventual ascendancy of Greek culture, at its best and its worst, throughout the former empire, has been exhaustively chronicled elsewhere, Cumont reminds us that "the civilization of the Greeks had never succeeded in establishing itself among the Persians.... The significant fact which dominates the entire history of Hither Asia is that the Iranian world and the Græco-Latin world remained forever unamenable to reciprocal assimilation...."[15]

That is not to say that both sides did not continue to imitate and learn from each other, as they had all along in a long-standing cultural feedback loop. At the same time, an increasingly polarized opposition developed between east and west (or as the Greeks would have it, between civilization and barbarism), and that opposition is still a central, organizing dynamic running straight through our Western cultural identity. We may argue about exactly where to draw the line today (for example, whether Turkey belongs in the European Union), but we are well aware that it still exists, and many are still as willing to fight to defend it as the Greeks or the crusaders.

In actual practice, the Greeks weren't that different from the Persians. This fabled line between them grows increasingly indistinct with each new analysis, as recent works by Western scholars such as Walter Burkert and M.L. West have emphasized. The Seleucid and Ptolemaic dynasties that succeeded Alexander were hardly models of enlightened democracy and science, nor champions of freedom, but the myth of their cultural superiority has fueled Western chauvinism ever since, and continues to do so; for instance in the monstrous stereotypes of the popular film *300*.

So what became of the Magi after Alexander? The loss of Achaemenid support could have spelled their doom, but the Magi proved surprisingly resilient instead. They carried on, for as Cumont puts it:

> ...after the dismemberment of the empire of Alexander (323 BC), there were established in Pontus, Cappadocia, Armenia, and Commagene, dynasties which the complaisant genealogists of the day feigned to trace back to the Achæmenian kings. Whether these royal houses were of Iranian extraction or not, their supposititious descent nevertheless imposed upon them the obligation of worshipping

the gods of their fictitious ancestors. In opposition to the Greek kings of Pergamon and Antioch, they represented the ancient traditions in religion and politics. These princes and the magnates of their *entourage* took a sort of aristocratic pride in slavishly imitating the ancient masters of Asia.[16]

The Magi served these new masters, never ceasing to agitate for the return of the divinely ordained empire of old, and becoming, in general, a real thorn in the side of the Greeks.

The Magi were well-positioned for such work. Although the bulk of their population was still concentrated in the traditional Median territories, and in Babylon and Persis, they were also well-established in communities all along the Mediterranean and throughout Asia Minor. They may have originally had been sent abroad to serve the Empire in administrative or religious functions, but the *Magoi* also possessed a particular penchant for proselytizing, and were not averse to going forth and spreading their message among strangers. In Yasna 42, which presumably dates from the Achaemenid period, we find the request that loyal Persians offer sacrifices for the safety of the *Magoi*, "as they go from afar to those who seek righteousness in the lands."[17]

Pliny the Elder listed some of the lands where the *Magoi* were settled: Persis, Arabia, Ethiopia, and Egypt. To his list can be added Armenia, India, Syria, Cappadocia, western Anatolia, Ephesus, Elephantine in Egypt, Susa in Elam, Sardis in Lydia, Pontus, Galatia, and Phrygia.[18] Eddy adds that "The magoi lived under a special law which, like the Holiness Code of Leviticus, maintained the ritual purity of a select group; consequently, they maintained their separate identity far into the historical period, living apart from the rest of society in their own groups...."[19]

St. Basil, the fourth-century Bishop of Caesarea, confirms this, for he reports in his letter to Epiphanius on the presence of sequestered Magian communities in Cappodocia even in his day:

> The Magussaeans...are here in considerable numbers, scattered all over the country, settlers having long ago been introduced into these parts from Babylon. Their manners are peculiar, as they do not mix with other men. It is quite impossible to converse with them, inasmuch as they have been made the prey of the devil to do his will. They have no

books; no instructors in doctrine. They are brought up in senseless institutions, piety being handed down from father to son. In addition...they object to the slaying of animals as defilement, and they cause the animals they want for their own use to be slaughtered by other people. They are wild after illicit marriages; they consider fire divine, and so on....[20]

Even as late as the fourth century CE, we can still recognize many of the customs attributed to the Magi by ancient writers; for instance, their seclusion and ritual purity, the worship of fire, abstention from the slaughter of animals, reliance on oral tradition, the hereditary inheritance of the priesthood, and of course, their most controversial characteristic: the illicit marriages the good bishop says they were "wild after."

To the consternation of the rest of the ancient world, the Magi insisted on marrying within the family. To some extent, they maintained the same royal marriage customs of the Achaemenids and the Egyptian dynasties, whose kings married their own sisters whenever possible, to keep their bloodlines pure and reduce fighting over inheritance and succession. In fact, the Magi were routinely accused of marrying not only their sisters, but their mothers and their daughters. Whether this was true, or yet another example of Greek propaganda, is still debated, but, as they say, where there's smoke, there's sacred fire.

At this point, it would be fair to ask exactly what the Magi believed and what sort of doctrines they held, for the teachings attributed to them are quite diverse. They traveled widely, sought out, and were much sought out themselves, and as wise men and professional sages, probably maintained an interest in all useful knowledge. At the same time, there were distinct Iranian traditions of their order that set them apart.

Traditional Median Beliefs?

We have no primary sources on the earliest Magian religion. The best we can do is speculate upon a possible Median origin for some of the more unique features of the Medo-Persian religion, in which a fusion of native Magian and ancient Iranian beliefs can be assumed. For instance, A.T. Olmstead maintained that the "Antidemonic Laws" contained within the *Vivedat,* or *Vendidad* (literally, the laws, *datem,* against the *daevas,* or demons) still "retain the essential features of this prehistoric culture."[21]

The world of the *Vivedat* was teeming with wicked demons of every stripe—all the creatures of Angra Mainyu, ready to torment man and his useful animals at any opportunity. The strictest precautions had to be maintained to foil the constant threats of death, disease, and crop failure. These precautions usually combined elaborate Magian rituals along with basic public health measures such as mandatory quarantine and a good scrubbing.

The worst demon of all was *Nasu Druj*—the corpse demon, who enters a body as the soul departs. Precise measures had to be taken to protect the community—as well as the earth, water, and fire—from the defilement of a corpse, and it is from this dread fear of *Nasu Druj* that the Magi's distinct burial customs evolved. To this day, orthodox Zoroastrians refuse to bury or burn their dead, but instead expose their corpses on isolated hilltop towers where wild animals and birds eventually pick the bones clean of all potential contaminants.

Olmstead claims that this material is depressing and permeated with the taint of the charnel house, but I beg to differ. There is an astounding mix of ritual magic and public sanitation throughout, along with what are perhaps the most primitive insights into the germ theory of disease. Although the Magi believed demons were responsible for causing death and disease, they were still trying to do a lot of the right things to stop it from spreading (even if their insistence on ritual washing with sacred ox urine may have been somewhat counterproductive).

The purity codes of the *Vivedat* reveal that Magian dualism was not entirely capricious or esoteric. Some things were good, such as sunshine, fresh air, and clean water, and led to health and prosperity. These were the gifts of Ahura Mazda. Other things, such as decomposing corpses and menstrual blood were not, and spread death and disease by contact. That putrid state was the work of Angra Mainyu and his demons, and every effort had to be made to separate the community from their evil effects. There was a lot of common sense at the bottom of this mountain of rules and rituals, even if it was taken to fanatical extremes by the faithful.

The Magi in Babylon

The Magi were also closely identified with the Chaldeans, the famous seers and wise men of Babylon, and the two names were often used interchangeably by Classical authors. The meeting of the Magi and the

Chaldeans dates from at least the late seventh century BCE, when the Medes joined forces with the Chaldeans to battle the Assyrian Empire. The two nations forged a close alliance, with royal intermarriages and diplomatic exchanges that would have, in all likelihood, brought the Magi and the Chaldean holy men together on numerous brilliant occasions. This same period—the late seventh and sixth century—was unique in the development of mathematical astronomy and the use of the zodiac to track planetary positions. The combined wisdom of both cultures can be seen in the rapid advances taking place in that sphere.

Although this alliance eventually fell apart, as all alliances do, the Magi and the Chaldeans drew even closer during the Persian period. Once Cyrus captured Babylon (539 BCE), the great city became a center of Persian administration, and the Magi were stationed in positions of supervisory authority over the Chaldeans. As Cumont describes it, "Babylon, in particular, being the winter residence of the sovereigns, was the seat of a numerous body of official clergy, called *Magi*, who sat in authority over the indigenous priests. The prerogatives that the imperial protocol guaranteed to this official clergy could not render them exempt from the influence of the powerful sacerdotal caste that flourished beside them."[22]

The Chaldeans' mysterious preoccupations with magic, as well as their skill in the sciences (astronomy, mathematics, and music), would have all been familiar to the Magi, and this proved to be a fruitful and lasting collaboration.

So from the sixth century on, the Magi are frequently identified by foreign authors not only with the Chaldeans, but with Babylon, and accounted as masters of all the magic and mystery to be found there. Thus, Iamblichus, in recounting the education of Pythagoras, says that after spending 22 years studying astronomy and geometry in the temples of Egypt: "At length, however, he was taken captive by the soldiers of Cambyses, and carried off to Babylon. Here he was overjoyed to be associated with the Magi, who instructed him in their venerable knowledge, and in the most perfect worship of the gods. Through their assistance, likewise, he studied and completed arithmetic, music, and all the other sciences."[23]

Van der Waerden believed that all the sacred geometry, music, and number mysticism attributed to Pythagoras was actually derived from the teachings of the Babylonians and the Magi, and that he served as one of the most important links between the teachings of the Magi and the later Greek schools.[24]

The identification of the Magi with the Chaldeans in Babylon is even more apparent in this excerpt from the Menippus by the second-century C.E. author Lucian: "I resolved to go to Babylon and address myself to one of the Magi, the disciples and successors of Zoroaster, as I had heard that with certain charms and ceremonials they could open the gates of Hades, taking down in safety anyone they would and guiding him back again.... On my arrival I conversed with one of the Chaldeans, a wise man of miraculous skill, with grey hair and a very majestic beard; his name was Mithrobarzanes."

Although Lucian went to Babylon in search of the Magi, he was content to find a Chaldean bearing a Persian name. As is evident here, the Magi and Chaldeans were reputed to have the magical ability to lead souls down to the underworld, as well as up, through the ascending planetary realms, into the empyrean. The freeing of the soul from its material case, and its journey through forbidden realms, figures into many later magical and hermetic texts, attesting to the influence of both the Magi and the Chaldeans throughout the philosophy and mystery cults of the Hellenistic and Classical world.

The Teachings of the Prophet Zoroaster

According to Mary Boyce, "Zoroastrianism is the oldest of the revealed world-religions, and it has probably had more influence on mankind, directly and indirectly, than any other single faith."[25] Still, "Zoro-what?" is the response of your average Westerner, but if you believe in, or have ever believed in, (1) God and the Devil, (2) Heaven and Hell, (3) the Last Judgment, (4) the Resurrection of the Dead, (5) Angels and Demons, (6) the Holy Spirit, (7) the Virgin Birth of the Savior, or (8) the Ultimate Battle between Good and Evil at the End of the World, then you can thank the Persian prophet, Zoroaster, and the Magi for that. Also, you may have a lot more in common with Muslims than you realize.

Many different people practiced some form of Zoroastrianism, or "Mazda-worship," for a long time over a very large territory. There was tremendous diversity in practice and development, but that is equally true of Christianity, Judaism, or Buddhism. So, when describing the Zoroastrian religion, and the beliefs and practices of its adherents, we want to avoid the reductionist tendency of speaking in broad generalities as if some kind of orthodoxy prevailed, and, whenever possible, try to be specific regarding time and place.

The prophet Zoroaster presents several unique problems to any historian. To begin with, he was perhaps the most influential sage of the pre-Socratic age. The astronomer Eudoxus of Cnidos was often credited with introducing Zoroastrian philosophy and its cosmic implications to the Greeks, along with the idea of its almost inestimable antiquity. Diogenes Laertius recounts that:

> From his age to that of Alexander, king of the Macedonians, were forty-eight thousand eight hundred and sixty-three years, and during this time there were three hundred and seventy-three eclipses of the sun, and eight hundred and thirty-two eclipses of the moon. Again, from the time of the Magi, the first of whom was Zoroaster the Persian, to that of the fall of Troy, Hermodorus the Platonic philosopher, in his treatise on Mathematics, calculates that fifteen thousand years elapsed. But Xanthus the Lydian says that the passage of the Hellespont by Xerxes took place six thousand years after the time of Zoroaster, and that after him there was a regular succession of Magi under the names of Ostanes and Astrampsychos and Gobryas and Pazatas, until the destruction of the Persian empire by Alexander.[26]

No one takes those dates very seriously now. In fact, the trend among scholars in the mid 20th century was to date the prophet Zoroaster as late as the sixth century BCE, or just before the rise of Cyrus the Great! There is no mistaking the arrival of Mazda worship on the world stage with the advent of the Achaemenids—particularly Darius the Great—and some place the prophet at the court of Hystapes, the father of Darius.

Hystapes, or Vistaspa, was a fairly common name, and legends tell of an earlier king Vistaspa, who, as the first patron and protector of the new religion, sheltered the prophet at his court. Whether this same king was the father of Darius is still open to debate.

As there is no denying that the reign of Darius the Great coincided with a surge of official Mazda worship, it is not unreasonable to assume that his family may have housed such a teacher. However, it has also been proposed that there were several Zoroasters, or that "Zarathushtra" became a title that gifted prophets claimed; one of whom may have held sway in Darius's childhood home.

The evidence of the Gathas is critical here. The Gathas are a collection of hymns, or sacred, mantic poetry, believed to have been composed by Zoroaster himself. The Gathas are a window into the mind of the man, and express the earliest form of the Zoroastrian ideas of heaven and hell, of a last judgment and resurrection, of the coming world saviors, and of the idea that the inevitable course of time and human destiny is leading up to an apocalyptic battle between good and evil at the end of the world.

The Gathas are radiant in their vision and simplicity. In these achingly personal revelations, we witness the passion of a prophet seeking justice in a primitive, violent society. Zoroaster is alone and abandoned, an exile, driven out from his kin for his radical religious beliefs. His personal problems are legion: no home, no herds, no honor, no future—but these are nothing compared to his concern for the suffering of his people.

The author of the *Gathas* obviously lived in an archaic society recently converted from nomadic wandering to a settled life of domestic herding and primitive agriculture. His people were subject to constant, brutal attacks from roving bands of cattle rustlers. These predators held to an older, polytheistic nature religion that Zoroaster desperately sought to supersede. Zoroaster calls them Daeva-worshippers, because of their ritualistic devotion to diverse nature spirits (the Vedic Devas).

In contrast, Zoroaster strove to uplift men's minds in contemplation of an overarching grand deity, the epitome of truth, justice, and wisdom. His constant exhortations to live peaceably in a community of laws, and to tend carefully to the needs of domestic animals, provide a startling glimpse into this turning point in human civilization.

Mary Boyce, one of the most renowned scholars of Zoroastrianism and early Iranian languages, pointed out that the old Avestan language of the *Gathas*, which was preserved in oral tradition long after it fell out of general use, is so similar to the language of the Indian *Rigveda* that they must have been composed around the same time. The combination of this archaic social context, and the linguistic evidence, convinced Boyce to argue that the Zarathustra who wrote the *Gathas* must have lived no later than about 1200 BCE, and possibly even earlier, between 1400 and 1200 BCE.[27]

Zoroastrian Priests

Once the Persian Empire had settled down under Darius the Great, the Magi also settled into their role as the official priests of the Persian

Zoroastrian religion. It's entirely possible that the Zoroastrian religion had its own separate history, originating long before the introduction of the Magi. It's equally possible that the *Magoi* had been a priestly caste for many generations before they assimilated into Zoroastrianism. Their absorption into the fold probably had some significant impact on the future development of the Zoroastrian religion, and vice versa. In their role as official priests, they became forever identified with the dualism, the messianism, and the apocalyptic eschatology of Zoroastrianism, as well as with the political support of the divine rights of the Achaemenid Empire.

Achaemenid Imperial Ideology

Even though Babylon and the Iranian territories fell under the dominion of the Seleucid dynasty (311 BCE) after the death of Alexander, there was always resistance—particularly religious resistance—to Hellenistic rule. The legitimacy of the Achaemenid kings had been founded in their all-encompassing imperial religion, for they ruled only as regents for Ahura Mazda, the high god of heaven, as part of his divine order. The wholly secular impositions of Greek rule meant that evil had triumphed over good, and all good men should fight it. A pervasive religious resistance ensued, often peacefully coexisting with political and economic compliance. The Magi led the way, spearheading the opposition to the Greeks, and the Romans after them, never ceasing to assert the god-given rights of the fallen Achaemenids, and prophesying their return to glory.

The Magi's reputation as astrologers and diviners was put to good use in this cause. Employing the great cycles of Jupiter and Saturn within their own unique astrological millennialism, their prophecies rang throughout the Hellenistic world. Wherever Greeks ruled, hope reigned as well, as word spread of the imminent coming of the promised one—part Zoroastrian world savior, part Achaemenid emperor—who would free the faithful from the bonds of foreign rule and restore the world to its rightful order.

Samuel Eddy, in *The King Is Dead: Studies in the Near Eastern Resistance to Hellenism, 334–31 BC,* a genuinely insightful work detailing Persian religious propaganda against Hellenistic rule, assesses the role of the *Magoi* in its origin and spread:

> The royal prerogatives of the *magoi* and the very close association of these priests with the Persian dynasty show that they were the source of the obviously religious

propaganda and prophecies. Since all of it deals with the re-establishment of the Persian kings as representatives of Ahura Mazdah, it must have been the work of a group deeply interested in kings and Ahura Mazdah. Furthermore, since similar Persian propaganda appears in Anatolia, Babylonia, and Judah, it must have been disseminated by Persians who had a common background of ideas and interests and who were at the same time located in these places. The only Persians who could have met these prerequisites were the *magoi*.[28]

It is in this capacity that the Magi appear in Matthew, seeking a heaven-sent king to overthrow the hated Romans, and wielding sufficient astrological acumen to know that his time had come. Whether or not these gift-bearing priests actually had the foresight to seek out the baby Jesus, it was well worth it for Matthew to include them.

Chapter 4
Empire of the Soul

The Masters of Religious Propaganda

Even though the Persians fielded the mightiest armies on earth, their greatest conquests lay in the hearts and minds of subject peoples. History teaches an important lesson in the fact that Babylon fell to Cyrus the Great (539 BCE), and Egypt to Darius the Great (c. 518 BCE), with only token resistance, after the skillful onslaught of Persian propaganda. As Berquist describes it, "Like Cyrus before him, Darius used religion and native traditions to construct an image of the Persian emperor as beneficent ruler, causing significant portions of the local population to ally themselves with Persia without military expenditures."[1]

Upon entering Babylon and Egypt, both Cyrus and Darius were proclaimed the rightful ruler, chosen by the traditional gods. Olmstead remarked on how the famous oracles of Apollo, and their priests, came over to the Persian cause: "...the fact remains that both Apollo of Miletus and Apollo of Delphi for the next half-century remained consistent friends of the Persians."[2]

The two emperors claimed to be restoring the ancient, ancestral ways, in contrast to their vanquished predecessors.[3] They were actually establishing something quite new and different, but historiography worked to their advantage. Of course it also helped that their massive armies were waiting in the wings, but contemporary warlords could still learn a lot from these two.

Cyrus the Great built skillful alliances with various interest groups in Babylon long before his troops ever entered the city. One of his more strategic moves was to enlist the support of the priests of Marduk, the traditional chief god of Babylon. Nabonidus, the ruling Chaldean king, had alienated this powerful priesthood, and proved to be something of a religious dabbler, more intent upon advancing the cult of the moon god, Sin, instead of Marduk. Cyrus seized the opportunity this presented.

Portraying himself as the friend of Marduk, and as the one chosen by the gods to liberate Babylon from the sacrilegious outrages of mad Nabonidus, Cyrus and his troops were welcomed into the great city.[4] By promoting and restoring the traditional religion, and visibly participating in the major festivals and rituals, Cyrus redirected all religious attention his way, fulfilling and remaking the expectations of the priesthood and the faithful at the same time.

Cyrus and Darius have been described as religious chameleons, posing as faithful adherents to any set of beliefs that would advance the causes of their empire. Of course, there are other ways to interpret this behavior, which Thomas M. Bolin describes as "a continual interplay between political motives couched in religious terms and religion used for political ends."[5] These two leaders both possessed a remarkably universal perspective on religion and politics; a grand, overarching worldview into which other nations and their gods were easily slotted into place. Tom Thompson has aptly termed it "inclusive monotheism,"[6] as opposed to the later "exclusive monotheism" of Judeo-Christianity. This inclusive, all-encompassing ideology led the Persians to conquer and stitch together the diverse nations of the ancient world into one, embracing all the fractured pantheons of polytheism into a greater global vision of the first truly universal world empire.

The God of Heaven

The high god of the Persians, Ahura Mazda, reigned supreme over heaven and earth, but also allowed to each his own, as did the emperors. Although plainly distinguishing their universal god of spirit from the tribal, regional, and lesser local deities, the Persians initially accepted these other "gods" as manifestations of, or "regional refractions"[7] of their "god of heaven."

We know very little about Cyrus's personal beliefs. The evidence is simply lacking. But the fact that he had a tomb is evidence that he did not follow the Magi's unique funerary rituals, and the theological language of the Cyrus cylinder seems directed at reassuring the priests of Marduk and their traditional Babylonian coreligionists. However, Darius's own inscriptions repeatedly declare his personal dedication to Ahura Mazda. In his official biography, he credits Ahura Mazda for all his success; or to be more specific, "Ahura Mazda and all the gods."[8] By repeatedly using this phrase, he gives the impression of a new kind of hierarchy; not another Canaanite Divine Council, but something more along the lines of a theological Persian Empire, complete with divine satrapies. Ahura Mazda was the universal, heavenly creator god, ruling over all, like the Emperor, and "all the gods," the local deities, had more limited duties in respect of their traditional tribes or regions. These local deities had their proper place in the grand scheme, but they could no more aspire to be God, or Ahura Mazda, than the governor of Yehud could hope to be emperor.

To the extent that the local deities maintained and promoted the good works of Ahura Mazda—protecting the Truth, resisting the Lie, and demonstrating loyalty to the empire—then they were participating in the grand plan to increase good and destroy evil, and all creation would benefit over time. On the other hand, if the local deities and their religious followers did evil and told Lies, especially against the empire, then they had obviously gone over to the dark side, and like snakes and scorpions, warranted extermination. Consequently, we find the Persians both restoring and destroying temples throughout their realm, even ones they had previously restored. The bottom line was the good behavior of the priests; in other words, their loyalty to the empire. This was as true in Yehud as anywhere else.

As Samuel Eddy described it in *The King is Dead*, the Persians' empire ruled one world, within one state, under one God—Ahura Mazda. Preserving the integrity of that state, under Ahura Mazda, was the theological rationale behind both Darius's and Xerxes' attempts to invade Greece and suppress the Ionian revolts. These were not the usual wars of aggression. The Persians came, not for loot or tribute necessarily, but rather to fulfill the will of their one god that there be one, peaceful world state.[9]

This was the *pax Achaemenica*, as Richard Frye so deftly put it: "If one were to assess the achievements of the Achaemenid Persians, surely the concept of One World,...the fusion of peoples and cultures in one 'Oecumen' was one of their important legacies."[10] The Achaemenid successors of Cyrus and Darius felt a duty to enforce respect for their one god throughout that *Oecumen*. Any form of revolt had a theological origin in some lesser, local deity raising a "'would-be Imperial head.'"[11] At the same time, as long as the local deities remained well-behaved, in respect to their proper place in the *Oecumen*, the "inclusive monotheism" of the Persians exercised its influence by allowing their cults to carry on.

Cyrus as Messiah

The priests of Marduk were not the only clergy to help the Persians into Babylon. Cyrus also worked his skills on the community of Judean exiles, receiving their enthusiastic support. So much of this fascinating process has been lost to history, but it still survives in the biblical canon, if you know where to look. The best place to start is the second part of the book of Isaiah, Deutero-Isaiah, chapters 40–56. Here, the prophet Isaiah proclaims Cyrus as a messiah, and Yahweh's chosen instrument in His plan to free the Jews. This is one of the most naked examples of Persian religious propaganda still extant.

"Redactors" tried to pass these writings off as the inspired utterances of the famous eighth century prophet, Isaiah. That is how it is presented in the Bible, even to this day. In fact, these chapters were probably composed in Babylon sometime around the time of Cyrus's conquest (538 BCE), specifically to whip up Judean support for his reign. The texts would have been worked over to make them fit into the context of the other Isaiah material. They got away with it for more than 2,000 years.

Both Christianity and Judaism have long taught that Cyrus himself read these "prophetic" words of Isaiah, and that's how he was inspired to free the Jews.[12] The Jewish historian, Josephus, writing in the first century CE, obviously still believed this:

> This was known to Cyrus by his reading the book which Isaiah left behind him of his prophecies; for this prophet said that God had spoken thus to him in a secret vision: "My will is, that Cyrus, whom I have appointed to be king over many and great nations, send back my people to their own land, and build my temple." This was foretold by Isaiah one hundred and forty years before the temple was demolished. Accordingly, when Cyrus read this, and admired the Divine power, an earnest desire and ambition seized upon him to fulfill what was so written; so he called for the most eminent Jews that were in Babylon, and said to them, that

he gave them leave to go back to their own country, and to rebuild their city Jerusalem, and the temple of God, for that he would be their assistant, and that he would write to the rulers and governors that were in the neighborhood of their country of Judea, that they should contribute to them gold and silver for the building of the temple, and besides that, beasts for their sacrifices.[13]

"Isaiah," Josephus, and Ezra all omit the fact that Cyrus liberated many captive peoples and their gods from Babylon, without any particular prompting from Yahweh. The Jews do not even appear among the extensive lists of liberated peoples that Cyrus published to commemorate the act. This freeing of slaves and captive peoples, and the return of captured idols to their native sanctuaries, is magnanimous in comparison with the bloody-minded policies of previous conquerors, but was all part of the Persians' long-term plans for their empire.

Cyrus the Great was a humanitarian and progressive leader, obviously way ahead of his time. Still, if he presented himself as the fulfillment of a subject people's religious expectations, the bottom line is that he did so largely in order to get them to do what he wanted. What Cyrus wanted was to fortify his new empire's far-flung borders with loyal colonies. In accomplishing this, Cyrus and his successors also left an indelible Persian stamp on these colonies, particularly on Judean culture and religion.

The very act of returning the captured gods to their native sanctuaries was a religious revolution in its own right. For how did all these gods come to be in Babylon in the first place? They came as captives when their territories were conquered and absorbed into the greater empire. This was the tradition, since at least the time of Ashur, the Assyrian Empire's great "King of the Gods."

In the wake of Assyrian victories, the head deities of conquered territories were demoted in status and carried away. The Assyrians would then inform the local populace that their gods had "been defeated and were now subservient to Ashur, or that their gods had abandoned them either out of anger or in submission to the superior might of Ashur."[14] The Assyrians would even occasionally return a captured idol to its owner, but only after it had been reinscribed and rededicated to the service of Ashur. In this way, the various local pantheons and divine councils were scattered and broken up in the service of empire; their chief gods demoted to second-rate servants in the train of the imperial high god, and their lesser deities forever lost in the process. This was a significant step on the long road to monotheism, and one that, as of 722 BCE, directly affected the gods of Israel and Judah and their divine councils. Throughout this process, Ashur, the high god of the empire, by the late eighth century, had evolved into "Ashur, father of the gods, lord of all countries, king of all heaven and earth, progenitor [of all], lord of lords...."[15]

When the Assyrian Empire eventually fell, the neo-Babylonians (Chaldeans) continued in the same vein, although they proclaimed the Babylonian god Marduk, "King of the gods," in place of Ashur. By the time of King Nabonidus, the Chaldeans had an extensive collection of gods gathered in submission to Marduk in Babylon; among them, Judah's Yahweh. For Cyrus to decree their return and order the rebuilding of their sanctuaries, was an extraordinary act; a stroke of genius revealing his unique character as a ruler. For now, unlike his Assyrian and Chaldean predecessors, he need not fear the restoration of their cults, for those cults would be forever in his debt, and continue to pray for him for ages to come. He not only bought himself a lot of love, but he also leveraged a lot of input into exactly how those cults would be restored.

Historically, the Persian kings retained that right, and continued their input into "...the cults within the state, over which the Great King could exercise control. Artaxerxes intervened in the dispute between his governor Tattenai and the elders of the Jews. Dareios II authorized the keeping of the Festival of Unleavened Bread by his Hebrew mercenary soldiers at Elephantine. The satrap Pherendates, an officer of Dareios I, supervised the appointment of priests for the Egyptian god Khnum."[16]

What began with acceptance usually ended in a makeover, as the Persians' superior foresight, insight, and influence were brought to bear, gradually bringing their subjects' beliefs more in line with their own. Ahura Mazda was not unaffected in all of this, and in adjusting to his ever-expanding role, took on more and more of the imperial iconography of the Assyrian high god, Ashur.

We still live with the results today. With time, and in the service of ever-expanding empires, the elaborate pantheons of polytheism gradually collapsed and coalesced around a single, masculine head deity—the high god of heaven, who was not merely the "king of the gods" but "the great god who gave [us] this earth, who gave us this sky, who gave us humanity, and who gave his worshippers prosperity."[17] This was the incalculable influence of the Persian combination of imperialism and inclusive

Ahura Mazda, from the Behistun inscription. *Image in public domain.*

A stone relief of the Assyrian imperial god, Ashur. *Image in public domain.*

monotheism, and it is as evident in the emergence of Zeus and Jove, as of Jehovah. Even M.L. West, in *The East Face of Helicon*, remarks on the appearance in the fifth century, in Aeschylus's later plays, the *Supplices* and the *Oresteia*, of "predicates and attributes of Zeus that do not appear earlier, and which derive from Near Eastern theology."

The Axial Empire

Persian inclusive monotheism marked both the culmination and the resolution of a growing political and spiritual crisis. Somewhere between the twilight of the Assyrian Empire and the death of Darius the Great came the dawn of the Axial Age, that well-defined historical pivot point, which, as did Cyrus and Darius, pierced right through the middle of the sixth century BCE.[18]

At this crucial juncture, humanity was collectively awakening to all the greater possibilities of being more fully human and truly divine, and of housing an immortal soul within the trappings of our mortality. The awareness of an infinitely more "real" world of spirit and ideals, of timeless truths and moral values, was taking hold, forming a stark contrast to the major preoccupation of polytheism: the petty wrangling of men and gods. Mankind was coming of age; outgrowing the cluttered polytheism of the ancient world, with its ever-changing arrays of gods in human form, its divine councils, incestuous pantheons, and thronging armies.

This crisis between old and new, between the death of the gods and the birth of philosophy and religion, took many centuries to work itself out. The pivotal religious and philosophical developments of the period still bear witness to it; for example, the emergence of Greek philosophy and literature, openly questioning and critical of the gods of Hesiod and Homer; the emergence of Buddhism and Jainism as alternatives to the elaborate polytheism of India; the emergence of both the Confucian and Taoist schools in China; the emergence of a mathematical, rather than mythological, astronomy in Assyria and Chaldea; and the eventual emergence of an exclusive monotheism from the Second Temple in Jerusalem.

The rise of the Persian Empire, and the policies employed in its administration of the multitude of provinces and cults under its jurisdiction represent the very apotheosis of the Axial Age, both temporally and thematically.

And yet, even though Persia was the dominant culture at this most crucial turning point in human development, Persia is still the least acknowledged, least understood, and, at least in the West, the most ignored world empire ever. For example, Tom Holland, in *Persian Fire*, admits: "This is a field in which almost every detail can be debated, and certain themes—the religion of the Persian kings, most notoriously—are bogs so treacherous that even the most eminent scholars have been known to blanch at the prospect of venturing into them."[19] Indeed, M.L. West, in undertaking his groundbreaking examination of Mesopotamian influences on Greek literature declared upfront that "...Persia itself lies beyond the purview of this work...."[20]

Axial Age authors such as Jaspers and Armstrong may have waxed eloquent on the topic of the Hebrew prophets, but they gave Zoroaster and the Persian religion comparatively short shrift. The implication is that real religion began in Judea, and Persia's relevance is limited to that of some dim precursor. Robert Bellah sums up the problem in his otherwise worthwhile article "What is Axial about the Axial Age?" He states that even though the Achaemenid Persian Empire was the largest and most powerful empire of its time; even though it profoundly influenced Judea in the post-exilic, Second Temple period; even though it profoundly influenced the Greeks in their homeland, with lasting "cultural consequences"; even though it profoundly influenced India "at just the moment of axial efflorescence in the Ganges Valley," coinciding with the birth of both Buddhism and Jainism—still, Persia and the Persian religion must remain outside of his discussion of Axial cases.

Why? He cites the enormous disputes over the dating of Zoroaster, about the contents and dating of the Zoroastrian scriptures, about "the degree to which and the way in which Zoroastrianism was institutionalized in Achaemenid Persia," and the very limited sources available. He concludes that although we are left in the "uncomfortable position of recognizing a significant Persian impact" on all aspects of the Axial Age, "Persia itself remains largely a historical cipher."[21]

But Persia is not a cipher. It was absolutely central. The Persian impact on the Axial Age, and on religion itself, is not only as plain as the nose on our faces; it *is* the nose on our faces. The problem is, our eyes are in the wrong place to see it.

Most of the disputes and enormous problems to which Bellah refers as arising from limited sources, have arisen mainly because the material in these limited sources contradicts the very foundations of our Western Judeo-Christian myth. Much of the confusion concerning what Bellah terms "the degree to which and the way in which Zoroastrianism was instituted in Achaemenid Persia" is a direct result of our highly mythologized misunderstanding of the degree to which and the way in which Judaism was instituted in Judea. We have long assumed an ancient and lasting institution for Judean monotheism that never really existed. Consequently, we do get a bit overwhelmed when faced with all the complex historical and sociological facets of Persian religion, spanning so many centuries and so many different cultures. It all seems so messy compared to our myth, but once we grasp that, we have come face to face within that magic mirror, and can begin to see ourselves as we really are.

There is nothing in Bellah's claims that could not be just as appropriately, if not more appropriately, said of ancient Judaism. There is tremendous dispute about the dating of the origins of Judaism, the contents and dating of the Jewish scriptures, and the degree to which and the way in which Judaism was institutionalized in Judea, stemming in large part from the limited sources available. These are the conclusions emerging from contemporary biblical scholarship.

I contend that we really don't want to know the Persians, because everything we learn about them contradicts what we want to believe about the Greeks and the Jews, and, of course, about ourselves. Even now, the most straightforward enquiry into the Persian period can quickly be derailed by meaningless arguments raised by otherwise highly qualified individuals who, for whatever reason, still feel compelled to maintain the streamlined, monolinear myth. The Persian side of the story seriously complicates that simple truth, but we have to come to grips with it. Otherwise, we will remain at war with people we claim we can't understand, but who are actually a lot more similar to us than we care to know. As long as the center remains a cipher, the whole system is unbalanced. If we restore the Persian Empire to its historical role as the central, organizing culture of the Axial Age, all the other pieces suddenly fall much more naturally into place.

The Spread of Persian Ideas: Yahweh Meets Ahura Mazda

Samuel Eddy claims that proselytizing was one of the chief jobs of the Magi,[22] but whether that is true or not, the power of their ideas (let alone their armies) would have been sufficient to spread them. Again, it is Deutero-Isaiah that provides us with some of the best remaining examples of this process, for these same books (Ch. 40–56) that prepared the Judean exiles for the advent of Cyrus and his resettlement plans, also significantly refine and redefine Yahweh's image.

For instance, Yahweh, the Bedouin warlord *cum* guardian of Judea, is exalted in Deutero-Isaiah as a sky-god, a god of heaven, and repeatedly extolled as a universal creator who rolled out the heavens like a curtain, and before whom the great princes of the earth are but willing pawns. The attributes ascribed to Yahweh distinctly parallel Persia's universal sky-god, Ahura Mazda.[23] At the same time, Deutero-Isaiah is oddly lacking in specific references to the presumably earlier creation stories of Genesis.[24]

Further, there is no mistaking the emphasis in Deutero-Isaiah on the sins of idolatry. The author complains at length about the Babylonian practice of making and bowing before idols, insisting that devotion to the abstract, creator sky-god is not only theologically superior, but also guarantees better results. Surprisingly, in all of this instruction against idolatry, there is no appeal to the authority of Mosaic Law or the Ten Commandments. The second commandment plainly states, "thou shalt not make unto thee any graven images, etc.," and yet Deutero-Isaiah makes no mention of this, even when it would undoubtedly have strengthened his arguments.

The "minimalist" position is that the Jews of that time had no Law of Moses. That all came later. Even the historian A.T. Olmstead believed that Ezra introduced the still unknown Law (Torah) of Moses to the Jerusalem colony when he arrived with his new book of laws, some 100 years after Deutero-Isaiah.[25]

Regardless of when the Jews received the Law of Moses, while Solomon's First Temple was reputedly brimming with graven imagery, the people most famous for eschewing idolatry in the ancient world were the Persians. The Greek historian, Herodotus, wrote reams about the Persians in his *Histories* (circa 430 BCE), but one of the first things he says in describing them is this: "The customs which I know the Persians to observe are the following: they have no images of the gods, no temples, nor altars, and consider the use of them a sign of folly. This comes, I think, from their not believing the gods to have the same nature with men, as the Greeks imagine. Their wont, however, is to ascend the summits of the loftiest mountains, and there to offer sacrifice to 'Zeus,' which is the name they give to the whole circuit of the firmament."[26]

Despite his obvious Hellenizing (Zeus?), this overt reference to the "God of Heaven," makes the Persian aversion to idolatry plain. It is the folly of idolatry that Deutero-Isaiah rails against, not Mosaic, legal injunctions against it. Thus, by proclaiming Yahweh a universal, creator sky-god, and condemning idolatry, within the same document that hails Cyrus as God's messiah sent to liberate the Jews, Deutero-Isaiah definitely marks an important developmental stage in the history of Jewish monotheism.

Finally, in making his case for Cyrus to the Judean exiles, Deutero-Isaiah embraces the topic dearest to the hearts of Christians and Jews alike: the "messiah," the one who is to come. In chapter 53, after admonishing the Judeans to hasten back to Jerusalem by the path their god has laid, in language so touching and tender it still moves hearts to confession today, the author introduces the "suffering servant" who is to come:

> (2) He grew up before him like a tender shoot, and like a root out of dry ground. He had no beauty or majesty to attract us to him, nothing in his appearance that we should desire him. (3) He was despised and rejected by men, a man of sorrows, and familiar with suffering. Like one from whom men hide their faces he was despised, and we esteemed him not. (4) Surely he took up our infirmities and carried our sorrows, yet we considered him stricken by God, smitten by him, and afflicted. (5) But he was pierced for our transgressions, he was crushed for our iniquities; the punishment that brought us peace was upon him, and by his wounds we are healed. (6) We all, like sheep, have gone astray, each of us has turned to his own way; and the Lord has laid on him the iniquity of us all (NIV).

Who is Deutero-Isaiah talking about? Christians are sure they know, and have picked up this imagery wholesale in their definition of Jesus and his role, but most Jews are still undecided. Still, there is no mistaking the urgent ascendency of the messianic ideal during the early Persian period. I can't escape the impression that the Jews were somehow encouraged by the Persians in this, especially because many of these references occur in literature that originated in Persian Yehud, such as Deutero-Isaiah, Haggai, and Zechariah.

In referring to the "servant" as a young plant, and as a root out of dry ground, the author may be echoing the prophetic tradition of the "branch," an offshoot of the royal family of David, which we find in the presumably earlier verses of Isaiah 11:1 and Jeremiah 23:5. I must say *presumably*, because with all the redaction going on, it becomes harder and harder to separate the pre- from the post-exilic literature. Any of the writings of the earlier prophets could have been thoroughly shot through with the Second Temple agenda, so it pays to be cautious in dating these references.

This code name, "The Branch," was frequently, although not exclusively, used as a symbol for a "kingly messiah." This hope of a conquering hero to come simmered among the returning exiles, boiling over into widespread revolts well into Matthew's time and beyond. The idea of a monarchical messiah was not limited to Judea, but could be found anywhere Persian propaganda ran up against Seleucid rulers, or indeed, wherever proud men chafed under the rule of strangers. Nor was it an entirely political messianism. The line between church and state was so thinly drawn as to be nonexistent. In many cases, each defined the other, for traditional Near Eastern kingship was god-given, by definition. As many disaffected minorities throughout the Seleucid, Roman, and Parthian territories harbored messianic hopes ranging from a heaven-sent home rule to a return to the full glory of the Achaemenids, the Judeans had their own variations on this theme.

Unlike Persia, Judea had no empire to rule, and no tolerance to extend. Their monotheism, perhaps as a consequence, took a rather self-limiting and self-absorbed turn. The greatest aspiration of their god of heaven was the restoration of the throne of David to unrivaled grandeur, and the conquest of Judea's traditional enemies. To this end, God would send a savior king to Judea, born of David's line. Under his glorious reign, Judea would conquer the world and all other nations would be subject to them—the Persian Empire, redux.

The Persians may have accidentally raised these expectations themselves, when they appointed Zerubbabel the first governor of Yehud. Zerubbabel was thought to be a lineal descendant of David,[27] but any monarchical messianists among the returning exiles would have been deeply disappointed to learn that the Persians had no intention of ever restoring the throne of David. For reasons that have been lost to us, Zerubbabel did not last long in the job. He disappears after building the temple, and Yehud was ruled by loyal Persian governors after that. We can only imagine what happened,[28] but a restored Judean monarchy in Yehud would certainly not have been in the empire's best interests.

But there is another kind of messiah who emerges parallel to the kingly messiah of the monarchists. This messiah is not so much a warrior, as a savior; one who will spread the worship of the One God throughout the world.[29] This was perhaps more in keeping with Zoroastrian expectations of a *Saoshyant*, but as both the Jewish and Persian expectations were subject to various interpretations as time went on, there is no singular, or even straight line of development for us to follow.

Still, the obvious coincidence of messianism and the building of the Second Temple makes me wonder if there was not considerable dialogue between the Persians and the Judeans on this subject. Although the Persians probably discouraged the idea of a Davidic kingly messiah, they may have encouraged the belief in a coming Jewish Saoshyant; one who would vanquish evil and spread the good religion throughout the world.

Even in Matthew's time, the Persians were still an integral part of Jewish messianic hopes, as he plainly depicts in the opening to his gospel. Although the Judean temple cult was developing into an exclusive monotheism that denied any debt to other religions, patriotic Jews still expected Yahweh to cooperate with their Parthian Persian neighbors to the east to bring about the advent of their long-awaited redeemer.

Parthian Persians

"...R. Simeon b. Yohai taught: If you see a Persian horse tethered to a grave in the land of Israel, look out for the coming of the Messiah."

Nearly 600 years before Matthew wrote his gospel, the Persians and their Magi saved Judea from extinction. They protected the colony and oversaw its development for two centuries, exercising great influence in the reconstitution of the Jewish religion. The conquests of Alexander the Great in 331 BCE were the beginning of hard times for both the Persians and the Jews. The Achaemenid years were remembered as the good times, and both the Jews and the Iranians shared a common messianic dream: the coming of a savior king who would destroy the invading foreign powers and restore the rightful rule of God.

The Iranian dream of empire revived under the Parthian Arsacid kings, circa 246 BCE. The Arsacid dynasty eventually liberated much of the old Achaemenid territory from the Greeks, fulfilling the messianic expectations of many Iranian nationalists, while frustrating others; for instance, the more "orthodox" Persians around Pasargadae, who would never be satisfied with anything less than an Achaemenid revival.

The rapid expansion of the Parthian Arsacid kingdom into an empire under Mithradates I (165–140 BCE) tied the hands of the Greeks sufficiently to make the Jewish Maccabean revolt possible—and vice versa. In fact, the year 165 BCE proved pivotal for both houses, as we shall see in later chapters. The Maccabees, a.k.a. the Hasmonean dynasty, ruled Judaea from ca. 140 BCE until 37 BCE. Even though they were not of the tribe of Judah, nor descendants of David, it was the only period of Jewish independence since the Babylonian captivity in 597 BCE. Jacob Neusner, in his seminal work on the Jews in the Parthian period, confirms that the common interests of the Parthian Arsacids and the Hasmoneans were clear and consciously coordinated.[30] Both sides furthered each other's aims during this period, at the increasing expense of the Greek rulers, even if they never staged a united attack.

No sooner had the Judeans and the Parthians succeeded in driving out the Greeks, than the Romans rushed in to take full advantage of the resulting vacuum of power.[31] Although their shared incentive in dismembering Seleucid territories had never resulted in united action, their opposition to the Romans did. As Neusner puts it, "From the middle of the first century BCE, there were Jews in Palestine who looked to Parthia for deliverance from Rome." These were theo-political hopes, intimately bound up with Jewish expectations that "the coming of the Messiah would be heralded by Persian conquest."

The King of the Jews

Consequently, it is a very loaded question that Matthew puts into the mouths of his *Magoi*: "Where is he that is born King of the Jews?"

Conservative Christians, trying to sidestep the astrology issue, contend that Matthew's *Magoi* were a subversive delegation of king makers, sent to rattle Herod, and provoke a potential border incident.[32] After all, the first century historian Strabo says in his *Geographies* that the Magi formed part of the Council of the Parthians, and that one of their duties was the appointment of the king. Incidentally, the Parthians of Matthew's time may have been experiencing a Zoroastrian revival of sorts under the first century Arsacid king Vologeses (r. 51–80 CE). He and his brother, the Magus Tiridates, reputedly began to recompile the Avestan scriptures Alexander had destroyed.[33]

The Magi's visit would have been provocative, all right. The Parthians were the empire's worst enemy, and worst nightmare, in the east. The crack Parthian cavalry units had done what precious few could: beat the Romans in battle, dealing the legions a humiliating defeat at Carrhae in 54 BCE, and forcing Mark Antony into retreat not 15 years later. The Parthians had the best cavalry in the world, and their highly trained archers were famous for turning back in their saddles while galloping off at full speed, and firing off their famous "parting" or "Parthian" shots with deadly accuracy—something to which the Romans were in no hurry to expose more legions.

There are definite political implications behind Matthew's choice of words, which hint at the ongoing alliance of Judean and Persian interests against the Romans. For one thing, there already was a king of the Jews reigning in Jerusalem—Herod the Great—but the crown did not sit easy his head. The Jews hated him. For one thing, he wasn't even Jewish, but Idumean. Herod owed everything to Rome.

It was Mark Antony who made Herod king, in 40 BCE, and as soon as he did, the Parthians invaded and restored a Jewish king to the throne, forcing Herod into exile. Herod wandered far, through Egypt and eventually onto Rome, where in his defense, both Antony and Octavian welcomed him, and the Senate officially declared him "King of Judea" in absentia.

Returning with an army, Herod staged a determined campaign and eventually retook Jerusalem in 37 BCE from the Parthian/Jewish coalition. The restored Herod reigned supreme as *Basileus* thereafter. Some 30 years later, the *Magoi*'s question, as the author of Matthew puts it, would have been a direct affront.

All of this history would have been common knowledge to Matthew's intended audience, but nowadays, most of us need reminding. The fact that the Parthian Persians and their Magi were the allies and supporters of the Jews in their struggle against Roman occupation only underscores the longstanding interdependence of Jewish and Persian interests: religious, political, messianic, and otherwise.

Nothing could have been more calculated to spark that resurgent nationalist fire in the hearts of Judeans than the image in Matthew of Persian Magi confronting the hated Herod with the promise of a real "King of the Jews," chosen by God and written in the stars. The Persians, guided by the same divine wisdom that designed the heavens, had once again come to save Jerusalem, just as they had under Cyrus the Great, the first messiah.

Still, it beggars belief to think that these *Magoi*, presumably wise men, would have the temerity to show up at Herod's place asking, "Where is he that is born King of the Jews? For we have seen his star in the east and are come to worship him."

Herod was a notoriously hard man, who had not scrupled at killing off his own sons at the barest suspicion of any threat to his reign. Had these Persian Magi actually done what Matthew describes, I rather doubt that this second chapter of his gospel would have extended on through verse 16 to Herod's infamous "Slaughter of the Innocents," without at least some mention of his dramatic slaughter of the Magi.[34]

Chapter 5
The Magi and Astrology

The Magi, like the Chaldeans and Druids, serve as a powerful reminder that the origins of modern science lie deep within the machinations of primitive magic. According to Philo Judaeus, an Alexandrian Jew and a contemporary of Christ, the Magi were among the "numerous companies of virtuous and honourable men.... Among the Persians there exists a group, the Magi, who, investigating the work of nature for the purpose of becoming acquainted with the truth...initiate others in the divine virtues, by very clear explanations."[1]

The contemporary astrophysicist Percy Seymour, in *The Birth of Christ, Exploding the Myth*, believes that the Magi: "...initiated an approach to mathematical astronomy that was to influence all later aspects of the subject.... Because they travelled a great deal, they assimilated the astronomical ideas of their neighbouring cultures and blended these ideas with their own...and so were also the transmitters of the ancient wisdom of astronomy, astrology and the religious beliefs based on these subjects."[2]

Astronomy, Astrology, and the Religious Beliefs Based on These Subjects

To understand the Magi, and how they used astrology in both their "science" and religion, we first need to consciously acknowledge that our modern attitudes about what astrology is, and what it is not, differ greatly from the way astrology was perceived in the ancient, classical, and medieval worldview. We make a very firm distinction between astronomy and astrology nowadays, but that was not always the case. In the time of Christ; indeed, up until the time of Newton, anyone who measured the heavens usually divined its meanings as well. More often than not, the very reason they measured the heavens in the first place was to better divine that meaning. We also make a very firm distinction between astrology and religion nowadays, but again this was not always the case. These three— science, religion, and astrology—were intricately intertwined through- out much of human history. Francesca Rochberg makes the same point in *Babylonian Horoscopes*: "Celestial divination, astronomical obser- vation, and astronomical computation represent interdependent parts of a multifaceted and complex tradition of celestial science in ancient Mesopotamia."

Astronomers and Astrology

"Astrology—belief in the physical influence of planetary rays on earth— is one of the most important historical contexts in which astronomy devel- oped. Astrology served as a motivation as well as a means of gainful employment for astronomers."[3] This statement, from the Website for the department of the history and philosophy of science at the University of Cambridge, applies to many of the giants of western astronomy, from Hipparchus and Ptolemy, to Brahe, Kepler, and Galileo.

Johannes Kepler, the mathematical genius who finally solved the mys- tery of planetary motion, was both a devout Christian and a passionate astrologer. As he declared in his masterpiece, the *Harmonices Mundi*, or *Harmony of the World*: "I was merely thinking God's thoughts after him. Since we astronomers are priests of the highest God in regard to the book of nature, it benefits us to be thoughtful, not of the glory of our minds, but rather, above all else, of the glory of God."

Kepler served successfully as court astrologer to the Holy Roman Emperor, a position he inherited from Tycho Brahe, and also as an astro- logical advisor on the military campaigns of General Wallenstein.[4]

Galileo, who made his famous stand against Ptolemy's geocentric (Earth-centered) universe in the 1630s, initially ran afoul of the Church much earlier in his career. In 1604, the Inquisition charged Galileo with practicing excessive fatalism in his astrological forecasts. His high-handed manner in predicting the death of his clients was a specific concern. Galileo served as court astrologer to the Medici family and was much sought after by the nobility for his astrological services. He also taught astrology at the university level. We still have copies of the astrological charts Galileo calculated for the birth of his own daughters, complete with his fatherly notes on their personalities and character.[5]

This kind of information often goes missing in science books, even though astrology was a driving force behind many important developments in astronomy and mathematics. "Mathematicians" such as Brahe, Kepler, and Galileo, were retained by the rich and powerful at great expense in prestigious posts, but the medieval *mathematicus* was quite different from a contemporary "mathematician." Instead, he was an expert in the mathematics and astronomy necessary for the practice of *astrology*. The good ones strove to incorporate the latest advances into their work.

It was an urgent need for greater accuracy in astrology, not some modern dedication to pure science, that inspired many of the mathematicians' most significant discoveries. This was as true for the Magi and Hipparchus as it was for their later European successors. For instance, one of Kepler's and Brahe's jobs as "Imperial Mathematician" to the Holy Roman Emperor Rudolph II was preparing accurate tables of planetary positions and orbits. Now why would the emperor want to pay for that? After all, he wasn't trying to send up a communications satellite or put a man on the moon. What the emperor *needed* was accurate political and economic forecasts. He needed the kind of information rulers have always sought from astrologers, such as the best time to start a war or sign a treaty, whether the price of wheat would rise or fall, and which of his children should succeed him.

However, it was the production of the *Rudolphine Tables* of planetary motion, a job Brahe started and Kepler inherited (and brought to completion in 1627) that ultimately made possible Kepler's most important discoveries. The *Rudolphine Tables*, compiled from many years of painstaking observations, provided Kepler with the data he needed to reach his historic realization that the planets actually moved in elliptical orbits, not perfect Aristotelian circles. Kepler's work as an astrologer not only made his groundbreaking laws of planetary motion possible, but it also made him quite famous. Many of the predictions he made as Imperial Mathematician regarding the weather, the economy, and political events proved to be surprisingly accurate, and so his reputation grew.

"The History of Wretched Subjects"

Nevertheless, the widespread use of astrology by Westerners, particularly Western scientists, has often been willfully excluded from history, especially from the history of science.[6] In 1951, Otto Neugebauer, a true pioneer in the history of the mathematical sciences, threw down the gauntlet on this issue in his landmark essay, "The History of Wretched Subjects." Neugebauer was responding to a scathing review by Professor George Sarton of the Mandean *Book of the Zodiac* by E.S. Drower. Sarton, "a recognized dean of the History of Science," had characterized the text as "a wretched collection of omens, debased astrology and miscellaneous nonsense;...the superstitious flotsam of the Near East."

Neugebauer was outraged, and in this timeless demand for freedom of inquiry, he proclaimed, once and for all, the scientific, historic, and cultural value of "the study of wretched subjects like ancient astrology." Paying tribute to the work already done in the field by the likes of Franz Cumont, Lynn Thorndike, and the Warburg Institute, he emphasized that their contributions had given us rare insight into the "daily life, religion, superstition, astronomical methods, and cosmogonic ideas" of the very fathers of science. He thanked Ms. Drower for her investigations into the Mandean sources, which can only help us to better understand "...all phases of Mediaeval learning, Medicine, Botany, Chemistry, etc."

Neugebauer ended this historic essay with a ringing indictment for all who profess to practice science, reminding Sarton that he was, in fact, undermining the very essence of the scientific method, and destroying the very foundations of any genuine history, instead of pursuing "...the recovery and study of the texts as they are, regardless of our own tastes and prejudices."

The sad truth is that many who claim to be scientific are actually professing *scientism*. Scientism is the belief that modern science is the ultimate and only legitimate form of knowledge. Scientism is often paired with a dogmatic materialism, which automatically dismisses religious, spiritual, psychic, or even emotional experiences as meaningless delusions. That is not science, it's *scientism*. Genuine science recognizes that certain aspects of human experience lie beyond the range of the scientific method, and limits its scope accordingly, even while constantly seeking to expand those limits.

Where scientism has encroached upon the history of science, the result has been a heavy-handed revisionism. Blind faith in *scientistic* dogma led true believers to falsify their own history from day one. Isaac Newton is a case in point. A dedicated Protestant Christian, self-proclaimed Arian heretic, and passionate alchemist, Newton could hardly be accused of scientism. In fact, he had a particular passion, during the latter half of his life, for researching and reconciling ancient chronology with biblical prophecy.

Frank Manuel, who has published extensively on Newton's life and work, elaborates on Newton's public image as an enlightened, thoroughly rational, modern scientist: "That part of the Newtonian system which was related to his puritanical bibliolatry and to his interpretation of prophecy was, of course, rejected by most eighteenth-century intellectuals and for many years was kept hidden as a shameful weakness in their new god."[7]

Shortly after Newton's death in 1727, rumors began to circulate insinuating that Newton suffered a complete breakdown in 1693, and that all of his later works were the products of mental illness. These stories have been traced back to the French astronomers Marquis de Laplace and Jean-Baptiste Biot, two dedicated positivists who were convinced that public knowledge of Newton's real interests would be dangerous to the cause of science.[8] In Cambridge, although Newton's scientific manuscripts in the Portsmouth Collection were readily available for study, access to his materials on chronology and theology was restricted. Even writers of the caliber of Edward Gibbon were prevented from studying Newton's historical and theological manuscripts.[9]

The Western mind remains tragically polarized in the wake of this kind of revisionism. Unable to maintain a balanced, inclusive viewpoint, many still believe it has to be one or the other—science vs. religion, or even science vs. feeling. We must choose which side we are on, and then throw stones at each other across the great divide. In that sense, scientistic fundamentalism has proven as divisive as religious fundamentalism, as in the work of Richard Dawkins, who preaches that science is perfectly good, and religion, its polar opposite, is *The Root of all Evil*, and all right-thinking people should rise up against it.[10]

The reality is that many of our most original scientists, men such as Newton, Roger Bacon, Descartes, or even Einstein, experienced great spiritual satisfaction in their work. There was a poetic, soulful side to their scientific personality that sought expression in astrology, alchemy, magic, or more conventional religious behaviors. They would have had their differences with institutional or orthodox religion, but they certainly didn't experience the split that later revisionists have since projected upon them.

So it was with the Magi and their contemporaries in the ancient world. They had never experienced modernism, or logical positivism, or a Catholic education. The Magi beheld a more holistic, "premodern" cosmos, if you will, but it's best to avoid such labels altogether, lest we fall into the same trap of revising history in our own image. Consequently, in coming to terms with the astrology and ancient science of the Magi, we must first recognize, and then consciously step outside of, our own prejudices and limitations.

Astrology and Religion

Our current split between religion and astrology is also a relatively recent, post-Reformation development. Astrology was Christian cosmology for the first 1,600 years of the Church. It was practiced, taught, and published at the highest levels by priests, monks, abbots, bishops, cardinals, popes, and saints.[11] Many contemporary Christians would hotly dispute the idea of any connection between their religion and astrology, but that is an entirely modern delusion.[12]

A Short List of Famous Christians Who Taught, Published, and/or Practiced Astrology

Pope Sylvester II	Roger Bacon
St. Albertus Magnus	Guido Bonatti
Adelard of Bath	Cardinal Pierre d'Ailly
St. Aldhelm, Bishop of Sherborne	Johannes de Sacro Bosco
	Peter of Albano
Alcuin of York	Catherine de'Medici
Charlemagne	Nostradamus
Roger of Hereford	William Lilly
Geoffrey Chaucer	Christopher Columbus
Michael Scot	Phillip Melancthon

Among the earliest Christian writings, there was considerable argument about astrology, but not about whether the heavenly bodies exercised any influence. That they did was considered common knowledge. The argument was generally over *how*, and *how much*, and what was right and proper to do with that knowledge. "Natural astrology," and the wholesale influence of the sun, moon, and stars over everything from the weather to the infirmities of the body, was rarely the cause of contention. St. Thomas Aquinas, the prince of theologians, patently confirmed this point in his *Summa Theologica*:

> The majority of men follow their passions, which are movements of the sensitive appetite, in which movements of the heavenly bodies can cooperate: but few are wise enough to resist these passions. Consequently astrologers are able to foretell the truth in the majority of cases, especially in a general way. But not in particular cases; for nothing prevents man resisting his passions by his free-will. Wherefore the astrologers themselves are wont to say that "the wise man is stronger than the stars" [Ptolemy, *Centiloquium*, prop. 5], forasmuch as, to wit, he conquers his passions.[13]

Christians saved their invective for *astrologers*, those scandalous rascals whose vain attempts to forecast the future not only made planets into deities and duped the general public, but who also threatened in their boldness to usurp the prerogatives of an almighty God.

Consequently, thinking Christians found themselves in a bit of a dilemma. They wanted to differentiate themselves from the gullibility and excesses of their Pagan neighbors, who were generally quite fond of horoscopes, but Christians also coveted the cosmological implications of astrology's overarching worldview, and not only sought to attribute that orderliness to the hand of God, but also to read the preordained sanctification of their own faith into the cosmic order. Their attempts to reconcile and reattribute these conflicting drives animate many early texts, in which Christians had long-running arguments with fatalistic star worshippers, but the astrological order of the universe, as designed by the hand of God, remained the standard, accepted Christian cosmology.

For instance, the delightful plot of *The Recognitions of Clement*[14] (approx. third century CE) mounts a Christian literary attack on astrologers that confounds the Pagan determination to read an unalterable future in the stars. However, Book 8 of *The Recognitions* contains in chapters 45–46 a most tidy description of natural astrology, attributing to the motions of the sun and moon the causes of everything from good and bad weather to plague and pestilence, accordingly as God chooses to use these, the instruments of his design.

Further, Book 1, chapter 32 contains this most intriguing reference to Abraham: "From the first this same man, being an astrologer, was able, from the account and order of the stars, to recognise the Creator, while all others were in error, and understood that all things are regulated by His providence." In this implication that monotheism itself was born of astrology, within the same work that damns the predictions of horoscopy, the author straddles the very crux of the Christian dilemma.

According to Theodore Wedel, the most influential source of "patristic condemnation of astrology" was the seventh century *Etymologiae* and the *De Natura Rerum* of Isidore of Seville. Isidore, who was recently proclaimed the patron saint of the Internet, continued the same confused stance, both for and against astrology, as his predecessors. He toed the company line in chapter XXVI of the *Etymologiae*, "On the Difference Between Astronomy and Astrology," describing but dismissing the claims of superstitious astrology. However, as Wedel puts it, "Isidore's logic is hardly equal to his learning," for quite a bit of astrology shows through the rest of his work. For instance, Wedel summarizes Isidore's views on medicine, and other natural sciences:

> The good physician, he says, will study astronomy as well as his own art, inasmuch as it is well known that our bodies change with the varying state of the weather and the stars. In the *De Natura Rerum*, Isidore ascribes to the moon an influence over fruits, over the brains of animals, and over oysters and sea-urchins. He even refers to it, in a phrase of unmistakable astrological coloring, as the *dux humentium substantiarum*. The dog-star is said to be a cause of sickness. As for comets, Isidore accepts them without reserve as the prognosticators of revolution, war and pestilence.[15]

Jim Tester, in his *A History of Western Astrology*, adds that in chapter IX of Book VIII of *Etymologiae*, Isidore includes such enticing descriptions of "the fascinating but illicit subject of astrology" that "The idea, at least, of a potentially valid science of astrology was kept alive by the very authorities who condemned it."

Remember, the Inquisition didn't indict Galileo for practicing or teaching astrology. If the Inquisition wanted to prosecute astrologers, they would have had to start with the pope. Urban VIII, the pope who oversaw Galileo's eventual condemnation, was openly dependent upon astrological advisors, but so were a great many occupants of the Chair of St. Peter, including those, such as Sylvester II, who were adept practitioners themselves. In the *Catholic Encyclopedia*, the Church describes its own use of astrology accordingly: "Emperors and popes became votaries of astrology—the Emperors Charles IV and V, and Popes Sixtus IV, Julius II, Leo X, and Paul III." Describing astrology as "the regulator of official life" and "characteristic of the age," the author, Max Jacobi, adds that at the papal and imperial courts, "ambassadors were not received in audience until the court astrologer had been consulted."[16]

Then there were the universities and medical schools. No one practiced medicine without first learning astrology, including Copernicus. Galileo stepped out of line with his excessive determinism, by proudly declaring that his predictions would inevitably come to pass—and that was going too far. The charges were eventually dropped anyway.

Until quite recently, astrology represented the highest expression of religious cosmology. It was universally "holy," whether the "astrologers" in question were Jews, Egyptians, Greeks, Chaldeans, Magi, Hindus, Muslims, or pre-Reformation Christians. This is what Percy Seymour meant in that quote at the beginning of this chapter, when he said the Magi "were also the transmitters of the ancient wisdom of astronomy, astrology and the religious beliefs based on these subjects." For the Magi and their contemporaries, astrology was an integral part of both their religion and their science.

The Magi and the Dawn of Science

The rise to power of the Medes and their Magi in the sixth to eighth centuries BCE coincided with a scientific and religious revolution in Mesopotamia, as the ancient world awoke to newer, more "universal" ways of perceiving the cosmos. The teachings of the prophet Zoroaster, combined with the *Magoi*'s own uniquely dualistic beliefs, directly impacted the development of astronomy and mathematics in its earliest and most critical stages.

The Median Magi were close to the Persians, both culturally and geographically, but they had another important ally in the Chaldeans. The Chaldeans occupied the territory southeast of Babylon, between the rivers. Chaldeans were keen astronomers, and according to J.D. North, "The Greeks were already in Plato's century giving due credit to the 'Magi' or the 'Chaldeans' and throughout the world of classical antiquity these epithets stuck, as synonyms for 'astrologer.'"[17]

The Chaldeans were on the rise by the late eighth century BCE, during the same period when the Medes were coming into their own. The simultaneous development of these two new powers, Media and Chaldea, was no coincidence. Both nations were expanding at the expense of the waning Assyrian Empire; the same Assyrians who destroyed the nation of Israel in 722 BCE. Their empire peaked in the eighth century, and held sway over all of Mesopotamia, but as the seventh century unrolled, it was fast losing its grip over its formal vassals.

The Chaldeans truly arrived on the world stage in 626 BCE when they wrested control of the city of Babylon from the Assyrians, establishing the Chaldean, or Neo-Assyrian dynasty, under their king, Nabopolasser. It was this Chaldean dynasty, specifically their second king, Nebuchadnezzar, who built the Hanging Gardens of Babylon, one of the Seven Wonders of the World. Nebuchadnezzar was also (in)famous for destroying the Judean capital, Jerusalem, and leading the Jews into captivity in Babylon (597 and 586 BCE).

By the late seventh century BCE, the Medes and the Chaldeans recognized that the time was right to drive the Assyrians into the ground. It was all a question of when and how, not if, as the two united in a determined political and military alliance bent on hastening Assyria's demise. In 614 BCE, a crack army under the leadership of the Median king, Cyaxares, advanced and surrounded the Assyrian capital of Ninevah. The Medes couldn't quite take Ninevah that first time, but they made a lasting impression when they withdrew to the south and stormed Ashur, the Assyrian religious capital, instead.

The Medes took this opportunity to further their alliance with the Chaldeans by arranging a dynastic marriage between the granddaughter of Cyaxares and Nebuchadnezzar, the heir to the Chaldean throne in Babylon. This Median princess may well have been the same Amytis for whom Nebuchadnezzar later built the famous Hanging Gardens. Legend has it that he wanted to console her when she grew homesick for the green mountains of Media.

The two upstart empires then renewed their joint assault on Assyria. Ninevah fell to the Medes in late August of 612 BCE, while the Chaldeans were still marching to join them. Together,the Chaldeans and Medes pursued the fleeing Assyrian leaders west into Syria. That was the end of the mighty Assyrian Empire, and the victors carved up the remains between them into a new world order.

In light of all this political and military turmoil, it is not surprising that an astronomical and religious "revolution" swept through the region as well. The changes had begun at the height of the Assyrian Empire, when the king had legions of astronomical observers and advisors at his service; but with the expanding influence of Median and Chaldean culture, the emphasis in astrology/astronomy shifted away from the more primitive mythological models to something new and different: an increasingly abstract and mathematical approach. In this same period, the seventh to eighth centuries BCE, we also find the first use of the zodiac.

Of course, by that time, the astronomer-priests of Sumeria, Assyria, and Babylon had been cataloging their observations of the sky for many centuries, and had built up a vast collection of celestial "omen-lore." The very dawn of scientific inquiry arose from the ongoing efforts of these ancient Mesopotamians to systematically link signs in the heavens to events on earth, but as J.D. North describes it, "The old Mesopotamian stellar religions had encouraged only a crude astrology of simple omens."[18]

These earliest astrologers were not doing horoscopes—that came considerably later. They focused on the big picture: the king, his troops, his enemies, the economy, the weather, the height of the river, and how these events on earth correlated with the ever-changing signs in the sky.

The *Enuma Enlil Anu*, a series of omen texts preserved on 68 clay tablets, grants a unique entrée into the way these earliest astronomers made sense of their sky. Recovered from the ruins of the library of the Assyrian king Assurbanipal, at Nineveh, the *Enuma* was inscribed by the Assyrians sometime during the seventh century BCE, but the observations and interpretations it contains are considerably older, possibly dating back to the Old Babylonian period (1600–1800 BCE). The *Enuma* employs a particular if-then formula to correlate celestial phenomena to earthly events. Here, for example, is a description of what to expect after a specific type of lunar eclipse, especially if accompanied by westerly winds:

> If on either the 13th or 14th [of the month] Ulûlu, the moon is dark;...his features are dark like lapis lazuli; he is

obscured until his midpoint; the west quadrant—as it covered, the west wind blew;...[the significance is] the son of
the king will become purified for the throne but will not
take the throne. An intruder will come with the princes of
the west; for eight years he will exercise kingship; he will
conquer the enemy army; there will be abundance and
riches on his path; he will continually pursue his enemies;
and his luck will not run out.[19]

Here is another example using the same formula to describe a different kind of celestial event and its expected results:

"If in month 1 the Demon with the Gaping Mouth [Cygnus, the Swan]
rises heliacally [just before the Sun]: for 5 years in Akkad at the command
of Irra there will be plague, but it will not affect cattle."[20]

Correlation was everything, and in the heights of the heavens, these
ancient astronomers instinctively sought celestial concomitants—whether
causes, coincidence, or just dumb luck—for all those defining moments;
all the terrors and triumphs of time. Vast catalogues of these painstaking
correlations remain preserved for us today, revealing ongoing and widespread research that involved thousands of scribes and observers for periods of thousands of years. Guided by an inner impetus we can scarcely
hope to fathom—part insecurity, part inspiration—their primitive genius
was stumbling through the darkness towards a great light, for, as Franz
Cumont put it, "from this mass of documents, laboriously collected in the
archives of the temples, the laws of the movements of the heavenly bodies
were disengaged with increasing precision."[21]

These desert stargazers were already using some of the same constellations we do, but they employed different, and relatively inefficient,
schemes for tracking the paths of the stars and the planets. In the years
circa 600–730 BCE, astronomical attention definitely shifted to the ecliptic,
the apparent path of the sun and the planets through the heavens. The
stars marking this pathway, and the constellations they formed, proved to
be the best way to pinpoint the exact positions of the sun and the planets in
their orbits. We know these constellations today as the zodiac, the circle of
animals. Coinciding with the rise of Chaldean and Median influence and
the decline of Assyrian power, this dramatic change in the heavens did not
take place in a vacuum, but accompanied important changes in the religious culture as well.[22]

Mesopotamian sky watchers had long believed that gods and goddesses controlled the stars and other natural phenomena, and used them to communicate their intentions to man. Circa 1800 BCE, the planets had been assigned to specific Babylonian gods and goddesses, and given their names. This was an important and widely influential development in stellar religion that was later adopted wholesale into Greek and Roman religion. This is why, to this day, our planets still bear the names of the gods and goddesses of the Greco-Roman pantheon.

In Babylon, Jupiter/Zeus was Marduk, their chief god. Mercury/Hermes was Nebu, Mars/Ares was Nergal, Venus/Aphrodite was Ishtar, and so on. However, an important distinction must be made here. These planets were not just *named for* the gods. In many respects, they *were* the gods. In their motions, they communicated their adventures, warnings, and intentions to man below. Any attempt to read mythology (or alchemy) without acknowledging this dimension is missing quite a bit.

Anything unusual or out of the ordinary in the heavens was interpreted as a warning of some kind. If the news from a planet wasn't exactly what the king wanted to hear, the deity could be propitiated through the appropriate sacrifices and rituals and the future made a bit brighter. This was fundamental Mesopotamian stellar religion. The same basic principles still apply today in Indian, or Vedic, astrology. Contemporary Vedic astrologers offer a range of planetary gems, remedies, and rituals designed to pacify the less-than-desirable intentions of the planetary deities.

But big changes were on the horizon, in the period between 600 and 730 BCE, as Mesopotamian astronomers began to shift their focus to the ecliptic, and to the zodiac. It was the beginning of mathematical, rather than mythological, astronomy. The use of the zodiac made the new mathematics possible, and, for the first time, astronomers could predict what the planets would do in advance, rather than wait for omens from the gods.

As Franz Cumont put it, suddenly the gods of heaven were subject to the laws of mathematics.[23] David Brown, throughout his important work, *Mesopotamian Planetary Astronomy-Astrology*, compares this transition to a Kuhnian "paradigm shift"; perhaps the first in recorded history. The old Assyro-Babylonian mythological order was passing away, and a new mathematical paradigm was emerging in its place.

Persia was still a relatively insignificant vassal at this point, filling in the southern corner of the Medes' growing empire, but the "scientific" revolution that began under the Assyrians and Chaldeans got a tremendous boost in the following (sixth) century with the rise of the Medo-Persian Empire of Cyrus the Great. Under Persian rule, mathematical astronomy received a whole new impetus. One tablet, dated to 523 BCE, shows how far this new science had advanced since the fall of Assyria. Suddenly, the positions of the sun and moon were calculated well in advance, and dated. The upcoming conjunctions of the moon with the planets, and the planets with each other, were all neatly located within the signs of the zodiac, revealing astonishing new levels of skill in calculation and prediction.[24]

Apparently the new Persian leadership had a consolidating effect on the celestial sciences, pulling together and systematizing all the disparate elements. Some of the most important developments in astronomy and celestial divination occurred between 600 and 300 BCE—the Persian period.[25] For one thing, our earliest extant individual birth chart dates to 410 BCE, for "It was not until the Persian period that omens for the lives of individuals were derived from celestial phenomena."[26] J.D. North describes the rare combination of reason and religious imagination propelling these rapid advances:

> The establishment of a system of celestial co-ordinates— in this case the division of the zodiac into twelve signs of thirty degrees each—was of the greatest importance for the advance of mathematical astronomy. Accurate planetary periods can be found within it...[and] for an analysis of the finer points of planetary motions such a system is essential. The motives for making that analysis must have been in part intellectual, but they also had much to do with religion and astrological prediction.[27]

North believes that the religion with the most bearing on this process was Persian Mazda worship; what we have come to know as Zoroastrianism; the revolutionary, dualistic form of monotheism that came to the fore during this same period. Although there is still disagreement on when the prophet Zoroaster lived, we can definitely trace the arrival of Persian Mazda worship, as a dominant religious and social force, to the period in question, and to the Persians and the Magi.

Whereas the mingling of the Chaldean and Median religio-scientific traditions began at least as early as their seventh-century military alliance, now the Chaldean astronomers in cities such as Babylon and Nippur were working under the supervision of the Persian Magi. According to Cumont: "Thus, as the period of the Achaemenid Kings, in the official procession of Babylon, there walked first the Magi, as Quintus Curtius states—that is to say the Persian priests established in the conquered capital, then the Chaldaei—that is the native sacerdotal body...."[28]

Although Ahura Mazda, the high god of the Persian Empire, already owed much to the earlier Assyrian imperial deity Ashur, in many respects, Persian Mazda worship picked up where the Assyrians left off, moving even further away from primitive polytheism and forsaking the worship of lesser deities in favor of the one good god. Ahura Mazda had no divine council or pantheon. Instead, he was traditionally accompanied by a consort of "Bounteous Immortals," abstract beings or entities who represented ethical principles, such as Holy Spirit, Justice, Truth, Righteous Thinking, et al.

This same period also saw the emergence of early Zurvanism, a decidedly cosmic form of Mazda worship. Zurvanism exalted and deified the abstract principle of infinite time, and was both an outgrowth of and influence on astronomy and math during the Persian period.[29] Compared to the polytheistic cosmologies of the Assyrians and Babylonians, both Mazda worship and Zurvanism were thinking-man's religions, emphasizing universals and abstract principles. Although the origins of these belief systems remain obscure, and are discussed in more depth in other chapters, we know that they shared an enduring common bond: the priesthood of the Magi.

Time: The Beginning and the End

The dawn of astronomy, astrology, and the stellar religions that both inspired and sprang from them can all be traced to this same revolutionary period. Naturally, these innovations inspired speculations on the big picture, on grand overarching religious cosmologies and chronologies that encoded the ultimate meaning of it all. Two competing systems eventually evolved—two completely different ways of understanding time and human destiny—and both left their mark on history and prophecy for ages to come: the fatalistic chronology of the Chaldeans, and the apocalyptic eschatology of the Magi.

The influence of Chaldean astrology spread far and wide, and with it, an increasingly deterministic cosmology and chronology. It held that Fate, or Necessity, ruled over all, and bound even the planetary gods to its bidding. In Fate, time was cyclic and endlessly repetitive. At the start of each new cosmic era, the planets in their orbits all massed together at the beginning of the zodiac. After a specific number of aeons, perhaps 432,000 years or more, the planets would all regroup at that same point, and the whole cycle would start all over again. All human destiny was ultimately encoded within the planetary movements through the zodiac; a grand cycle that repeated endlessly. Any real progress or purpose was optional. This was the fatalistic Pagan astrology that so offended the early Christians. It lent itself to all manner of interpretation, echoing down through the ages within the subsequent chronologies of the Hindus, the Stoics, the Romans, the Muslims, and on into medieval Europe.[30]

But another system arose out of the same revolutionary ferment, and it went in an entirely different direction. This was the chronology of the Magi. It held that within the imponderability of infinite time, we inhabit only a very finite sequence of limited time. That finite time was decidedly linear. Finite time was going from point A to point B, and it was all adding up to something. In fact, finite time had only been created and called into being for one specific purpose: to house the ongoing battle between good and evil, between the good god Ahura Mazda, and his evil counterpart, Angra Mainyu. Finite time was completely astrological in nature, and everything within it was either on one side or the other: good or evil, light or dark, Truth or the Lie. Everyone was free to choose. After the completion of an appropriate number of astrological ages, finite time would come to its inevitable conclusion in the final showdown, the ultimate battle between good and evil, where good was destined to win, and evil would be vanquished forevermore; in other words, the apocalypse. This was the chronology of the Magi, and of Zurvan Zoroastrianism.[31]

And for the remnant of the Jews who survived the holocaust of 586 BCE and lived in exile in Babylon, these two worldviews made a lasting impression. The doctrine of Fate and Necessity, of infinite return and repetition, was the chronology of their captors, the Chaldeans. The Chaldeans destroyed the Jewish temple and homeland, and led them away into captivity. The doctrine of the apocalypse, of the ultimate battle between good and evil at the end of time, was the chronology of their liberators, the Persians and their Magi. Cyrus the Great freed the Jews from their Babylonian captivity and insisted they return to the burned-out site of old Jerusalem and rebuild their nation and their temple. So which system do you think the Jews preferred?

Jewish Astrology?

The assumption that Second Temple Jews or early Christians were not interested in astrology was never based upon evidence, but instead, as Dr. Kocku von Stuckrad puts it, was the result of "...a preconceived and misleading opinion about the basic ideas of astrology, which led to an astonishing disregard of Jewish and Christian evidence for astrological concerns. This evidence has either been played down—if not neglected entirely—or labeled 'heretic,' thus prolonging the polemics of the 'church fathers'...."[32]

Dr. Lester Ness includes a comprehensive overview of Jewish astrological efforts in his landmark work on Jewish astrology, *Written in the Stars: Ancient Zodiac Mosaics*. Ironically, in referring to the Jewish writers Artapanus and Eupolemus (late third or early second century BCE), Ness describes them as not being especially interested in astrology per se:

> But wanted, rather, to improve the image of the Jews by showing that they were an ancient people who had made important contributions to "modern" culture. Artapanus and Eupolemus took a "scientific" practice which they believed true and tried to make it look Jewish by associating it with Jewish heroes. This was the approach of most of the Jewish astrological writers.... A great variety of astrological treatises ascribed to angels or biblical heroes survive in Greek and in Aramaic or Hebrew.[33]

A famous astrological text attributed to Abraham was known to exist in the third century BCE and is one of the oldest works in Hellenistic astrology. Even classical astrologers such as Vettius Valens list Abraham, along with Egyptian authorities Hermes and Nechespo, as one of the earliest astrologers. Church fathers, such as Clement of Alexandria, also refer throughout their works to the widespread Jewish and early Christian belief that Abraham not only discovered astrology, but taught it to the Chaldeans, indicating general acceptance of that very dubious tradition.[34]

As both Ness and von Stuckrad repeatedly emphasize throughout their work, Jewish astrology did not necessarily contradict Jewish religion. The Jews who studied and composed astrological texts did so within a monotheistic framework, wherein their God ruled over all and the stars and planets did his bidding. In the words of Rabbi Joel Dobin, "...our ancestors considered Astrology to be the hand of God written across the heavens."[35]

There were always those who objected, but it was entirely possible to be a good Jew and a good astrologer at the same time; judging by the growing number of extant texts, there were quite a few of them. For instance, in the 1989 article "Astrological and Related Omen Texts in Jewish Palestinian Aramaic," the authors, J.C. Greenfield and M. Sokoloff, introduce an astonishing variety of texts revealing the Jewish fascination with "Mesopotamian" stellar religion, lunar omens, astrological physiognomy, and natal and predictive astrology.

Further, it now seems that astrology was integral to the life of the community at Qumram that left us the Dead Sea Scrolls. Qumram astrology, as with all aspects of community life, was permeated with a raging dualism, in anticipation of the ultimate battle between the sons of light and the sons of darkness. From the fragmentary material that remains, it appears the community may have used a "physiognomic" astrology to determine which side one was on, and hence, an individual's eligibility for both membership and leadership.

The cryptic text known as "4Q186" details a system for determining both the physical appearance and the balance between light and darkness within the individual: "His spirit has six parts in the house of light and three parts in the house of darkness. He shall be born under the haunch of Taurus and he will be poor. His animal sign is bull."[36] There is even an ongoing debate about whether the community used a similar system for predictions about the physical appearance of the coming savior and his adversary. Whether or not that was the case, these fragments from Qumram certainly leave the impression of a strong Persian apocalyptic and dualist influence on the Jewish practice of astrology.

The growing amount of extant material reveals that even though the Jews were not as mathematically inclined as the Mesopotamians or the Greeks, they were just as interested in astrology and all its implications. The modern idea that Jews and Christians were immune from astrological interests has evolved more as a result of scholarly emplotment than from an objective examination of the evidence.[37] It is yet another aspect of the orthodox, or normative myth, which von Stuckrad terms "a theological project of legitimization carried out in ancient and early modern times," in which the need for centralization and the creation of a monolinear history were the overriding concerns.[38]

The Magi in Matthew's Gospel open our eyes to the other side of the story.

Chapter 6
Which Star Was It?

At this point, informed opinions diverge. So much work has been done, spanning the centuries, by such diverse contributors as Origen in his third-century *Contra Celsium*, the eighth-century Baghdad astrologer Masha'Allah, and Johannes Kepler (1614). The efforts of the first 18 centuries are but small in comparison to the mountain of published opinion arising in the modern era, the result of the combined efforts of scientists, religious scholars, and historians, all inspired by the promises of modern astronomy. Despite all the claims to the contrary, no definitive answer has ever emerged.

Of course, there is a certain irony to this, apparent even in the 15th century. In 1465, Jacob von Speyer, the royal astronomer to Prince Frederic d'Urbino, asked Regiomontanus, the greatest astronomer and mathematician of his day, to try to determine the birth of Christ. Regiomontanus declined, declaring that this was a task for astrology, not astronomy.[1] Not that Regiomontanus was disinclined to do astrology. On the contrary, he was quite adept and made significant contributions to the practice (for instance, his ephemerides and system of house division), but he was making an important distinction, and one that has gone largely unacknowledged in the modern search for the Star.

It is worth pointing out that with the notable and very recent exceptions of the work of Michael Molnar and Percy Seymour, astrology has been effectively sidelined in the modern quest for an astronomical answer. It's not exactly news that modern astronomers and theologians don't care much for astrology, but the unspoken corollary to their distaste is that they don't know all that much about it, especially about how it applied to religious beliefs and messianic expectations in Matthew's time. The tendency then is to mistakenly assume there really wasn't much to it; certainly nothing worth investigating.

Not Astrology

The astronomer Ferrari d'Ochieppo decided that the religious background and astrological reasoning of the Magi could not be known with any degree of certainty. Instead, he theorized: "Yet the following basic concept is plausible: Jupiter, the planet of their highest deity, Marduk...was considered to be the Star of the Messiah proper." He then declared, "...Saturn, the celestial representative of the Jews."[2]

Bulmer-Thomas, writing in the *Quarterly Journal of the Royal Astronomical Society*, claims that because the *Magoi* were seeking a "King of the Jews," they must have been following Jupiter, because it was the most regal planet. He offers, in defense of his position, the explanation that the Greek word Σωτηρ (*Soter*) and the Latin word *Servator*, which both mean "Savior," were used in some unnamed classical sources as epithets of Jupiter.[3]

Hughes also avoids any primary sources in deciding on the Jupiter-Saturn conjunction, and instead quotes New Testament scholar Raymond Brown as saying, "Pisces is a constellation sometimes associated with the last days and with the Hebrews, while Jupiter, an object of particular interest among Parthian astrologers, was associated with the world ruler, and Saturn was identified as the star of the Amorites of the Syria-Palestinian region."

Or Kidger, forsaking any sources at all, says, "Let's speculate. One possible interpretation of the events would be the following. Jupiter is a royal and benevolent planet, while Saturn is malign and Mars invokes thoughts of war. The encounter between Jupiter and Saturn could have suggested to the Magi that a great ruler (the awaited Messiah) would arise, challenging a malign one (the Roman Empire) and liberate his country by the sword (as signified by the bloody color of Mars)."[4]

This kind of mythological mish-mash is not astrology, and that's why you will never see these claims sourced to the work of any ancient astrologers. They didn't talk that way. As ancient astrology, this barely even scratches the surface. In spite of all the evidence to the contrary, there remains this persistent assumption that the work of ancient astrologers involved juggling these jumbled myths, as opposed to, say, cataloging their systematic observations of the heavens, identifying their cycles, and correlating them to the ebb and flow of the tides of human history.

Even when astronomers think they are using real astrology, they can be sadly deceived in their efforts. Hughes is yet another case in point. In 1972, Rabbi Roy A. Rosenberg wrote a paper called "The 'Star of the Messiah' Reconsidered," in which he elaborated upon the importance of Saturn and Jupiter to the Jews. In quoting Rosenberg on the work of the 15th-century Jewish scholar Don Isaac Abrabanel, Hughes believed he was presenting Jewish astrology and a Jewish messianic astrological tradition: "Rosenberg claims that Matthew is probably reflecting what was essentially at that time a Jewish astrological tradition. From what we know of traditional Jewish astrology,...the Jews did link the appearance of the Messiah, and other great events, with the conjunctions of Jupiter and Saturn."[5]

Rosenberg was a great man in many respects, but he was not a particularly good source on ancient astrology. His Abrabanel, apart from being a rather late source, was blatantly recycling much older methods, couching his Jewish messianism within the extravagant trappings of earlier Persian astrology, imported into Europe through the medieval Moorish schools in Spain. Hughes continues in that same vein, without so much as a backward glance, and no mention of the real source, or scope, of this tradition.

At the same time, there were good Persian sources available in the 1970s that could and should have been consulted, including Pingree and Kennedy's landmark translation of Masha'allah's *On Conjunctions, Religions, and Peoples*, or Kennedy's classic "Ramifications of the World-Year Concept in Islamic Astrology," both of which reveal the broader, pan-monotheistic implications of Abrabanel's borrowed methods. The fact that they weren't consulted only goes to show how hard it is to crack the "Classical" and "Judeo-Christian" mindset of the West. Even science is bound by the limits of the culture in which it is practiced.

Paffenroth sums up the problem nicely, concluding that the plethora of different "scientific" explanations of the Star is itself indicative of a basic problem in the "scientific" methodology. A methodology that produces "new explanations for a given question each year must strike anyone as...less than helpful."[6]

There is a much more straightforward approach to solving the mystery of the Star, one that begins with investigating what Persian, Magian astrologers actually believed. Still, it's not as if the astronomical approach has been entirely uninspired—far from it. The process has brought to light all kinds of fascinating mysteries and clues, and often succeeded in spite of itself, coming surprisingly close to the right answers, even if for all the wrong reasons. So let's explore some of the most interesting and controversial work to date.

A Triple Conjunction

Many theories, but by no means all, focus upon the triple conjunction of Saturn and Jupiter in the constellation Pisces that occurred during the year 7 BCE. Johannes Kepler, who began his studies of the Star of Bethlehem in approximately 1603, was one of the first Western, Christian astrologers to refocus attention on this particular conjunction, but others have proposed theories on it as well, including the astronomers Dr. K. Ferrari d'Occhieppo, David Hughes, August Strobel, Hans Sandauer, Percy Seymour, and Rabbi Roy A. Rosenberg.

A "triple conjunction" is not an uncommon phenomenon, and occurs when two planets appear to meet up on three separate occasions. It's all due to the planetary "reverse gear" we call retrograde motion. We know that the planets orbit regularly around the sun, just as we do here on Earth. So why is it that they sometimes appear to be going backwards? This nagging question perplexed sky watchers for millennia, and it was the same Johannes Kepler, mathematical genius and court astrologer to the Holy Roman Emperor, who finally solved the problem in the 17th century.

Because Earth is the third planet from the sun, two of our fellow planets (Mercury and Venus) are traveling within our orbit, and the rest are traveling outside of it. The planets all travel at different rates of speed, and that speed decreases with their distance from the sun. Although Jupiter and Saturn are next-door neighbors in the solar system, Jupiter, being closer to the sun, moves faster than Saturn. Jupiter orbits the sun in approximately 12 years, and Saturn's orbit takes anywhere from 27 to almost 30 years. Jupiter catches up with Saturn every 20 years, on a regular basis. When this happens, the two planets make a conjunction (literally, a coming together) in the same sign of the zodiac.

Usually they meet up just once, and Jupiter, the faster of the two, passes Saturn and moves on. However, sometimes Jupiter appears to catch up and conjunct with Saturn, and then passes it and goes retrograde. From our earthly perspective, we see Jupiter come to a stop (a station), turn around, and start moving backwards (retrograde). On its backwards course, Jupiter makes a second, retrograde conjunction with Saturn, which by this time also appears to be moving backwards, but more slowly than Jupiter. Jupiter continues in its retrograde motion for several months, then stations and goes direct; in other words, comes to a stop, turns around, and starts moving forward again. Saturn also makes a station, or stops, and starts moving forward again. Once again, for a third time, Jupiter catches up to the slower-moving Saturn, and makes the third conjunction, before heading off around the zodiac for another 20 years until their next meeting.

Of course, the planets are not actually going backwards. It just looks that way because we earthlings inhabit a speedier planet and have overtaken them in our orbit. At that point, we are watching them recede in our rearview mirror. This is what astronomers and astrologers mean when they speak of retrograde (backwards) motion.

The Jupiter-Saturn conjunction in Pisces in 7 BCE was one of these triple conjunctions, and undoubtedly, it was a spectacular sight. Jupiter made its first conjunction with Saturn in Pisces on approximately May 29, 7 BCE, passed it, and then went retrograde on approximately July 17. On approximately October 1, Jupiter made its second, retrograde conjunction with Saturn in Pisces. On November 13, Jupiter stopped and turned around, or stationed and went direct, and moving forward again, made its third and final conjunction with Saturn in Pisces on December 5.

This was Kepler's triple conjunction, and it is still one of the top contenders for the title "Star of Bethlehem." By the late 1970s, the theory was so popular that it had its own acronym: PCH, for planetary conjunction hypothesis.[7]

An Amazing Coincidence

Kepler did not believe the triple Jupiter-Saturn conjunction was the Star of Bethlehem, but that it precipitated the appearance of a nova, a new star, which then led the Magi to the child. A similar event had already happened in Kepler's time.[8] In December of 1603, Kepler observed a Jupiter-Saturn conjunction in fiery Sagittarius, which was followed the next autumn by a spectacular grouping of Mars, Jupiter, and Saturn in the same sign. This conjunction of the three outer planets was relatively rare, and highly anticipated. Astrologers were predicting great things for it, including the possibility that it might produce a comet.

All of Europe was watching closely as Mars made its conjunction with Saturn on September 26, and then moved on to join with Jupiter on October 9. Imagine their surprise when a new star suddenly appeared, like clockwork, on October 10, right between Jupiter and Saturn, and almost as big and bright as Jupiter itself! Kepler was deeply affected by this experience, and eventually wrote a book on it, entitled *De Stella Nova in Pede Serpentarti* (*About the New Star in the Serpent's Foot*).

Kepler realized that the triple Jupiter-Saturn conjunction of 7 BCE had also been followed by a massing of Mars, Jupiter, and Saturn, similar to the one he had witnessed. He reasoned that it must have also produced a nova, similar to the one he had seen, and that perhaps God had placed the nova there, specifically to guide the magi.

So Kepler did not necessarily believe that the triple conjunction of Jupiter and Saturn was the actual Star of Bethlehem. He believed that it, and the stellium of Mars, Jupiter, and Saturn that followed in 6 BCE had produced a new star, a nova, and that had alerted the Magi to the birth of Christ.

Ironically, ancient Chinese and Korean records indicate the appearance of a nova, or something similar to it, in the years 4–5 BCE. The modern nova theory was revived in 1977, in the work of David Clark and Richard Stephensen and has more recently been reworked by astronomer Mark Kidger in his 1999 book, *The Star of Bethlehem*. Although the Chinese "nova," if indeed that is what it was, was not nearly as timely, nor as perfectly situated between Jupiter and Saturn as Kepler's nova in 1604, it is still an amazing coincidence. If I were only looking for something that matched the description in Matthew, then the nova might fit the bill—but it doesn't answer the bigger question, of why this would be sufficiently meaningful to the Judeans for the author of Matthew to open his gospel with it.

Matthew's Words

The starting point for astronomical research on the Star is the account in the Gospel of Matthew. The problem with such a secure starting point is that it depends upon an underlying, and usually unstated assumption, such as, "everything Matthew wrote about the Star is absolutely true and should be interpreted as an astronomical description." There is even a repeated insistence throughout the scientific literature that this is the only way we can know anything about the Star. For instance, Colin Humphreys, a science professor at the University of Cambridge stated: "There are several specific characteristics of the star of Bethlehem recorded in Matthew's gospel which, if accepted, allow the type of astronomical object to be identified uniquely."[9]

Only the Star of Bethlehem could put scientists and academics in the same camp with fundamentalist evangelicals (even if only temporarily). According to the astronomer Mark Kidger, in *The Star of Bethlehem: An Astronomer's View*: "We can explore the idea of the Star as a true astronomical event more fully if we take the Gospel accounts to be almost literally true. Doing so will permit us to find more fascinating clues, although we risk over-interpreting the data."

Risk? Then, in *The Quarterly Journal of the Royal Astronomical Society* (1992), Ivor Bulmer Thomas says, regarding Matthew 2: "It claims to be a record of a historical event, and the onus of proof for those who regard it as a myth rests with themselves. If a simple, rational explanation of the 'star' can be given, such as is here proposed, the case for its historicity is strengthened."

Such a literal interpretation of the New Testament seems a bit out of place in a scientific journal. I suppose it goes without saying that these gentlemen do not apply the same standard of proof to Matthew's report of the Virgin Birth, which immediately precedes the Star, or to the miracle stories that follow.

This fundamentalist interpretation of the Bible, or, at least, a few very select chapters of it, is not only naïve, it is symptomatic of a much larger problem with the astronomical approach: Astronomers tend to see astronomy everywhere, even in the most unlikely places—the Gospel of Matthew, for instance. But isn't that typical historiography? The art of writing ourselves into the past, in the pursuit of the Star, has twisted the language of Matthew all out of proportion.

Anyone brave enough to venture through the labyrinth of previous research on the Star has already encountered one unavoidable problem. Among the many authors who claim that Matthew is talking astronomy, there is a glaring lack of consensus on exactly what it is he is saying. Now, before we get too deeply involved in quibbling over obscure Greek terminology, let us first briefly consider how very unlikely it is that the statements in the second chapter of Matthew were ever uttered by the *Magoi*, or spoken in Greek...or even spoken at all.

As we saw in Chapter 1, the Magi were probably a later addition to Matthew's Gospel, and may have been added by someone other than the original author—someone who preferred to remain anonymous. That might explain why the Gospels of Luke and John, which are presumably later, fail to mention them.

Further, whoever Matthew was, he obviously wasn't there at the time. He also does not reveal his source for the story. Bulmer-Thomas declared that we must presume the story came from Mary, but such a presumption would be more dogmatic than reasonable, as no reasons are given. The character of Mary, the mother of Jesus, receives considerably more attention from the authors of John and Luke, so if the story indeed came from her, then it is all the more conspicuously absent from their Gospels.

Even if we did accept that Matthew got the story from the Virgin Mary, we are left with the same problem: She obviously wasn't there when it happened either. She also would have lacked the astronomical knowledge necessary to provide any reliable details.

The only ones present in Matthew 2:7, when Herod "privily called the wise men" and "inquired of them diligently what time the star appeared" (KJV) would be Herod, the wise men, and Herod's closest courtiers. Unless the author of Matthew was directly quoting from one of them, which he clearly does not indicate, then this is hearsay evidence reported almost a century after the fact and translated beyond recognition. Not only does Matthew fail to provide us with a single date, time, degree or zodiac sign, but he also doesn't even answer Herod's question. I cannot see the point in treating this as a reliable description.

Balaam's Star

Many writers, both scientists and Christian apologists, have been quick to point out that Matthew's Star must have been intended as a fulfillment of the prophecy of the seer Balaam, found in the book of Numbers, chapter 24:

> 16: The saying of him who heareth the words of God, And knoweth the knowledge of the Most High, Who seeth the vision of the Almighty, Fallen down, yet with opened eyes:
>
> 17: I see him, but not now; I behold him, but not nigh: There shall step forth a star out of Jacob, and a scepter

shall rise out of Israel, and shall smite through the corners of Moab, and break down all the sons of Seth.

18: And Edom shall be a possession, Seir also, even his enemies shall be a possession, while Israel doeth valiantly.

19: And out of Jacob shall one have dominion, And shall destroy the remnant from the city (The Masoretic Text).

Most versions of this prophecy stop midway through verse 17, but I have continued Balaam's oracle through the next several verses to maintain both the continuity and the context of his words. I have some trouble relating this prophecy to Christ, who, aside from turning the tables at the temple, is not usually credited with any significant military successes against anyone—Moab, Edom, or otherwise. Even if we apply a more metaphorical or historical interpretation, the specific territories listed are traditionally Muslim, rather than Christian lands, so is this then a prophecy of the coming of Islam?

Either way, if Matthew did intend his star as a fulfillment of Balaam's prophecy, why doesn't he say so? Is this really the same author who so carefully links the Virgin Birth, the Flight into Egypt, and even Jesus's relocation to the town of Capernaum (4:14), to obscure passages in the Old Testament, stretching them all out of context to try to establish some prophetic authority for his claims? Why would he bypass this perfect opportunity to do the same? Why does he not say, as he does everywhere else, that all this was done that "it might be fulfilled which was spoken of the Lord by the prophet, saying a star shall come forth from Jacob"? I can't claim to know the reason for this curious stylistic departure, but it is an annoying discrepancy.

Even after all of that, we are still faced with the nagging problem of why the Magi would tell all this to Herod. Of all the people in Jerusalem, shouldn't Herod have been the last to know? As Molnar points out, "It is odd that the Magi told a king about the birth of another king without expecting serious repercussions."[10]

So, I have a number of problems with the historicity of the account in Matthew. I also have to wonder whether it does not more accurately reflect the conditions and concerns of both the Jews and the Persians during the years 70 to 90 CE, rather than those prevailing at the time of the birth of Jesus. However, many authors disagree and have published some fascinating work as a result.

En te Anatole

The Greek phrase *en te anatole* occurs in Matthew 2:2, and is generally translated to mean that the Magi saw the Star in the east, or rising in the east. That simple definition is probably the best, but it has gotten very complicated in recent years. In 1977, Professor Ferrari d'Occhieppo of the Astronomical Institute of the University of Vienna, published *Der Stern der Weisen-Geschichte oder Legende*, followed in 1978 by an article in the *Quarterly Journal of the Royal Astronomical Society*. In both, he claimed that *en te anatole* was actually an astronomical reference to the acronycal rising (meaning rising at sunset and setting at sunrise), specifically of the Saturn-Jupiter conjunction in 7 BCE. To more fully define the term, an acronycal rising occurs when the object in question is 180 degrees from, or in opposition to, the sun. Thus, as the sun sets in the west, the object rises in the east.

British astronomer David Hughes popularized d'Occhieppo's theories in his book, *The Star of Bethlehem Mystery*, published in 1979. Referring to the use of *en te anatole* in Matthew 2:2, Hughes said: "The word *anatole* has a special astronomical significance meaning the acronycal rising. It can also be translated as 'rising on high' and was in common use for the sun. It is more suitable for the acronycal rising. Here the star or planet in question rises in the east just as the sun sets in the west."[11]

Both d'Occhieppo and Hughes concluded that the Magi regarded the evening of the acronycal rising of the Saturn-Jupiter conjunction (Sept. 15, 7 BCE) as the birth date for Jesus.[12] The astrophysicist Percy Seymour, in his book, *The Birth of Christ: Exploding the Myth*, also dates the Star to the evening of September 15, 7 BCE. On that night, as the sun (in the sign Virgo) set in the west, it was in direct opposition to the Saturn-Jupiter conjunction rising in the east in the opposite sign of Pisces. Seymour quotes Hans Sandauer, the author of *History Controlled by the Stars*, for the alternate date

> λεχοντες που εστιν ο τεχθεις βασιλευς των ιουδαιων ειδομεν χαρ αυτου τον αστερα εν τη ανατολη και ηλθομεν προσκυνησαι αυτο
> —Hort and Westcott
>
> **Where is he that is born King of the Jews? For we have seen his star in the East and are come to worship him**
> —Matthew 2:2 (KJV)

of September 17, 7 BCE, which also features this same Virgo-Pisces oppo-sition, albeit about 2 degrees of longitude further along.[13]

However, the astronomer Michael Molnar, in *The Star of Bethlehem: The Legacy of the Magi*, says, referring to Matthew 2:2: "The phrase 'in the east' is a literal translation of the Greek Phrase, en te anatole, which actually means at the rising. But more important, in Greek astrology it means specifically that a planet rises before the Sun as a morning star; that is, it undergoes a heliacal rising. Thus, although en te anatole trans-lates literally as 'in the east,' in the parlance of astrologers it really means 'at the heliacal rising' or 'at the morning appearance.'"

Further, in 1999, astronomer Mark Kidger published *The Star of Bethlehem: An Astronomer's View*. He claimed that:

> The biblical text, as translated traditionally, was so ambigu-ous in its reference to the east that this brief statement only serves to confuse the issue of the Star and the Magi. How-ever, in the mid-1970s, David Hughes, a scholar and writer with considerable interest in the Star who wrote an authori-tative review of the Star mystery for the journal *Nature*, cast considerable doubt on the traditional interpretation of the phrase in Matthew 2:2. He pointed out that the origi-nal Greek text says "en te anatole" (in the east, in the sin-gular). However, the correct grammar in Greek, if you want to say that an object is in the east, is to use the plural "en tai anatolai" (literally "in the easts"). Hughes points out that the phrase "en te anatole" has a special meaning in Greek, that is, it denominates the "heliacal rising" of a star or planet.

Relying on no other sources for his decision (or at least, none that he reveals), Kidger ignores the use of the acronycal rising throughout the rest of Hughes's work, and uses the heliacal rising throughout his own book. Ivor Bulmer-Thomas also interprets *en te anatole* as the heliacal rising; in his case, of the planet Jupiter, as it separated from its conjunction to the sun in May of 5 BCE and began to visibly rise before it at dawn. Bulmer-Thomas concludes that the *Magoi* were following the planet Jupiter, and confidently dates the birth of Christ to the the latter part of September in 5 BCE.

All these gentlemen seem to be reading way too much into this and are struggling to find some science in the Bible that was probably never there in the first place. The fact that they can't agree on the definition implies that there isn't enough information in Matthew to draw any reliable conclusions. However, that is just my opinion, and I would be the first to admit that my own knowledge of biblical Greek is so exceedingly limited that I didn't dare make that kind of determination on my own. I needed help from someone who knew enough about both ancient Greek astronomy and Greek astrology to deliver a genuinely informed opinion. Fortunately, I knew exactly where to go.

Robert Schmidt is perhaps the premier translator of ancient Greek astrology into contemporary English. The many translations to his credit include the works of Vettius Valens, Hephaistio of Thebes, Ptolemy, Antiochus of Athens, Paulus Alexandrinus, and more.[14] So I brought the question to him: What does Matthew mean in 2:2 when he says that the Magi saw the star *en te anatole*? Is it the heliacal rising, or the acronycal rising, or perhaps something else? Schmidt replied:

> I will say straight off that the expression en teh anatoleh is not standard astrological language for either kind of rising. Heliacal rising is normally denoted by the phrase epi' anatolehi (at rising) using the preposition epi without an article instead of en with the article. The phrase en teh anatoleh would read much more naturally as "in the east." But we can always suppose that the writer of the Matthew text didn't get his preposition right. Also, when the expression epi' anatoleh is used in astrological texts, it is usually modified by the adjectives heohios or hesperios, of the morning or of the evening respectively, which is not the case here.... Furthermore, the use of the definite article here is uncommon when talking about planetary phases relative to the Sun.

I specifically asked Schmidt if this same passage implied the acronycal rising, as described by Hughes and d'Occhieppo, to which he replied:

> This is simply incorrect. The term anatole does not in itself mean acronycal rising. When it does not mean rising relative to the horizon, it means rising relative to and in proximity to the Sun, as a morning or evening heliacal rising. In every astrological text I have seen, and the astronomical

texts I remember, the writer explicitly uses the term akronuktos, an adjective meaning rising at nightfall (the implied noun for this adjective being phasis, meaning phase), when referring to acronycal rising. To my knowledge they never use this adjective with the verbal noun anatole. My conjecture is that someone with very little Greek looked up the anatole in the Greek lexicon, found the cross-reference to epitole, which defines it as the rising of a star "as the Sun rises or sets," and then misinterpreted this definition. He certainly could not have studied this word in the context of astrological or astronomical texts in Greek and come up with such a notion.

Dorian Gieseler Greenbaum, who has translated the astrological works of Paulus Alexandrinus and Olympiodorus,[15] said in response to the same questions:

> When the magi say that they see a star *en tê anatolê,* it means that they see a star rising ahead of the sun at dawn or setting after the sun at sunset (as we see the newest crescent Moon, which is in higher longitude than the Sun, visible near the western horizon at sunset; that is called the phase of *anatolê*—or, as I describe it in Paulus, as "emerging"— by the Greeks). *Anatolê* can mean heliacal rising, but it can also mean just rising ahead of the sun, far enough away from the sun to be visible.... But *epitolê* is used by Ptolemy to mean specifically "heliacal rising," that is, the first appearance of a star after conjunction with the sun. Schmidt is correct in saying that *en tê anatolê* is not consistent with the usual phraseology in Greek astrological texts. A heliacal rising phase would more likely be described as *heoia anatolê*, and an acronycal one a *Hesperia anatolê* (this can also be used of the first visibility of the Moon in the west after conjunction with the sun).

So there simply is not enough information given in Matthew to justify either conclusion—heliacal or acronycal—or anything beyond simply "rising in the east," and that is why there is this continuing disagreement among the various authors. As Schmidt put it, "they are all chewing more than they bit off."

Ton Chronon tou Phainomenou Asteros

Ironically, the heliacal rising may figure into verse 7, in which the author of Matthew says that Herod asked the Magi what time the star appeared. According to Dorian Gieseler Greenbaum, "Literally, this says, 'the time of the appearance [coming into being or visible appearance] of the star'—in other words, the time when the star was far enough away from the sun to be seen, thus not combust. As I said, this could be heliacal rising, but also could be acronycal rising, and these terms refer to different phases for the inner planets, Mercury and Venus, than they do for the outer planets Mars, Jupiter and Saturn. The term is not specific enough to mean, unambiguously, heliacal (or acronycal) rising."

> τοτε ηρωδης λαθρα
> καλευας τους μαχους
> ηκριβωσεν παρ αυτων τον
> χρονον του
> φαινομενου αστερος
>
> —Hort and Westcott
>
> **Then Herod, when he had privily called the wise men, enquired of them diligently what time the star appeared**
>
> —Matthew 2:7 (KJV)

Schmidt was more emphatic on this point: "This Greek phrase does strongly suggest heliacal rising, the time the star made an appearance or *phasis*, having emerged from under the beams of the Sun."

However, this does not tell us anything about the star the Magi saw. It appears instead in a question that Herod asked, and Matthew fails to answer.

Esteh/Estatheh

According to Michael Molnar, Matthew 2:9 is full of astronomical terminology and should be paraphrased as follows: "And behold the planet which they had seen at its heliacal rising went retrograde and became stationary above in the sky [which showed] where the child was."

Following the claims of Ivor Bulmer-Thomas, Molnar says that the Greek term *proegen,* which is usually translated as "to proceed, or lead the Magi" is actually a technical astrological reference to retrograde motion. According to Molnar, *proegen* is derived from the astrological term *proegeseis*, which means "to go before" or "to go in the same direction as the sky moves." That's what a planet does when it goes retrograde; it stops going eastward through the zodiac and begins to move in the same westward direction as the sky.

He was firmly taken to task for this by J. Neville Birdsall, a biblical scholar with a passion for Greek grammar, in a review of Molnar's book that appeared in the *Journal for the History of Astronomy*. According to Birdsall, "it quickly becomes evident that the author's Greek is very insecure." I will graciously spare the reader the bulk of Birdsall's very sound grammatical arguments, and jump straight ahead to his conclusion; namely that Molnar's attempt to derive *proegen* from *proegeseis* is misguided and "cannot be used to link this item of Matthaean vocabulary with astrology." Indeed, Birdsall says that Molnar's "lack of terminology reveals the absence of philological formation!"[16]

Now before I am justly accused of the same, Greenbaum had this to say about it: "Birdsall is right that they [*proêgen* and *proêgêseis*] are...from two different roots." She further noted that *proêgêseis*, the noun that does not appear in Matthew, is derived from *proêgeomai*, and: "It's *proêgeomai* that is the technical astronomical/astrological term (meaning) planets in 'leading' zodiacal signs, i.e. in lower zodiacal longitude, leading in diurnal motion. Its opposite term is *hepomai*, follow, meaning behind or following the Sun in diurnal motion, in higher zodiacal longitude."

> ...και ιδου ο αστηρ
> ον ειδον εν τη
> ανατολη προηχεν
> αυτους εως ελθων
> εστη/εσταθη
> επανω ου ην
> το παιδιον
>
> —Hort and Westcott
>
> **...and lo, the star which they saw in the East went before them, till it came and stood over where the young child was**
>
> —Matthew 2:9 (KJV)

In other words, even if *proegen* were related to *proegeseis*, which it is not, it still does not necessarily mean retrograde motion, but rather, going before, or leading, in the zodiac.

Further, despite both Molnar's and Bulwer-Thomas's claims that Matthew 2:9 describes a planetary station, both Birdsall and Greenbaum agree that the technical term for a station, *sthrigmos*, is conspicuous in its absence. The terms that are used are more appropriately translated as they always have been, and we are left with a charming story of a star leading the Magi to Bethlehem. All of which does not mean that there is no astrological tradition behind this story; just that we have been looking for it in all the wrong places.

There is magnificent astrological and astronomical import in this story, but my guess is that the author of Matthew would be the last person to know how to explain it. My perspective is no doubt tempered by my many years studying astrology, but at the risk of projecting that perspective onto Matthew, I have to add here that people love to talk about astrology, even when they have no idea what they're talking about. They're happy if they can remember some snippet of something an astrologer once told them, and share it. You hear these conversations all the time, such as "I'm a Pisces with Mercury in Scorpio, and my husband is a Leo with the Full Moon in Taurus." Now I know that's astronomically impossible, but they're just enjoying themselves.[17]

That's how I see the author of Matthew. He knew that Magi and their adherents were around. He had probably met them, and talked deep into the night. They told him all about their wonderful theories, and it all sounded very important and meaningful, even if he barely understood a word of it. He was trying to share it with us as best he could, but he wasn't a qualified stargazer. He was one heck of a storyteller though, and he knew his audience.

Molnar and the Ram of God

In his 1999 book, *The Star of Bethlehem: The Legacy of the Magi*, astronomer Michael Molnar concluded that the Star of Bethlehem was an occultation of Jupiter by the moon in the sign Aries. He touted a date of April 17, 6 BCE for the birth of Jesus Christ, when the sun, moon, Jupiter, and Saturn were all in Aries. In arriving at these conclusions, Molnar was one of the first astronomers to attempt to factor in the principles of ancient astrology. I think he deserves a lot of credit for doing so, and hate to have to criticize his methods, but, unfortunately, it has to be done.

First, lacking any appreciation of the role of Persia and Persian religion in the ancient Near East in general, and in Judea in particular, he gives very short shrift to the Magi. According to Molnar, the title *Magoi* was: "...originally given to a caste of Zoroastrian priests who, in a struggle to take over the Persian throne, were beaten and slaughtered by King Darius (521–519 BC). Over time the title lost its connection to Zoroastrianism and was given to seers who predicted the future from omens and dreams."[18]

Molnar presents the Magi as effectively dismantled by Darius, and then thoroughly Hellenized after Alexander, especially in their astrology. For instance, he claims that: "although they came from the East, they practiced not archaic Babylonian astrology but a newer Hellenistic astrology.... To understand the Magi's star, we must realize that the principles and practices of ancient astrology became Hellenistic throughout the Near East and Roman World before the birth of Jesus."[19]

There is no mention in Molnar's work of the Magi's role as the opponents of Hellenization, nor of the unique role that Persian astrology played in their resistance. In fact, there is no mention of Persian astrology, period. Apparently, Molnar believes that the use of the Jupiter-Saturn conjunctions relative to the birth of Christ began with Abarbanel in the 15th century, adding that "conjunctions between Jupiter and Saturn were not regarded as distinctly regal portents by astrologers of Herod's time.... Thus, it is apparent that Abarbanel drew his conclusions from his personal beliefs, not from primary astrological sources of Roman times."[20]

Having set his face against Persia, Molnar veers off into classical Western astrology, which, in my humble opinion, he stretches way out of context to fit his own theories. For instance, I have any number of technical objections to the way that Molnar applies excerpts from the *Mathesis* of Firmicus Maternus to his chart for Jesus. But these are small potatoes. What does any of this have to do with the Magi?

If all of these different theories leave your head swirling in confusion, I assure you they do the same for me. But there is one constant here among all these authors: Not one of them appears to know anything about the astrological and religious traditions of the Magi. It seems so simple, but every last one of them is speculating without any reference whatsoever to what the Magi believed, what kind of astrology they practiced, or why the birth of a child in far-away Judea would be of any interest to them. There is no better demonstration of the blind side of Western scholarship than this shocking omission. Western authors don't even think enough of the Persians to ask, much less find out.

In my humble opinion, we really have no way of knowing either the exact date or time of Christ's birth. It is an exercise in futility, and in the futility of intellectual pride. I also believe that we should be wary about accepting the word of someone who claims to be Matthew as evidence. However, we might want to carefully consider the conjunctions of Jupiter and Saturn, because the Magi would have been watching them closely. Unlike Greek and Roman astrologers, the Persian Magi had very highly developed traditions about the cycles of Jupiter-Saturn conjunctions; specifically about how these cycles presaged the rise and fall of empires, dynasties, prophets, and new religions.

Chapter 7
The Legacy of the Magi

It was the Persians who first developed the astrological use of the cycle of Jupiter and Saturn conjunctions. They believed that these conjunctions were instrumental in timing the rise and fall of new dynasties, prophets, and world religions. In the Persian tradition, specific Jupiter-Saturn conjunctions heralded the birth of Christ and Christianity, and the birth of Mohammed and Islam. Although anchored in the ebb and flow of the tides of ancient Persian history, the cycle's use only increased with the passing of time. These exotic Persian chronologies traveled well, and made as profound an impact on astronomy and astrology in Judaea and the Christian West as they did throughout the vast Muslim empire.

We can trace a long line of influence, stretching from the Magi to Christopher Columbus, and beyond. Our starting point lies somewhere deep within the exotic courts of Sasanian Iran.

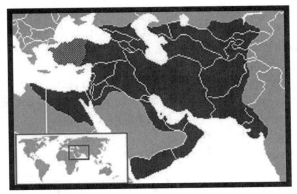

The Sasanian Empire in approximately 610 CE, under Khosrau II. Image in public domain.

The Sacred Fire

The evidence gleaned so far links the use of the Jupiter-Saturn conjunctions to the kings of the Iranian Sasanian Dynasty and their *wazirs* (circa 531 CE). However, as the Sasanian kings were enthusiastic collectors of the ancient knowledge of Persia, the tradition itself could be considerably older. According to authors Yamamoto and Burnett, "The Persians appear to have been particularly enthusiastic about historical astrology (which had been banned in the Roman Empire), and it is unfortunate that no text in Persian has survived. What we have are texts on conjunctional astrology dating from the mid-eighth century onwards.... The text most relevant...are those of Masa'allah and Umar ibn al-Farruhan at-Tabari [sic]."[1]

The founder of the Sasanian Empire, Ardashir, son of Papag, conquered the last of the Parthian Arsacid kings circa 226 CE. Ardashir hailed from Persis, the very heartland of ancient Persia, and was descended from the hereditary priests of the fire temple of the goddess Anahita at Istakhr, near the ruins of Persepolis. Ardashir and his partisans represented those ardent Persian nationalists who, even 500 years after the coming of Alexander, remained committed to a Persian revival, and to resurrecting the glory of the Achaemenids and the Persian, Imperial religion. The flame never died for these true believers, and at long last, their time had come.

By conquering the former Parthian territories, Ardashir (the Pahlavi version of "Artaxerxes") amassed a formidable empire for his descendants, an empire that would stand firm against both Rome and Byzantium until 651 CE, when the Sasanians were finally undone by the coming of the Arabs and Islam.

In styling themselves, and their empire, after their Achaemenid forebears, the Sasanians initiated an era of "high" Persian culture; a culture so distinct, so compelling and aristocratic, that even the Islamic conquest of Iran was itself ultimately conquered, and transformed into a "Persian Renaissance." Much of what we now recognize as Islamic culture, especially the architecture, literature, and scholarship of its Golden Age, were taken from Sasanian Persian traditions and then spread throughout the wider Muslim world.

The Sasanian kings were great defenders of the faith. During their reign, the Persian religion, under the leadership of the Magi, or Mobads,[2] developed further along the lines of an orthodox church, into what we recognize as Zoroastrianism today.

The Persian Revival

Dimitri Gutas, the author of *Greek Thought, Arabic Culture*, says:

> The Sasanian empire of Persia (226–642), with its state religion of Zoroastrianism, saw itself as the heir of the Achaemenid empire, of hoary antiquity and matchless civilization, and developed an ideology and culture to reflect and promote this self-view. An imposing succession of Sasanian emperors actively engaged in collecting, recording, and editing the historical and religious record of this civilization.... This treasure-house of Zoroastrianism and Persian civilization also contained an account of the transmission of learning and the sciences in Persia, from the earliest times....

The Sasanian emperors made an all-out effort to reclaim the rightful glory of Persia, and to put the painful memories of Alexander's conquest to rest. The Sasanians believed they had lost the greatest treasure of Persia to Alexander's armies: the fountain of all wisdom and knowledge contained in the original *Avesta* scriptures. Torn from its Persian storehouses, this inspired and encyclopedic compendium of all the knowledge of the ancient world had been sent as a hostage to Greece and Alexandria. There, Hellenistic scholars succeeded in passing it all off as Greek, but the Sasanians knew better, and were determined to recover what was rightfully theirs. To this end, they initiated their ambitious translation and recovery projects.

Relief showing Ardashir II (center) receiving the sacred crown from Ahura Mazda. Both stand upon defeated enemies, while Mithra stands to the left, upon a sacred lotus, crowned with the sun's rays and holding a priestly barsam. Image in public domain.

Descriptions of these extensive projects still survive, for instance, in the *Denkard* (Book IV); which was most likely written during the reign of Khosrau I ("Chosroes," r. 531–578 CE). In this version, just prior to the coming of Alexander, Darius II Codomannus, the last of the Achaemenid line, ordered two copies each of the complete *Avesta* and all its commentaries. By the command of the king, these copies of the sacred texts of Zoroastrianism, in the ancient Avestan language, along with the *Zand*, the collected commentaries, were deposited in the royal treasury, and in the Fortress of Archives.

This story in the *Denkard* also refers to the first-century Parthian Zoroastrian revival. It says that the Arsacid king Vologases (I? Ruled ca. 51–80 CE.) sent out through all the provinces a memorandum, requesting that all surviving fragments of the *Avesta* and the *Zand* that had been scattered throughout the kingdom, as well as every teaching deriving from it, whether in written or oral form, be gathered together for collection.

Ardashir, the first Sasanian king (ca. 226 CE), at the instigation of Tansar, his chief mobad, or mage, continued what Vologases had begun, and called for all the fragments to be gathered together at his court. His son Shapur (r. 241–271 CE) went even further in recollecting all the non-religious knowledge derived from the *Avesta*, including medicine, astronomy, logic, movement, time, space, "becoming," all the useful arts and crafts, and so on, rejoining them to the pure teachings of the Mazdean religion. Khosrau I, known as Anushirvan ("of the immortal soul"), furthered the process by proclaiming that all such useful knowledge had ultimately been derived from the original *Avesta*, and was therefore integral to the Mazdean religion.

This Sasanian Imperial ideology, in which all learning ultimately derived from the *Avesta*, stands in healthy contrast to our own, equally unbalanced, Helleno-centric and Judeo-centric narratives in the West. In spite of all our pretensions, the Greeks did not, in some unique cultural assertion of rationality, singlehandedly invent science and philosophy, and the Jews did not, as the chosen people of God, singlehandedly invent monotheism. Of course, neither did the Persians. Ultimately, the whole truth lies somewhere between the two extremes, bridging that classical impasse between East and West.

Still, in reconstructing their Persian heritage, the Sasanians forged a renewed Persian identity and ideal; that of a universal body of God-given knowledge. Even though the Sasanians eventually fell to the Muslim invaders, their ideals proved stronger than the sword, ultimately winning over the leaders of the Islamic empire, which, grasping and newborn, would soon find its own sure footing amidst the glories of ancient Persia.

The Islamic Translation Movement

After the death of the prophet (peace be upon him) in 632 CE, the Islamic Empire experienced a period of rapid conquest and expansion, converting by the sword and quickly taking over the territories of Persia, Asia Minor, Syria, Palestine, Egypt, North Africa, Gibraltar, and Spain. A mere century after the prophet's passing, a popular uprising rooted in Persia overthrew the reigning Muslim dynasty, the Umayyads, and the new 'Abbasid caliphs boldly came to power in 749 CE.

In 762 CE, the 'Abbasid caliph al-Mansur moved the empire's capital out of Damascus and back into Persian territory when he founded Baghdad, his *Madinat al-Salam*, the shining new City of Peace on the Tigris. Baghdad's proximity to the nearby ruins of ancient Babylon, Ctesiphon, and Seleucia, the crumbling capitals of the former Parthian, Sasanian, and Seleucid empires, lent the new city the credibility the caliphs craved, but the 'Abbasids had other good reasons for burrowing deep into the heart of Persia. As Richard Hooker explains it, "The overwhelming majority of foreigners who rallied to the Hashimiyya ['Abbasid] cause were Iranian.... When the 'Abbasids took power, the center of Islamic culture shifted from the Semitic world in Arabia and Syria to the Iranian or Persian world in Iraq."[3]

The rule of the 'Abbasids brought about a resurgence of Persian high culture, as the 'Abbasids turned to the past to legitimate their power and unite the various factions under their rule, assuming the glories of the former Persian Empire as their own. Initially, the new leadership undertook a program of deliberate "re-Persianization" in which both astrology and Persian ideology played a central role in establishing the cultural identity of the Islamic Empire. Dimitri Gutas describes this transition in *Greek Thought, Arabic Culture*:

> Indispensable for the 'Abbasid victory over the Umayyads in 750 were people from Persia. These...included Arabs who had lived in the area...and had become "Persianized." ...Arabized Persians who had converted to Islam, Persians who remained Zoroastrians, and people of other backgrounds... who were natives of territories formerly occupied by the

Sasanian [Persian] empire.... Strong elements of Sasanian culture...survived among these peoples and their elite occupied prominent positions in the 'Abbasid administration.... The Sasanian culture carried by these elite had two components that proved of immense significance to [the caliph] al-Mansur in helping him to consolidate the 'Abbasid cause: Zoroastrian imperial ideology and political astrology. Fused together, they formed the cornerstone of al-Mansur's 'Abbasid dynastic ideology.

Hence, the need for further translation and recovery projects. The vast compendium of Sasanian literature, which had come under attack during the first Muslim invasions, needed to be preserved and made available in Arabic for use throughout the Muslim world. Once started, the translation movement boomed, for the 'Abbasids displayed the same royal zeal for knowledge as their Sasanian predecessors, and soon all the authorities of the ancient world were finding their way into Arabic.

The result was a cultural renaissance, an Islamic Golden Age, centered in Baghdad. The refinements in the arts of civilization, and the virtual explosion of science and learning that occurred in the next two centuries, can only be compared, in its scope and lasting influence, to the later Italian Renaissance.

Unfortunately, when the Arabs came, almost all of the literature of the Zoroastrian Sasanids was destroyed. This includes their astrological works. However we do have a strong clue as to what their astrology must have been like. Most of the greatest astrologers in the Arab era were Persians!

And the astrology they taught is quite different from both the Hindu and the Greek. It had orbs of aspect, the Great Cycles of Jupiter and Saturn, all of the elaborate systems of planetary interactions....

While Arab era astrology clearly owes a large debt to Hellenistic astrology, it is also clear that...something new had come into the stream. This...was the Persian stream of astrology. And Arab era astrology is the immediate ancestor of the Western astrology of today. Our astrology may be in fact the successor to that third stream of ancient astrologies.

—From Rob Hand,
The Astrological Record of the Early Sages in Greek (xiv)

In the West, we still tend to call this the new "Arabic" learning, as our medieval forebears did, but that is a gross oversimplification that unwittingly obscures the more significant cultural influences. "Arabic" was more of a linguistic distinction than a cultural one. Of the many scholars and translators who distinguished themselves during this period, there were very few Arabs. Most came from the former Sasanian territories, and would have seen themselves as carrying on the revered traditions of their Persian ancestors.

The Demand for Persian Astrology

Resurrecting Persian political astrology from the ash heap of the Arab invasions was a top priority in the early days of the 'Abbasid regime. Western scholars have typically focused on the importance of the Greek translations, but, in fact, the first translations under the 'Abbasids were actually from Pahlavi (the Sasanian Persian language) to Arabic. Three kinds of texts were of immediate interest: those of an administrative nature, which would facilitate the work of the new government; texts of literary or historical interest; and texts on Persian political astrology. As Gutas describes it, referring to this third set of texts: "These texts, which can be considered as carriers of Zoroastrian Sasanian ideology, ...were primarily of an astrological nature, dealing specifically with political astrology or astrological history.... The translations would appear to be related to the incipient 'Abbasid cause (*da'wa*) and to have played a significant role in the ideological campaigns of those groups aspiring to a return to the Sasanian past."

Persian astrology was in great demand by both the 'Abbasid rulers and their opponents. It offered divine justification for them both, and, in the right hands, could be interpreted as favoring either one of their competing agendas. This was the same Persian astrology the Magi developed during their long opposition to foreign rule, expressing all their hopes in a coming savior and king. It derived from centuries of observing the celestial correlates of their history, including the successes and failures of the Achaemenids, the Arsacids, the Sasanians, and theo-political allies such as the Judean Hasmoneans.

Persian astrology included specific techniques for predicting the rise and fall of dynasties and kingdoms, the advent of prophets and new religions, and even the Final Hour. After all, Mohammed, as had Jesus before him, left his followers with the distinct impression that the Last Day was just around the corner. In the heady mix of apocalyptic expectations swirling about Baghdad—whether Muslim, Christian, Jewish, Zoroastrian, Manichean, or otherwise—citizens were seriously concerned that time was running out. So whether, as did the 'Abbasids, you needed to establish that your reign was ordained by God on high—or as the Persian partisans conspiring against them that it was

> **Elect**
>
> A verb, derived from Electional Astrology: when an astrologer chooses the best time for a particular event, such as a marriage, grand opening, or in this case, the foundation of the capital of the world's newest empire.

not—whether you thought Mohammed was the seal of the prophets, or you were still eagerly awaiting the one who was to come, Persian astrology offered answers, and a powerful cosmic rationale.

Masha'allah!

We may never know his real name, but he will live forever in history as Masha'allah—an Islamic proclamation of faith meaning "God has willed it so!" He was born a Jew near Basra, but as Masha'allah, he lived and worked in the eighth century CE in the area of present-day Baghdad. He was one of a select group of astrologers, along with the Persian, al-Nawbakht, chosen by the caliph to elect the chart for the foundation of the city of Baghdad (July 762 CE).[4]

Among his many influential works, Masha'allah composed a book entitled *On Conjunctions, Religions, and Peoples*. This work has not survived intact, but a good bit of it remains embedded in another work, itself extant only in parts, by one Ibn Hibinta, a Christian astrologer who practiced in Baghdad in the ninth century.[5]

In this work, Masha'allah presented a series of horoscopes relevant to the birth of Jesus Christ and Christianity, and the birth of the prophet Mohammed and Islam. These are the earliest textual references still extant for the connection between the Jupiter-Saturn

The Four Elements	
Fire	Aries, Leo, Sagittarius
Earth	Taurus, Virgo, Capricorn
Air	Gemini, Libra, Aquarius
Water	Cancer, Scorpio, Pisces

conjunctions and the birth of Christ. Masha'allah clearly believed that the 20-year cycle of Jupiter-Saturn conjunctions was relevant to the arrival of great prophets and new religions, especially when the cycle shifted from the signs of one triplicity (element: fire, earth, air, water) to another.

Triplicities

The 12 signs of the zodiac are divided among the four elements: fire, earth, air, and water. Consequently, there are three fire signs (Aries, Leo, Sagittarius), three earth signs (Taurus, Virgo, Capricorn), three air signs (Gemini, Libra, Aquarius), and three water signs (Cancer, Scorpio, Pisces). Hence the term "triplicity."

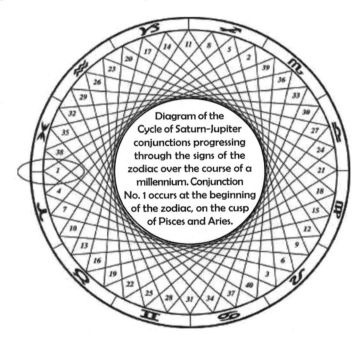

Diagram of the Cycle of Saturn-Jupiter conjunctions progressing through the signs of the zodiac over the course of a millennium. Conjunction No. 1 occurs at the beginning of the zodiac, on the cusp of Pisces and Aries.

Image created by Michael G. Conrad.

By a fortuitous combination of geometry and timing, the Saturn-Jupiter conjunctions move between signs of the same element, gradually tracing a compelling pattern of interlacing triangles. In principle, the entire cycle starts with the conjunctions in the fire signs (Aries, Leo,

Sagittarius), and Jupiter regularly meets up with Saturn every 20 years in one fire sign after another. This was known as the *small conjunction*— the period of time when the cycle stayed in the same triplicity.

After about 240 to 260 years, more or less, the conjunctions pass into the earth signs (Taurus, Virgo, Capricorn), and in another 240 years, more or less, they move into the air signs (Gemini, Libra, Aquarius), and then on into the water signs (Cancer, Scorpio, Pisces). This shift between the elements was known as the *middle conjunction*. Both the birth of Christ and the birth of Mohammed occurred at a *middle conjunction*, as the cycle was shifting between the elements.

However, there can be considerable overlap in these shifts. The conjunction could, and often did, hesitate, moving back and forth, for example, between the end of the water signs and the beginning of the fire signs, for 60 years or more before finally settling into the new triplicity.

There was an even larger cycle, the *great conjunction,* and that happened when the conjunctions had moved all the way around the circle of the zodiac, and the whole process began anew. The *great conjunction* cycle was believed to last almost 1,000 years, and constituted, or defined the millennium. We know now that the complete conjunction cycle is considerably shorter than that (approximately 800-plus years, depending on how you define the beginning and end of the cycle), but the millenniums were always the priority for the Persians. They held to a very ancient tradition of dividing time into distinct 1,000-year periods, each under the astrological rulership of a planet or zodiac sign, and they delighted in fitting the Jupiter-Saturn cycle into that scheme.

Astrological historiography was hardly an exact science, and astrologers such as Masha'allah were often quite creative with their chronologies. Personal and ideological agendas could always be factored in, along with some really awkward math. After all, Masha'allah and his contemporaries based all their calculations on an estimated mean, or average, rate of planetary motion. This means that their planetary positions became increasingly inaccurate the further backward and forward in time they went. Not only did they often have the wrong positions, but in all fairness, they rarely had the right ones. That's why we can still find any number of conflicting opinions on exactly how these systems meshed together, and when the cycle, and hence, the millennium, began.

Hardly a day goes by that I don't find myself chuckling over the words of the immortal Edward S. Kennedy, who said, regarding his own work in this vein: "...the matter is so diffuse, the elements so contradictorily compounded of religion, magic, and myth, and the sources so numerous that one often feels, as Biruni would say, that the only reason for studying the subject is to be able to warn the reasonable man away from it."[6]

And yet, if we want to understand Matthew's Magi, and why he depicts them finding Christ through their astrology, this is where we must look, for this is where their astrology survived. Even as late as the 11th century CE, al-Biruni could write of a man, Abu Abdallah al-Adi, "who is stupidly partial to Magism," who "wrote a book on cycles and conjunctions in which it is claimed that the eighteenth conjunction since the birth of Muhammad coincides with the tenth millennium, which is ruled by Saturn and Sagittarius."[7] So we're on the right track, but it can be pretty rough going.

The New Millennium

The Magi were of Chaldea, where astrology was born, of which this is a dictum: Great conjunctions of planets in cardinal points, especially in equinoctial points of Aries and Libra, signify a universal change of affairs; and a cometary star appearing at the same time tells of the rise of a king.

—Johannes Kepler, *Kepleri Opera Omnia*

Edward Kennedy, in the preface to his priceless book *The Astrological History of Masha'allah*, says that Masha'allah's work is based upon the theory that the most portentous time of all was the *great conjunction*, when the Saturn-Jupiter conjunctions completed their journey through all 12 signs of the zodiac and started a new round, or a new millennium. This heralded the most significant changes in world order; particularly, the arrival of a major prophet and a new religion. Kennedy also says that Masha'allah believed the *middle conjunction*, which took place approximately every 240 or 260 years, as the conjunctions shifted into the signs of the next triplicity, signified sweeping social changes, such as the rise of new nations or dynasties.

Far be it from me to argue with Kennedy, who is infinitely more qualified than I will ever be to comment upon such matters, but I'm not sure that I get this same meaning out of the material. Try as I may, I can't find any place in this work where Masha'allah or Ibn Hibinta ever says that, nor do they give any indication of when this great conjunction occurred, or will occur again. Reason would suggest that the new millennium would dawn as the conjunctions finished up in the water signs and shifted back into the fire signs. The great conjunction would occur in the beginning of fiery Aries, the first sign of the zodiac. But remember, this is astrology; reason is optional.

In fact, in another work, *De Revolution Annorum Mundi*, Masha'allah described the middle conjunction as that "in which there is a change from one triplicity to another, by which a change of religions and dynasties occurs."[8] This would be more in keeping with the system advocated by later Baghdad astrologers such as Abu Mashar, and explained at some length in Yamamoto and Burnett's classic, *Abu Ma'sar on Historical Astrology*. There, greater significance was generally accorded to the middle conjunction, especially in the rise of new religions.[9]

Engraving by Albrecht Dürer, from the title page of **Massahalah, De Scientia Motus Orbis** *(1504).*
Image in public domain.

It would be pointless to seek some kind of scientific consistency among medieval astrologers, but given that the birth of Mohammed and Islam took place at the time of a middle conjunction; the shift into the water signs in 571 CE, this emphasis among Muslim astrologers upon the middle conjunction is not surprising. After all, this material would have been produced under an Islamic regime. Even though it was an especially open-minded and intellectually curious Islamic regime, the 'Abbasids were also notoriously heavy-handed in repressing ideological opponents. Therefore, it is only natural that these interpretations of Persian astrology tend to confirm the Islamic revelation.

In contrast, emphasis on the priority of the great conjunction could have been construed as support for Christianity, for it was Jesus who was born as the conjunctions shifted from the water to the fire signs. The early days of the Christian Church coincided with the first Saturn-Jupiter conjunctions in Aries. Again, it is too much to expect consistency on these points, but it's entirely possible that Magian astrologers in Matthew's time were more inter-

> **Vernal Equinox**
>
> The first day of spring, when the days and nights are of equal length, halfway between the longest and shortest days of the year (the solstices). Also, the day when the sun crosses the threshold of the zodiac, moving from the last degree of the last sign, Pisces, into the first degree of the first sign, Aries.
>
> It was traditionally celebrated as the first day of the New Year in Persia and Iran.

ested in the significance of the great conjunction, and the presumed start of a new millennium, than Islamic astrologers working under the 'Abassids. These discrepancies do prompt a closer look at Masha'allah's methods to see exactly what he believed and how he operated.

The Revolution of the World Year

In Masha'allah's messianic astrology, the shift from the water to the fire signs is an important indicator of the birth of Christ. His method was to cast charts for the exact date and time of the Vernal Equinox, or "year-transfer," preceding the Saturn-Jupiter conjunctions. The three astrological charts he claims indicate the coming of Christ are set for:

1. The Vernal Equinox preceding the Jupiter-Saturn conjunction in Sagittarius in 45 BCE, marking the shift from the water signs into the fire signs.[10]

2. The Vernal Equinox preceding the first Jupiter-Saturn conjunction in Leo in 25 BCE.

3. The Vernal Equinox of 12 BCE, which he claims was the year of Christ's birth.

His reasoning in all of this is a bit contradictory, especially as it comes down to us through the hand of Ibn Hibinta. For instance, Kennedy and Pingree point out that if we check his math relative to the birth of Mohammed, we get a date of 1 BCE for the birth of Jesus. So although

Masha'allah may have known of the more traditional date, he apparently set great store by that conjunction in the royal sign of Leo and had his reasons for linking the birth of Christ to it; reasons that will become clearer as we go along.

Saturn, Jupiter, and Islam

Masha'allah uses the same methods for the birth of the prophet Mohammed. A chart for the Vernal Equinox preceding the shift of the Jupiter-Saturn conjunctions from air to water signs in 571 CE is introduced for the birth of the prophet of Islam. Mohammed was born around that time, but exactly when is hard to say, precisely because later Islamic astrologers kept moving his birthday to make it match more closely with the Jupiter-Saturn conjunction in Scorpio of 571 CE. His traditional birth date of April 20, 571 CE, which features the sun in opposition to that Jupiter-Saturn conjunction, was certainly contrived.[11]

The Great Conjunction

So even though it is claimed that Masha'allah believed that the great conjunction heralded the rise of great prophets and new religions, he seems to place the rise of two great prophets and two new religions at the middle conjunction, or the shift between the elements, without specifically saying whether one marks the beginning of the millennium or not.

Reason suggests that this problem might be easily resolved if we only knew where Masha'allah believed the whole cycle began. But in fact, knowing this only complicates the matter. Ibn Hibinta does say that Masha'allah begins his astrological history with the very first Jupiter-Saturn conjunction ever. This initial conjunction occurred at the very beginning of planetary motion at 7° of the constellation Taurus. And when was the beginning of planetary motion? According to Mash'allah, it began halfway through the millennium of Mars, some 2,400-and-something years before the Great Flood in the year –5782. Let's be clear about this—Masha'allah says that the millenniums preceded planetary motion, and that more than 500 years of the millennium of Mars had already passed before the planets even started moving. In Persian astrology, the millenniums were always the priority.

But why Taurus? Kennedy and Pingree are of the opinion that "The choice of a conjunction in Taurus was probably influenced by the role played by the sacrifice of the Primordial Bull in the creation of the material world." That may well be, for this particular myth is prevalent throughout Zoroastrian cosmogony, persisting even into the rites of the later Mithraic cults. Further, Taurus was the first sign in the earliest sidereal zodiacs, a fact that may also have had some reciprocal bearing on the origin of this creation myth.

Knowing all that still doesn't help us, for although Masha'allah fixes the beginning of the conjunction cycle in Taurus and the subsequent earth signs, we don't know why. There is also nothing in this work regarding any subsequent shifts to the earth signs, which should have initiated new millenniums. For instance, just such a shift would have taken place in the late second to third century CE, between the birth of Christ and Mohammed, but if Masha'allah did have something to say about that, it has not come down to us.

'Umar

However, there is a more purely Persian source available on this same subject, in the work of 'Umar ibn al-Farruhan at-Tabari, also known as Omar Tiberiades. 'Umar was a native Persian; in fact, Kennedy says that his family came from the Caspian provinces of Iran, formerly known as Media. 'Umar and Masha'allah were contemporaries. We can be fairly certain that they knew each other, and each other's work, and they may have even worked together on the chart for the foundation of Baghdad. It was al-Biruni who said that Masha'allah and 'Umar were "halfway between the Persians and Abu Ma'sar."[12]

Writing in the same tradition as Masha'allah, 'Umar says that once the Jupiter-Saturn conjunctions, which he calls "the conjunctions of the thousands," or the millenniums, had moved back into the fire signs, the first conjunction in the royal sign Leo was the most significant of the entire millennial cycle. It set the tone or pattern for all the changes and developments that would eventually unfold through the ensuing cycle of middle and small conjunctions, as the new millennium unfurled: "...This point of time indicates the sum of what happens in this period.... At this point of time there is a shift from one condition to another, a change in genera and shapes, and new matters, the like of which has never occurred before. No indication is like its indication, no period like its period, and there is no doubt about the change...."[13]

According to 'Umar's calculations, which are not exactly clear from his text, this happens only once every 959 years. What is clear, as Yamamoto and Burnett point out, is that 'Umar here relates the period of the great conjunction to the Zoroastrian cycle of a thousand years. This is classic Persian astrology, and probably not too far removed from Matthew's Magi.

Both 'Umar and Masha'allah set great store by that initial conjunction in Leo. Certainly Masha'allah ascribed great influence to it, even moving the date of Jesus's birth closer to it, but 'Umar goes even further and gives every appearance of hailing the first conjunction in Leo as the leader of the new millennium. A little background information should illuminate all that 'Umar has left unsaid.

Both 'Umar and Masha'allah lived and worked in the 'Abbasid boomtown of Baghdad in the latter half of the eighth century and the beginning of the ninth century CE. Both of them passed away in approximately 815 CE, just as the Jupiter-Saturn cycle was shifting back into the fire signs from the water signs. The year 809 CE saw the first conjunction of the shift into the fire element, in Sagittarius. The year-transfer chart for this shift is included in Masha'allah's astrological history. The next conjunction in 829 CE was the first one in Leo. Masha'allah also included the year transfer chart for that conjunction in his history—but, of course, by that time, both Masha'allah and 'Umar had passed on to their reward.

Jesus: The Jew Who Conquered Rome

In writing with such surety about the millennial power of that first conjunction in Leo, 'Umar was not speaking from experience, but was addressing times that were to come by referring to days gone by. The last shift into the fire signs, with its first conjunction in Leo, was the same one that Masha'allah used for the birth of Christ. Certainly, that was a pivotal event in religious history, and one that ushered in a whole new era, but it wasn't the only thing going on at the time.

That Leo conjunction was in force from November of 27 BCE until July of 26 BCE. The year 27 BCE was a momentous one in the annals of world history; one that saw the rise of a new empire—the Roman Empire—from which was born a new religion: the emperor worship of Imperial Rome. In January of 27 BCE, in an audacious move that heralded both the death of the old Roman republic and the dawn of the greatest empire the world had ever known, the Roman senate approved the consolidation of worldly power and might in the hands of one Octavian, the gangly grand-nephew of Julius Caesar. He would henceforth be known as the Imperator Caesar Augustus, and even his arch enemies, the Persians, would never forget how he boldly took the center stage in world history under the auspices of that Leo conjunction.

By connecting the birth of Christ to the same conjunction, Persian astrologers were inexorably linking the fortunes of the Christian Church with the power of Rome. So there was at least one ancient Persian tradition that linked both the advent of Christ and the Emperor Augustus with the cycle of the Jupiter-Saturn conjunctions, and the dawn of a new millennium, or a new world age. It is preserved in the work of 'Umar, and echoes through the work of Masha'allah. This tradition would conceivably predate the Sasanian era, and could have served as a springboard for their further chronological speculations. At the same time, the conjunction that heralded both Jesus and the empire of Augustus would have been perceived in its own time, by contemporary astrologers, as yet another manifestation of a well-established, older cycle.

This is Persian astrology, and it should be apparent by now that it was quite different from the way the Greeks did it. The Persians, true to form, were more intrigued with the big picture: kingdoms, dynasties, prophets, and religions. The Persians perceived a God-given orderliness to the vicissitudes of world history that is conspicuously absent in the more polytheistic Hellenistic astrology.

Jupiter and Saturn Through History

From its Persian beginnings, the use of the Jupiter-Saturn cycles as a chronological infrastructure for the ebb and flow of human history spread throughout later Islamic astrology, which was then imported wholesale into medieval Europe. There, the new Muslim learning, the intellectual harvest of the Islamic Renaissance and the Golden Age of Baghdad, provided the wake-up call that roused Christian Europe from its Dark Ages.

Ironically, astrology appears to have led the way in reigniting Christian curiosity. From the 10th century on, European clerics eagerly sought the work of the Islamic astrologers of the Golden Age, such as al-Biruni, Abu Mas'shar, and, of course, 'Umar and Masha'allah. By the 12th century, Islamic astrology was a permanent and pervasive fixture throughout the newborn Christian academy. Dr. Nick Campion, in his article on Islamic astrology and its impact on Christian Europe, says, "That the translation of astrological material occurred at the beginning of the period of translation of Arabic texts into Latin has caused a reassessment of the process by which Islamic astrology penetrated Christian thought."

Previously, historians believed that the translation process had been inspired by a Western desire to retrieve the lost science and philosophy of the ancient world. Astrology was just an unfortunate by-product of Islamic superstition, which somehow slipped in, along with the good stuff. If, as it now appears, the astrological texts were among the first to be sought out for translation, "this suggests that western scholars...may have been more interested in astrology than in astronomy or mathematics."[14]

Astrology, particularly "natural," or historical astrology, proved uniquely suited to the task of Christian eschatology, wherein educated churchmen sought to understand and anticipate the order of God's universe as it unfolded in sacred time. Christian scholars were especially keen to pinpoint when it all began, how it would end, and when Jesus could reasonably be expected to come again.[15] "Arabic" astrological eschatology, which freely incorporated Zoroastrian themes, was a natural complement to Christian eschatology, but in order to practice astrology and attain its remarkable medieval benefits, it was necessary to first become adept in mathematics and astronomy. Many great advances in science and learning immediately followed.

Europeans were fascinated with the history-making cycles of the Jupiter-Saturn conjunctions, and they were enthusiastically adopted by men such as Christopher Columbus, Cardinal Pierre d'Ailly, Roger Bacon, Kepler, and, of course, Don Isaac Abrabanel, whom we met in the last chapter, just to name a few.

Christopher Columbus, a gifted navigator, and therefore no stranger to applied astronomy, provides one of our best examples of how the Jupiter-Saturn conjunctions were employed in the causes of Christian Europe.[16] Columbus believed that his explorations ultimately served the higher purpose of spreading the gospel of Jesus Christ throughout the world, a prerequisite for the second coming. Using the cycle of Jupiter-Saturn conjunctions, Columbus calculated several possible dates for this much-anticipated advent, which he believed his voyages had considerably hastened. He described his astrological reasoning in his *Book of the Prophecies*, in the copious notes he made in the margins of the volumes in his personal library, and even in his letters to the king and queen of Spain.[17]

Columbus was influenced in this particular line of inquiry by the work of the French cardinal Pierre d'Ailly. D'Ailly's extensive use of Jupiter-Saturn conjunctions to apportion Christian history was the subject of L.A. Smoller's *History, Prophecy, and the Stars.* Smoller relates at length how the cardinal, inspired by his astrological eschatology, led the 15th-century Council of Constance in healing the Great Schism within the Church. D'Ailly's biggest influence in astrochronology was no doubt Abu-Mashar, whom he came to via the work of the Franciscan, Roger Bacon, particularly the *Opus Maius.* Of course, Abu-Mashar was deeply indebted in his work to Masha'allah. Once we understand the historical chain of transmission behind these ideas, we can place Hughes's and Rabbi Rosenberg's 15th-century Abrabanel and his "traditional Jewish astrology" in its proper context.

So, in the work of Masha'allah and 'Umar we find a Persian astrological tradition in which the birth of Christ is an event of the utmost significance, not because he was a Judean king, but because of his role as a prophet, founder of a new religion, and, presumably, the usher of a new millennium. Furthermore, Masha'allah uses the Jupiter-Saturn conjunction in Leo in 26 BCE, the first conjunction in Leo after the shift to the fire signs in 46 BCE, as his main harbinger for the birth of Christ, even moving the birth year closer to it. So what about the triple Jupiter-Saturn conjunction in 7 BCE upon which contemporary theorists have pinned their hopes? Masha'allah and 'Umar don't even mention it!

But would any of this have been relevant to the Magi in Matthew? Would they have attached any significance to the Saturn-Jupiter conjunctions, or did these Persian techniques originate only later, during the Sasanian dynasty? Tracing the influence of Masha'allah forward in time is a fairly simple matter, for the transmission of ideas is well documented. Tracing his influences backward is more difficult, for the opposite reason— lack of documentation: "No pre-Islamic Iranian astronomical documents, either in the Pahlavi original or in translation, are extant."[18] But it is not impossible.

We know the conjunction cycle was used during the reign of Khosrau I Anushirvan, after centuries of efforts to reclaim and revive earlier Persian traditions. His ascent to the Sasanian throne in 531 CE coincided with a Saturn-Jupiter conjunction in the sidereal sign of Gemini, but we can hardly claim that event, or any other single incident, as the origin of a theory of such scale and scope. Instead, the timing of Khosrau's ascension would have only been meaningful if it were construed as further confirmation of a long-standing pattern.

The close coincidence of the birth of the prophet of Islam with the shift in the conjunction cycle incited a lot of local interest in the subject. In fact, the conjunction cycle fit remarkably well with the fall of the Sasanians (651 CE), the birth of Mohammed, the rise of Islam, the Muslim conquests, and the dramatic change of dynasty under the 'Abbasids. As people struggled to make sense of all the transition and turmoil of their times, it was only natural that they sought some comfort and order in these earlier Persian traditions.

The popular perception of a correlation between Islam and the shift in the conjunction cycle gave rise to further speculation that important events in Islam's future would be linked to future shifts in the conjunction cycle. There is no shortage of evidence for this application of the theory, particularly by partisans seeking to overthrow the established Muslim leadership, beginning with the 'Abbasids.[19]

By most accounts, the first 'Abbasid caliph, al-Saffah, was publicly proclaimed in a ceremony at the mosque in Kufa on November 28, 749 CE; a date that featured not only a full moon, but also marked the heliacal rising of the Jupiter-Saturn conjunction in Scorpio. Since as early as the seventh century BCE, if not before, the heliacal rising, when Jupiter and Saturn emerged from the beams of the sun and rose before it at dawn, was held to be one of the most powerful points of the planetary cycle. As the Umayyads were not actually defeated until several months later, at the end of January, 750, there is probably a degree of astrological contrivance behind this official date. It's just a little too perfect, especially when you consider that the main backers of the 'Abbasid cause, particularly in Kufa, were militant Iranian millennialists.

Masha'allah may have had a Persian nationalist agenda of his own. As Kennedy and Pingree point out, he apparently anticipated a return to Persian rule and expected that the upcoming shift of the conjunction to the fire signs would fell the 'Abbasids in the year 813 CE. In fact, it was Masha'allah who died, around 815. Whether these two instances—his prediction and his passing—were at all related, we may never know.

But could the elaborate chronological systems employed by Masha'allah and 'Umar have evolved solely as a response to the dawn of

Islam and its new world empire, or do we simply lack the textual evidence for their earlier use? Further, if we assume a Sasanian origin for the Jupiter-Saturn tradition, one problem immediately presents itself: The fall of the Sasanians does fit the pattern, but the same cannot be said for their rise (226 CE).

In fact, of all the Persian dynasties, the Sasanians are the only ones whose rise to power did not markedly coincide with the Jupiter-Saturn conjunction cycle. For instance, the dawn of the Achaemenid dynasty, the dramatic coup d'etat of the false Magian, and the counterattack of Darius (522 BCE) all transpired under the unmistakable influence of a triple Jupiter-Saturn conjunction. This particular triple conjunction, in the constellation of Libra, was also an especially anomalous shift, moving the cycle temporarily from the earth element into air. I rather doubt the Magi would have missed that, and I even have to wonder if it didn't figure into their plans.

Alexander's dramatic installation as emperor in Babylon, followed by his sudden death and the breakup of his empire, were also uniquely heralded by a Jupiter-Saturn conjunction. So was the rise of the Parthian Arsacid dynasty (ca. 246 BCE), and its crucial expansion into an empire under Mithradates I. The revolt of the Maccabees (late autumn, 165 BCE), when Judah and his band of zealots, the ideological allies of the Magi, seized the Jerusalem temple and cleansed it of the Hellenistic abominations of the Greeks (an event still celebrated annually in the festival of Hannukah), was timed to the heliacal rising of the Jupiter-Saturn conjunction. Even Augustus and the Roman Empire fit the pattern. The only Persian dynasty that doesn't was the Sasanian. Ardashir defeated the last Parthian emperor ca. 224 CE, under a Jupiter-Saturn opposition, and the empire is usually dated ca. 226 CE. So can we safely assume an origin for the Persian Jupiter-Saturn tradition within the only dynasty that doesn't fit the model?

Remember, Mesopotamian astrologers were passionate observers, constantly contriving correlations between celestial and terrestrial events. The Magi had been teamed with the Chaldeans of Babylon since at least 539 BCE, if not long before. Their traditions regarding the Jupiter-Saturn conjunctions grew out of long centuries of meticulous observation and correlation. Even with all its faults, their work was considerably more sophisticated than all that cutting-and-pasting of mythological meaningfulness that modern researchers have tried to project upon them.

In my opinion, the evidence suggests the use of the conjunction cycle at least as early as the revolt of the Maccabees, and certainly during the reign of Augustus. Its relevance for astrologers in that era, including perhaps Matthew's Magi, remains enshrined in the work of Masha'allah and 'Umar. But the actual origins of such usage could go back to that pivotal year of 522 BCE, when the triple Jupiter-Saturn conjunction, shifting into the sidereal sign of Libra, oversaw the ascension of Darius the Great, and both the overthrow and the salvation of the Achaemenid throne. As always, the Magi were right there, in the thick of it.

Chapter 8
The Millennium and the Messiah

Grand Conjunction Theory

Masha'allah's methods raise a number of questions. For instance, why did he always use the chart for the Vernal Equinox before the conjunction? Why not cast the chart for the date and time of the exact conjunctions, or, for the matter, the heliacal rising? The most practical answer is that it was too difficult. After all, he was only using the mean motion for both planets in his calculations, so his planetary positions became increasingly inexact with each passing year.

He probably had other doctrinal considerations in mind as well; for instance, the idea of the Vernal Equinox as the annual "Revolution of the World Year." Many ancient chronologists believed that at the creation of the world, all the planets gathered together in a "Grand Conjunction" at the beginning of Aries, the gateway to the zodiac. This initial "Grand Conjunction" set all time and creation in motion. It also initiated the shorter cycles of Saturn-Jupiter conjunctions, which thereafter serve as the appointed timekeepers, transmitting the original impetus in a series of cascading resonances throughout history. Each new Vernal Equinox represented yet another revolution of the world year, and the chart would have been examined carefully to reveal what was in store.

Even though Masha'allah was obviously influenced by this line of thinking, I believe that Kennedy and Pingree are correct when they assert: "Masha'allah's chronology depends on a millennial theory rather than on a conjunction theory, for the intervals he gives are all from the midpoint of the millennium of Mars to a particular event. In this he differs from other astrologers, such as Abu Mas'shar in his *Kitab al-uluf,*

who begin their histories with...the mean conjunction of all the planets in
♈ 0° (zero degrees of Aries)."

World Ages and the Age of the World

The astrological chronologies of Masha'Allah and 'Umar are firmly anchored in earlier Persian millenarianism. 'Umar even refers to the Jupiter-
Saturn cycle as "the conjunctions of the thousands"—as an integral part
of the millennial system. But what were these zodiacal millennia, and
would they have meant anything to Matthew's Magi?

As Edward Kennedy puts it, "By Sasanian times (and perhaps since
the 5th century BC) the notion of a world-span of 12,000 years was current in Iran...one [millennia] for each of the zodiacal signs of Babylonian
astronomy...."[1]

This uniquely Persian version of the "World Year," in which historical
time is divided into 12 millennia, each ruled by a zodiac sign or planet, may
have originated as early as the Achaemenid era. The astrological order of the
Persian cosmos was created to accommodate the ongoing battle between good
and evil in all its phases, especially its dramatic conclusion. To fully penetrate
its mysteries, we need to come to terms with Zurvan Zoroastrianism.

Zurvan: God of Infinite Time

Zurvanism is often classified as a Zoroastrian heresy, but it endured
for more than a thousand years alongside the more normative "Mazda
worship," and remained an ongoing concern, even into the later Sasanian
era. Zurvanist ideas are especially evident throughout the Sasanians' "orthodox" Pahlavi literature, so perhaps it is better to think of Zurvanism
as an enduring sect, school, branch, or stream.

Although the sect's origins probably lie somewhere deep in the
Achaemenid period, the name "Zurvan" itself may have been borrowed
from an even earlier Phoenician deity.[2] Many ancient Near Eastern myths
and images may have been bound up into the Zurvan tradition as time
went on. Still, our best and most comprehensive sources for Zurvan
Zoroastrianism come from the later Pahlavi literature, thanks again to
the Sasanians' efforts to gather together the older Persian traditions. Here
the ancient god Zurvan emerges fully formed; a deified concept of infinite Time, and the sacred source of all creation.

Zurvan (Time) alone has infinite being, and it is Zurvan who gives birth to the good and evil twins, Ahura Mazda and Ahriman; thus the battle begins. This birth story, which appears in several forms throughout the Zoroastrian corpus, may have grown out of attempts to resolve the inherent theological difficulties arising from the religion's extreme dualism. In the earliest Avestan literature, the *Gathas*, presumably written by Zoroaster himself, and dating to perhaps as early as 1000 BCE, if not earlier, we find this quote from Yasna 30.3–4, which presents the contending duo as twins:

> (3) Now the two Primal Spirits, who reveal themselves in vision as Twins, are the Better and the Bad, in thought and word and action. And between these two the wise ones chose aright, the foolish not so.
>
> (4) And when these twain Spirits came together in the beginning, they created Life and Not-Life, and that at the last Worst Existence shall be to the followers of the Lie, but the Best Existence to him that follows Right.

The simple dualism of the ancient Yasnas may have inadvertently spurred thinking Zoroastrians on to envision a more ultimate source of good and evil. Obviously, Zurvanism would have gone through some important developmental stages after that, but much of that process is lost to us now. However, we do have the results, for at the other end of the spectrum, in the Muslim period, after a millennium of myth-making and accretion, we encounter the full-blown Zurvanist cosmology.

The following is a very late version of the Zurvan creation story from a document entitled *Ulema i Islam*, or the *Doctors of Islam*.[3] Here, the good doctors conduct a debate with "one who was learned in the Zoroastrian faith." Their debate explores the origin of the Zurvanite cosmos, in which finite time is set apart from infinite Time (Zurvan) and arranged into millennia, all to accommodate the ultimate battle between good and evil. Verse 8 contains this declaration: "In the religion of Zoroaster, it is thus revealed. Except Time all other things are created. Time is the creator; and Time has no limit, neither top nor bottom. It has always been and shall be for evermore."

Within the abode of Zurvan, or limitless Time, Ohrmazd (Ahura Mazda), the good god, the bright, pure, sweet-smelling, and beneficent, comes into being. But he eventually looks down into the depths and detects the presence of Ahriman (Angra Mainyu), the bad god—black, foul, stinking, and maleficent. Ohrmazd realizes he must destroy Ahriman before

Ahriman destroys him, and begins to consider how. In verse 12, Time comes to his aid, for "all the excellence that Ohrmazd needed had already been created."

> (12) And Ohrmazd made Time of the long Dominion manifest which has the measure of twelve thousand years, and within it he attached the firmament, the artificer (and heaven).
>
> (13) And each of the twelve Signs of the Zodiac which are bound to the firmament he appointed for a thousand years. During three thousand years, the spiritual creation was made, and Aries, Taurus, and Gemini held sway each for a thousand years.

Ahriman was so intimidated by this display of righteousness that he rushed back to hell empty-handed and could not move for 3,000 years, so that in verse 15: "...during these three thousand years material creation was made. The control of the world passed to Cancer, Leo, and Virgo. In this matter, much has been said."

This story in the *Doctors of Islam* is a relatively late recapitulation of the kind of material that is abundantly present throughout the Sasanian Pahlavi literature. It reveals the Zurvanite preoccupation with the origin of finite time from infinite Time, with its arrangement into millennial ages ruled over by the signs of the zodiac, and with its eschatological culmination in the ultimate battle between good and evil. All of these themes are described in unabashedly astrological detail. The astrology is not in any way separate from either the cosmogony or the eschatology; instead it permeates the entire theology in a surprisingly holistic manner. The good God created the material universe with an implicit astrological order that is there to assist him in his ultimate defeat of evil and to help keep track of exactly when that will come about.

The full system of zodiacal world ages is explained in several different places throughout the Pahlavi literature, but it receives particularly detailed treatment in both the *Bundahisn* and the *Greater Bundahisn*. Zurvan chronology was not an exact science either, for while the various systems are fairly consistent on the idea of 12 millennia, there are differences in the way pivotal events are parceled out among the millennia. For instance, in some versions, Ahriman, the Adversary, comes in to attack the world in the first millennium (Ch. XXXIII, Greater *Bundahisn*). In other versions, Ahriman first enters the world in the seventh millennium of Libra, after half the cycle has already passed (ch. Vb, *Greater Bundahisn*).[4]

> (15) Again, there is this that till the advent of the Adversary, six thousand years of time had elapsed: three thousand years in spirituality, and three thousand years of materiality in purity; and those six thousand years were from Aries to Virgo, and each constellation ruled a thousand years.
>
> (16) As the rule of the millennium came to Libra, which is the house of fall, the fall of the Sun, the Adversary entered from underneath.

The prophet Zoroaster makes his appearance in the Capricorn, or 10th millennium in chapter XXXVI of the *Greater Bundahisn*, whereas in chapter XXXIII, he comes in the fourth millennium. It is confusing to try to determine from this literature exactly where we stand on this millennial time scale, but one thing is certain: Zurvanism was always associated with the Magi. Consider the following quote from Plutarch, in which he cites an earlier author, Theopompus, who was born c. 380 BCE:

> Theopompus says that, according to the Magians, for three thousand years alternately the one god will dominate the other and be dominated, and that for another three thousand years they will fight and make war, until one smashes up the domain of the other. In the end Hades shall perish and men shall be happy; neither shall they need sustenance nor shall they cast a shadow, while the god who will have brought this about shall have quiet and shall rest.... Such is the mythology of the Magians.[5]

Compare this to what al-Biruni (d. 1048 CE) said in his *Chronology*. When referring to the religion of the Magians, he reported that they had a cycle of "12,000 years, corresponding to the number of the Signs of the Zodiac and of the months."[6] From age to age, there is this one constant with the Magi—the millennia.

The cosmological complexities of Zurvan Zoroastrianism may have arisen from the necessary confrontation between the dualism of the ancient Median Magi and the astronomy of their Mesopotamian neighbors. In this prolonged cultural comingling, the influences flowed both ways. While the universalism of the Persian religion helped to inspire significant developments in mathematical astronomy among the Assyrians and

Babylonians, Assyro-Babylonian astrology could not help but impact the Magi, who, from their position of authority within the Persian Empire, directed the work of Babylonian stargazers and had ready access to all of their best information. The Magi were then faced with the task of integrating it all into their own worldview. The result was this distinctly Mazdean stream of astrology—the Zurvanist cosmology and cosmogony preserved in the Pahlavi compilations.

This Persian astrology contained many of the same elements as Babylonian and Greek astrology—signs, rulerships, malefic and benefic planets, and so on—but it was also significantly different in that it actually sought to explain the reasons behind all the astrological rules. For instance, why are some planets malefic, such as Mars and Saturn, and why are some planets benefic, such as Jupiter and Venus? Why is the sign Libra the fall of the sun? Why does the first house represent the life of the native? The Zurvan astrological cosmology was a complete theological system that rationalized many of the traditional rules of astrology (still used by practicing astrologers today) while continually weaving all the astrological considerations into the ongoing and ultimate battle between good and evil.

So the Magi of Matthew's time, although certainly aware of Greek and Babylonian astrology, had a native system of their own; a system that was entirely relevant to their appearance in Matthew's narrative.[7]

The Zoroastrian World Saviors

The Persian Magi were also awaiting the virgin birth of their own promised messiah, or world savior—yet another reason they hold such pride of place within the Christian canon. In fact, Matthew may have been playing to Zoroastrian expectations in his use of Isaiah's "prophecy" about the virgin who would conceive and give birth.

The Magi were awaiting the coming of not only one, but three great saviors, who were expected during the next three world ages, or millenniums. In the course of the religion's long history, these Mazdean beliefs in the coming saviors, similar to their beliefs in Zurvan, passed through their various developmental stages. In the earliest Avestan literature, the *Gathas*, we do find a number of promising references to "one who is to come," a future deliverer, who will establish righteousness throughout the earth. For example, the *Ushtavaiti Gatha*, chapter 45, verse 11, refers to "...the holy *Daena* of the future deliverer...." Here, the Avestan term *Daena* means religious view, faith, doctrine, conception, or vision.

In the *Vahishtoishti Gatha*, chapter 53, verse 2, we find: "Then let them seek the pleasure of Mazda with thoughts, words, and actions, unto him praise gladly, and seek his worship,...making straight the paths for the Religion of the future Deliverer which Ahura ordained."[8]

Yasna 48 of the *Spentamainyush Gatha* contains two references to the hope placed by Zarathustra in the coming of future deliverers, who would be more victorious than he in spreading the good religion:

> (9) When shall I know whether ye have power, O Mazda and Right, over everyone whose destructiveness is a menace to me? Let the revelation of Good Thought be confirmed unto me; the future deliverer should know how his own destiny shall be.

And:

> (11) When, O Mazda, shall Piety come with Right, with Dominion the happy dwelling rich with pasture? Who are they that will make peace with the bloodthirsty Liars? To whom will the Lore of Good Thought come?

> (12) These shall be the deliverers [translator's note: *Saoshyants*] of the provinces, who exert themselves, O Good Thought in their action, O Asha, to fulfill their duty, face to face with thy command, O Mazda. For these are the appointed smiters of Violence.

The term *Saoshyant,* introduced here by the translator, Joseph H. Peterson, originally meant a benefactor, strengthener, or redeemer; literally, one who sets about benefiting. But early in the Avestan literature, *Saoshyant* emerged as a designation for the anticipated savior or religious leader to come. For instance, in the Avestan Yasna 59, verse 28, we find: "We worship Verethraghna, the Ahura-made, the victorious blow; and we worship the Saoshyant, who smites with victory...."

From these humble but distinct beginnings, the doctrine of a future deliverer spread; not only throughout Zoroastrianism, but everywhere the Persians went—and they went everywhere. It proved to be one of the most widely popular premises of the Persian religion, and found ready acceptance wherever people longed for redemption. Many other myths and legends accrued, and by the time of the compilation of the Pahlavi literature, the Sasanian Mazda-worshippers were expecting three world saviors, all sons of Zoroaster, who would bring his good works and righteousness to their ultimate completion.

Just as in Judean messianism, there was never complete agreement on all the particulars. In essence, the first two saviors, who in some sources go by the names of Aushedar and Aushedar-mah, were to be born at the dawn of each subsequent millennium. At the age of 30, their campaigns of righteousness would begin. They would both do much good, but by the end of their millennium, the powers of darkness would descend and undo much of what they had accomplished.

The third, the Saoshyant, the ultimate world savior, would come in the last millennium, and destroy the forces of evil forever, in the final battle between good and evil at the end of the world. Then he would usher in an everlasting aeon of peace, with a last judgment and the resurrection of the dead.

All three sons would be born from the seed of Zoroaster, which was spilled in some suitably pious manner. Thousands of angel-spirits watch over this precious seed, which lies hidden in the waters of the holy Lake Kasava, or Kayansah. A virgin would come to bathe in that lake, and being impregnated by the miraculous seed, would bring forth each son in his time. Chapter XXXIII of the *Greater Bundahisn* ends with this reminder of how these millennial sons of Zoroaster will come about:

> (36) As regards these three sons of Zartosht, such as Aushedar, Aushedar-mah, and Soshyant, one says, "Before Zartosht wedded, they had consigned the glory (khwarrah) of Zartosht for preservation, in the sea Kayansah to the glory of the water, that is to the Yazad Anahit."
>
> (37) They say "Even now they are seeing three lamps glowing at night in the bottom of the sea. And each one of them will arrive when it is their own cycle.
>
> (38) It will so happen that a virgin will go to the water of Kayansah in order to wash her head; the glory (khwarrah) will mingle within her body, and she will be pregnant. They will one-by-one be born, thus in their own cycle."

This virgin mother owes much of her imagery to the Persian goddess Anahita, or as the text calls her, the Yazad, Anahit. The lady of the waters, who insured the purity and abundance of fresh water, and therefore the life of the people, Anahita was the chief goddess of the Persian religion. She was often portrayed as an ever-virgin mother, who routinely renewed her virginity by bathing in the purist of waters; hence, her connection with the virgin mother of the sons of Zoroaster.

In the inclusive monotheism of the Persian religion, the worship of the ancient goddess Anahita remained popular throughout, along with other ancient Aryan gods such as Mithra, in much the same way that the Virgin Mary and the saint cults managed to hold their ground within the ostensibly monotheistic Christian churches. Remember, the family of Ardashir, the first Sasanian emperor, served as the priests of the temple of Anahita in Istahr. In Western terms, this might be akin to serving at the Cathedral of Notre Dame. From this background in Persian goddess worship, Ardashir emerged as a Zoroastrian conservative, bent on restoration.

Once we understand the Persian tradition of the coming world saviors and their virgin mother/goddess, Matthew's exaggerated claim that Isaiah prophesied a virgin birth starts to make a lot more sense, especially when he introduces the Magi immediately after. If the Magi were using astrology to seek a savior, then a virgin was necessary to complete the context.

So from the pages of the Pahlavi texts arises an astrological eschatology in which time is divided into astrological millennia. The revelations of new religions and the appearance of great religious leaders are timed to these astrological millennia, both in the original Zoroastrian concept of World Saviors, and in later Islamic millennial extrapolations. Zurvan Zoroastrianism would appear to be the specific context in which these ideas arose.

Persian Inclusive Monotheism

Let's return to Masha'allahs's rather awkward chronology in which he unabashedly mashes together the two systems, the conjunction theory and the "thousands." Although he was a Jew with Zoroastrian sympathies, he was writing about the birth of Christ under an Islamic regime. By combining the conjunctions and the millennia, he crafts a very happy marriage between all four religions, presenting Christ and Mohammed as the first two world saviors, or sons of Zoroaster. Kennedy and Pingree agree that with a little adjustment in his numbers, "...one finds perfect correspondence between the Zoroastrian doctrine and Masha'allah. The motion of the heavens commences in the fourth millennium (after 3509), the Deluge—a catastrophic event—occurs at the end of the sixth millennium (after 5932) and Christ and Muhammad, who defeat evil, were both born in the tenth millennium...."[9]

In his system, the first two sons of Zoroaster, Jesus and Mohammed, have each arrived on time. Maybe Mohammed arrived a bit early, but who's counting? In accomplishing this, or more likely, passing it along, we owe Masha'allah a genuine debt of gratitude. For here, he was serving as much more than a mere astrologer. He was presenting one of the finest examples of an all-inclusive monotheism still extant. Here is the big picture, the overarching God's-eye view, wherein all who worship the one God are one and always have been. We lost that thread a long time ago in the West, and stubbornly adhere to the orthodox, man-made myths of Christian, Jewish, and Islamic history, each claiming a separate and exclusive origin in divine revelation. Masha'allah's inclusive version is actually more in keeping with what we now know about the historical transmission of monotheism in the ancient Near East. On the question of whether or not we can live peacefully on the same planet with the people of Persia, Masha'allah's inclusive monotheism is more relevant now than ever.

Catholic Astrology

In his *Tetrabiblos*, Ptolemy made the distinction between *Katholikon* (*to kath'hola* in Greek), or Catholic astrology, and *genethlialogical* astrology. Catholic astrology deals with entire races, countries, and cities, whereas *genesis* deals with the birth of individuals, and the concerns of their individual lives.[10] According to Franz Cumont, the term *Catholic*, meaning universal and all-inclusive, actually originated in astrology.[11] It was introduced to distinguish between local, tribal gods, and celestial, planetary gods, who were not limited in influence to any particular place or people, but instead ruled over activities and experiences that affected the whole earth, or the whole human race. This represented a philosophical step forward from the pettiness of warring tribal gods to a more all-encompassing concept of divinity and order. How ironic then, that the term *Catholic* has, through the ages, in the pursuit of orthodoxy and the persecution of heresy, come to signify its own opposite.

The Magi specialized in the *Katholikon*. It's hard to be exclusive when you're focused on the big picture, and the Persians, as always, were uniquely concerned with the big picture: empires and dynasties, great prophets, world religions, and the ultimate meaning of time and the universe. Whoever it was that put the story of the Magi into the Gospel of Matthew must have believed that his claims for Jesus would carry a lot more weight and reach a lot more people if he framed them within the more Catholic monotheism of the Magi's astrological universe.

Chapter 9
Pisces and Precession

In his unique work, *The Birth of Christ: Exploding the Myth*, astrophysicist Dr. Percy Seymour remarks on the Magi and the Age of Pisces:

> Shortly before Christ's birth, the sun at the vernal equinox had moved into the constellation Pisces. The astronomical period which began just around the time of Christ's birth is called the Age of Pisces.... If...we accept that the Magi knew about the Great Year and the coming new Age of Pisces, and if, in common with the messianic expectations of the time, they therefore sought a messiah who would represent the new Piscean age, then the triple conjunction of 7 BCE would be important, not only because of its astrological meanings and it particular significance for Judea and Bethlehem, but also because of the sun at the vernal equinox in Pisces. Thus the Magi's search for the Messiah is put into the context of the age in which they lived....

Percy Seymour's work[1] is important, and I wish everyone would read it, but I still have to take issue with this particular point. The idea of astrological world ages based upon the precession of the equinoxes has been popular in New Age and theosophical circles for some time. The idea of astrological world ages originated among the Magi in Zurvan Zoroastrianism, but I have yet to see any firm evidence that Persian astrologers ever linked their astrological ages to the precession of the equinox, or that they had any expectation of a coming new Age of Pisces. If only it were that simple!

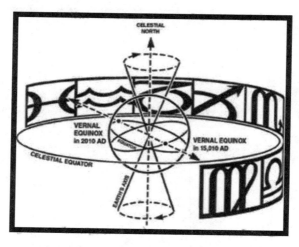

The tilt of the Earth's axis traces a circular path in the sky. The equinoxes follow a similar path, completing the circle every 26,000 years. So the Vernal Equinox points toward the cusp of Pisces in 2010 CE, *and it will be pointing at the cusp of Virgo (on the opposite side of the zodiac) halfway through the cycle, in the year 15010* CE. *Image created by Michael G. Conrad.*

Hipparchus

Let's start with the basic premise: Hipparchus of Rhodes discovered precession at some point in the mid-second century BCE. That's reasonable enough, isn't it? It was only a matter of time before someone, reading through the observations compiled by the Babylonians, would come to the unavoidable conclusion that the so-called fixed stars had moved.[2]

But was he the first to notice? This point has been debated at length, and the bottom line is: no, of course he wasn't. The ancient Egyptians aligned their buildings to fixed stars, so the next generation or two couldn't help but see that something had shifted—and that's only one example of many. As the authors of *Hamlet's Mill* demonstrated, people noticed this motion long ago, and entire bodies of myth and legend developed around it.

Hipparchus was the first astronomer working in the Greek scientific tradition to attempt to derive precession from a series of systematic observations, and to try to place a mathematical value upon it. That was original—or at least, we think it was. The fact is, we don't really know for sure, because almost none of the work of Hipparchus and his contemporaries has survived. Of the 14 books attributed to his hand, the only one still extant is his *Commentary on the Phenomena of Aratus and Eudoxus*, which doesn't really deal with the question of precession.

Consider this: Most histories of science proclaim Hipparchus the most important astronomer of the ancient world. He is credited with developing the first trigonometric tables, the first reliable method of predicting solar and lunar eclipses, the first star catalog of the Western world, the discovery of precession, and maybe even the invention of the astrolabe. And yet, every bit of this work was deemed unsuitable for transmission in the medieval monasteries.

We know his writings were widely published and survived at least into the fourth century CE. For instance, his influence is evident in the writings of Strabo (first century BCE) and the Roman author Pliny (first century CE). Ptolemy obviously had ready access to Hipparchus's most technical material in Alexandria in the second century CE, and relied on it in

compiling his *Almagest*. Pappus of Alexandria (third century CE) and Theon of Alexandria (fourth century CE) also knew his work, but after that, 13 of his 14 books disappear.

As it is, we have only a few very late, secondhand sources for this, the greatest astronomer of the ancient world; but of course, everyone knows that Hipparchus discovered precession. Further complicating the issue is the lack of any surviving references to precession from the period between Hipparchus and Ptolemy. Whatever anyone else thought about it at the time is also lost to us now. That's 300 years of silence on the matter. All we have is Ptolemy. Why?

Claudius Ptolemaeus, as portrayed by a medieval artist. Image in public domain.

Historians generally agree that the popularity of Ptolemy himself may have meant Hipparchus's undoing. Both Neugebauer and G.J. Toomer theorize that Ptolemy's *Almagest* was so dominant that it made the earlier astronomers and their work redundant, resulting in what Neugebauer called "an almost total obliteration of the prehistory of the Ptolemaic astronomy."[3] As Toomer puts it, "being obsolete, they ceased to be copied."[4]

Hipparchus and Astrology

That may well be, but perhaps there were other factors at work too, at least in certain quarters. Liba Taub, in his article on The Starry Messenger, the excellent Cambridge University Website on the history of astronomy, broadens the whole question by pointing out that "the work of Hipparchus...dealing with the calculation and prediction of celestial positions would have been very useful to those engaged in the sort of astronomy known as astrology"[5] In fact, the advances made by Hipparchus in observation and mathematics were driven largely by the need for greater accuracy in astrology. After all, no one was trying to send up a communications satellite or put a man on the moon in the second century BCE, but as a writer and teacher of astrology, Hipparchus would have had a lot of interested readers. Otto Neugebauer had this to say about it: "Hipparchus is often quoted in the astrological literature.... It was F. Boll who first emphasized that the ancient reports connecting Hipparchus with astrology have to be taken seriously...."[6]

Franz Cumont rather blithely pointed out that "It is remarkable that the great astronomer, Hipparchus...was also a convinced supporter of one of the leading doctrines of stellar religion."[7] Pliny extols Hipparchus in book 2, chapter XXVI of his *Natural History* as a man who "can never be sufficiently praised, no one having done more to prove that man is related to the stars and that our souls are a part of heaven." Or as Cumont has it, "that our souls are particles of heavenly fire." D.R. Dicks adds: "It would seem that Hipparchus' contemporary fame rested largely on his astrological works...."[8] G.J. Toomer, who authored both a biography of Hipparchus and a translation of Ptolemy's *Almagest*, is even more emphatic on this point, and believed that: "...astrology had no importance in the Greek world until after Hipparchus, and that his role, both directly as an advocate of astrology, and indirectly as a developer of astronomical methods which became an essential part of it, was pivotal."[9]

That's a pretty strong statement, and whether or not that is the case, it does cement Hipparchus's reputation as an astrologer; one who not only measured the motions of the heavens, but who also interpreted its meanings. And if he interpreted this meaning, is it not possible that he, and his students or associates, may have attached some astrological, chronological, or even quasi-religious meaning to the precession of the equinoxes, no matter how dimly they understood the mechanics?

If we consider the question of how Hipparchus's discovery of precession might have been received as an astrological doctrine, or how it might have impacted contemporary religious cosmologies and chronologies, we are suddenly faced with a startling realization. Shortly after the time of Hipparchus, in the first centuries BCE and CE, the ancient world experienced an explosion of radical new religious chronologies, based upon the idea of the end of the old world, and the beginning of a new age and a new world order.

The most lasting and influential of these was Christianity, which from the very beginning proclaimed the apocalyptic coming of the Kingdom of God. With its aeon (a world age) and imminent Parousia (the second coming), Alpha and Omega, and the Piscean symbolism of the Christ/fish, Christianity was the original "New Age" religion. This elaborate Christian eschatology did not arise in a vacuum, but fit well within the broader social spectrum, wherein the early Christians were surrounded by other cults and sects who believed along much the same lines; for instance, the Gnostics, the cults of the Aeon and Mithras, and of course, the solar/emperor worship at the very heart of the Roman Empire.

In 1989, David Ulansey published *The Origins of the Mithraic Mysteries*. In this work and related articles, Ulansey developed the idea that the symbolism of the Roman cults of the god Mithras, particularly their taurectonomy, the ever-present bull-slaying scene, represented a contemporary religious response to the discovery of precession. Ulansey's work raised some very good questions about how the discoveries of Hipparchus would have been received; questions that remain unresolved.[10]

Perhaps we have been looking in all the wrong places for the impact of the discovery of precession. Perhaps it is hidden in the symbolism of the Mithraeums (temples of Mithras). There, many of the older cosmological myths and deities were attached to the Mithraic iconography in a new way, and Mithras was increasingly portrayed as a composite of the gods in charge of a changing cosmos. Perhaps it survives in the fish stories in the Christian Gospels, or in the *Fisher of Souls Saga* of the Mandean cults of John the Baptist, in the symbolic guise of the Good Fisher who comes to save his fish. Perhaps it survives in the poetry of Virgil, who in the opening to his fourth Ecologue, written in 37 BCE, heralded the dawn of a new age, with the return of Saturn and the Virgin Justice: "Now the last age by Cumae's Sibyl sung has come and gone, and the majestic roll of circling centuries begins anew."[11]

All these breathtaking new visions of time, wherein circling aeons and swirling centuries were all cycling up to their inevitable conclusion and glorious rebirth, emerged in the wake of the discoveries of Hipparchus. And who is to say they were wrong? After all, we still organize time, whether BC/AD or BCE/CE, along these same lines. Perhaps at least one of the reasons the books of Hipparchus and his unknown commentators did not survive the copying process was because some of the ideas in them were too controversial, and too uncomfortably close to the emerging orthodox Christian eschatology.

But nowhere in all of this fascinating chronology do we find anything even remotely akin to the declaration in the rock musical *Hair* of the dawning of Age of Pisces—and there was very good reason for that. As excited as people were about all the religious and cosmological implications of the heavens in motion, they really did not understand the mechanics or the math sufficiently to think about it in that way.

The Misunderstanding

Regarding the lack of references to precession in the interval between Hipparchus and Ptolemy, Noel Swerdlow said, "...it is most likely that the precession was not mentioned for three hundred years because Hipparchus' description was so tentative, and so uncertain of what his observations showed, that no one paid any attention to it until Ptolemy demonstrated that it really existed."[12]

Hipparchus was uncertain about what he had observed. He even offered several hypotheses to both explain and test his observations. Ptolemy reports that Hipparchus's first hypothesis was that only zodiacal stars, particularly bright zodiacal stars such as Spica, moved with the equinoxes.[13] Hipparchus also questioned whether the fixed stars were really fixed at all. He proposed the possibility that they had other, independent motions, and included detailed descriptions of stellar alignments in his work so that later observers could check to see if any changes had taken place. Ptolemy did check them, and was able to show that all of the alignments were still in place, exactly as Hipparchus described them.[14]

Hipparchus was also unsure about the actual rate of precession. In fact, somewhere between Hipparchus and Ptolemy, the rate got hopelessly distorted, with long-term consequences. In the *Almagest* (VII.2), Ptolemy quotes Hipparchus himself from *On the Precession of Solstitial and Equinoctial Points* (no longer extant), for a series of observations of the star, Spica.[15] These observations would have yielded a precessional rate of 1° in a little more than 75 years, had Ptolemy checked the math. Instead, Ptolemy quoted another rate, 1° in 100 years, which Hipparchus had tentatively proposed in his *On the Magnitude of the Solar Year* (no longer extant). Even though Hipparchus only suspected this was the rate, subject to a number of conditions, this latter value was accepted by Theon of Alexandria and remained in use for centuries, confusing astronomers everywhere, while the former, and more accurate value had to be rediscovered many times over before it was finally accepted.[16]

The Fabulous Eighth Sphere

In the pre-Copernican, geocentric (Ptolemaic) cosmology, with its system of interactive planetary spheres, precession was believed to be a result of the motion of the fabulous "eighth sphere." This eighth sphere was the home of the fixed stars of the constellations, and it revolved somewhere beyond the seven planetary spheres. The misconception of the sphere, combined with Ptolemy's miscalculation of its rate of motion, created big problems in astronomy for more than 1,000 years.

There were always perceptive astronomers who came closer to the real figure in their calculations. Albategni (d. 929 CE) believed that the rate of precession was approximately 1° in 66 years, and al-Biruni (d. 1048 CE) calculated it to 1° in 68 years. Petro de Abano (13th century) refers to the precessional cycle of one "Azolphi" (25,200 years), which is remarkably close to the accurate rate.[17]

It was Isaac Newton, in the 17th century, who produced the first full theoretical explana-

> **The Rate of Precession**
>
> 1° of zodiacal longitude every 71.6 years
>
> One complete cycle of the zodiac in 25,765 years

tion of precession, and accurately calculated its annual rate.[18] Before Newton, much of the work in the intervening centuries quotes Ptolemy's nice, round number of 100 years. For instance, the *Sphaera Mundi* of

Rabbi Abraham bar Hiyya, published in 1546, contains a history of the theories of the eighth sphere, and opens with the assertion that it moves 1° in 100 years, and makes a complete rotation in 36,000 years.[19] Edward Grant notes that: "During the Middle Ages, numerous periods were proposed for the Great Year, the most popular being 36,000 and 49,000 years. The former was derived from Ptolemy's *Almagest*, based upon a value of precession of the equinoxes of 1° in 100 years."[20]

The Theory of Trepidation

Further adding to the confusion, ancient astronomers did not assume that precession was a simple, straightforward motion. Most of them believed that the eighth sphere not only precessed at a regular pace, but that it also periodically reversed itself and went back in the other direction, at various and confusing intervals. This was the *theory of trepidation*, and it too would plague the study of precession for more than a thousand years.

The origin of this theory remains a mystery, and still clouds our understanding of how precession was received in the ancient world. Swerdlow claims that Hipparchus may also have proposed "that the sphere of the fixed stars might oscillate back and forth over a short arc of eight degrees..." but there is little evidence that he did.[21] The earliest reference to trepidation is found in Theon of Alexandria's "small" commentary to Ptolemy's "Handy Tables" (fourth century CE). Theon claims that Ptolemy specifically did not ascribe to a theory of "the ancient makers of talismans" in which the Vernal Equinox oscillates back and forth between 0° and 8° of Aries at a rate of 1° every 80 years. Now just who these mysterious talisman makers were is anybody's guess. Later astronomers such as al-Biruni thought they were Babylonians, and Neugebauer believed the term was an oblique reference to earlier Greek astronomers.[22]

The most widely used theory of trepidation during the Middle Ages was that of the ninth-century astronomer Thabit ibn Qurra. Thabit hailed from Harran, a town famous for the stellar religion of the Sabians, but he lived and worked for most of his adult life in Baghdad under the 'Abbasids. I can't help but wonder if those old talisman makers may have, as had Thabit, come from the mysterious star cults of Harran. Nevertheless, in his *On the Motion of the Eighth Sphere*, Thabit postulated the theory of the progressive and regressive motion of the stars, also known as access and recess. He defined trepidation as an alternative, or substitute theory for the precession of the equinoxes, and it soon became common practice for astronomers to treat trepidation and precession as two separate and distinct motions.[23]

J.D. North claims that if Ptolemy had gotten the precessional rate right in the *Almagest*, the theory of trepidation might have never come into play, for it was a necessary adjustment astronomers had to make as they tried to square their own observations with Ptolemy's fictitious precessional rate: "The fact is that most of the best astronomers of the time believed that Arabic writers had established the reality of the phenomenon beyond doubt...[and were] not sufficiently careful readers of Ptolemy's *Almagest* to appreciate the source of the fallacy...."[24]

Whether the notion of trepidation arose before Hipparchus, with Hipparchus, or post-Ptolemy, is still a matter of debate. However, in the ceaseless, and ultimately thankless, efforts to refine the notion of trepidation, not only were various values proposed for the rate, and various intervals designated as recessional, or backwards periods, but also, whole new spheres were eventually required—the ninth, the 10th, the 11th, ad infinitum—to account for these varying degrees of motion.

St. Albertus Magnus, in his *Metaphysics*, book 2, attributed three separate motions to the eighth sphere of the fixed stars: (1) the obvious east-to-west motion observed every night, (2) the precession of the equinoxes, and (3) the trepidation, or motion of accession and recession described by Thabit.[25]

However, other astronomers disagreed, and believed that extra spheres, or orbs, were necessary to explain such complicated motion. Peter of Abano (Petro de Abano), in his *Lucidator*, argued for nine spheres, assigning the daily, east-to-west motion of the fixed stars to the eighth sphere and the precession of the equinoxes to the ninth sphere. An impressive contingent fell in behind the idea of 10 spheres, controlling the three separate motions of the fixed stars. These included Albert of Saxony, Roger Bacon, Themon Judaeus, and Pierre d'Ailly. Albert of Saxony assigned precession to the eighth sphere, trepidation to the ninth, and the daily motion to the 10th sphere.[26]

Europe's Medieval Magi

Even though astronomers completely misunderstood the mechanics and the math of precession, that never stopped them from speculating on what it all meant. Although there is no record of the use of astrological world ages such as Seymour described, medieval European astronomers entertained a whole range of astrochronological schemes using precession and trepidation, many of which employed distinctly Persian and Zoroastrian imagery. The idea that significant intervals in these movements coincided with turning points in world history certainly flourished. In describing the work of the 14th-century astronomer/historian Walter of Odington, J.D. North maintains that "...it would have been appropriate to include a discussion of precession and trepidation in a work on the age of the world; first, it was widely thought that vicissitudes of the world's history were linked with the periodicities of trepidation—notice how Alfonsine trepidation had a turning point near the time of Incarnation."[27]

Consider, for example, how the theory of trepidation was used by the 16th-century French astronomer Pierre Turrel. Lynn Thorndike quotes his work from an obscure French manuscript, the English title of which translates as: *The Period, That is to Say, the End of the World, Containing the Disposition of Terrestrial Things by the Virtue and Influence of the Celestial Bodies.*[28] Turrel used a regular precessional movement in which the entire sky revolved once in 49,000 years, against a periodic, or trepidational movement of 7,000 years.[29] Turrel believed that there were four stations in the trepidational period, occurring quarterly, or every 1,750 years, and to these pivotal stations he assigned the Flood, the Exodus, the destruction of Jerusalem, and the end of the world.

Thorndike maintains that Turrel probably derived his methods from the earlier, 15th-century work of Jean de Bruges, *De Veritate Astronomiae.* De Bruges, in turn, may have been influenced by the *Summa Astrologie* of John Ashenden (14th century), which also discusses trepidation and the theories of the highly influential Thabit ibn Qurra. J.D. North quotes from the *Lucidator* and *Conciliator* of Petro de Abano (13th century) the following tale in which the diminishing life span of man is linked to an ill-defined movement through the constellations of the zodiac:

> "The worlde is divided into 3 partes. The first from the Creation unto Noah his flod and after then untille 2,000 years...." The age to which a man might live was supposed to reduce in steps from 1,200 years (and that begane in the head of Sagittarius) to a mere 75. The top of the page has been torn away, and this might have given some clue as to what "it" was which was supposed to move steadily

around the zodiac, starting at the head of Sagittarius at the Creation, occupying each sign for 500 years, and finishing at the end of Scorpio at the end of the world, Anno Mundi 6000.[30]

Another famous 14th-century astrologer, Cecco d'Ascoli (d. 1327 CE, at the stake), in his commentary of the *Sphaera* of Sacrobosco, quoted from a work falsely attributed to Hipparchus, called *De Hierarchiis Spirituum*, for this strange story about the incubi and succubi who reside at the *colures* (the great circles on the celestial sphere that pass through the north and south poles and define the solstices and equinoxes). D'Ascoli recounts that at pivotal moments in world history, these spirits combine to produce great men "as of the Godhead." North describes how "Cecco then goes on to relate a similar account from a pseudo-Zoroastrian work...entitled *Liber de dominio quartarum octave spere*. A quadrant of the eighth sphere is said to dominate every historical period of 12,000 years and at the turning points of which men of divine attributes are born of incubi and sucubi...."[31]

In tracing these references back through time, two things become apparent. By all accounts, the precession of the equinoxes and its medieval concomitant, trepidation, were widely used in European astronomy/astrology to apportion history. Further, the influence of Persian and Zoroastrian ideas upon these efforts is obvious. Still, we don't find any astrologers or astronomers dividing time into zodiacal world ages based upon a steady precession of the equinoxes. The reason for that is that they didn't understand the phenomenon and the math sufficiently to do so. That understanding came in the age of Newton.

Certainly, Newton and his post-Copernican contemporaries had a great advantage in their more accurate understanding of the true nature and rate of precession. Newton put this advantage to use in *The Chronology of Ancient Kingdoms Amended*, his own contribution to the ongoing effort to measure the course of human history against the rhythms of precession. The lack of understanding never stopped their predecessors from trying, but in spite of all their efforts, the modern theory of astrological world ages based upon a steady precession of the equinoxes seems to have only come into play post-Newton. The earliest references for this kind of thinking appear in the late 19th century, in the lectures of Gerald Massey. These ideas were further popularized in theosophical circles by Madame Blavatsky and her associates.[32]

The Mighty Intiha

Just because Persian astrologers didn't divide time into zodiacal world ages based on a steady precession of the equinoxes doesn't mean they weren't thinking along those lines. The Persians had their own traditional ways of dividing up the millennia along both the ecliptic and the celestial equator; for instance, the *Intiha'at* and the *Tasyirat*.

As Kennedy describes these techniques, it is useful to think of them as the moving hand on a clock, with the ecliptic circling the dial instead of the hours. "At the beginning of the world year, all hands depart from 0° Aries and sweep around with different speeds. At any given instant a unique point on the zodiac will be designated by any one of the hands." These periods were used in natal astrology to determine the timing of an individual's fate, and they were also used on a much grander scale in mundane astrology to indicate significant turning points in the world year.[33]

As with the Jupiter-Saturn conjunctions, the *tasyirat* and *intiha'at* were classed according to their influence: mighty, big, middle, and small. The "mighty" world-*tasyir*, which travels along the celestial equator, moves 1° in 1,000 years. The "big" world-*tasyir* moves 1° in 100 years, with a rotational period of 36,000 years, corresponding to Ptolemy's rate of precession. The *intiha'at* moves along the ecliptic and is measured in zodiacal signs. The "mighty" *intiha* moves through a zodiac sign in 1,000 years, and its period is 12,000 years, corresponding to the traditional Persian millennia.[34]

Masha'allah's work is full of references to these systems. For instance, in commenting upon the chart for the Jupiter-Saturn conjunction proceeding the birth of Mohammed, he says, "Verily it [the divisor] reached Libra from the conjunction of the Deluge, and from the sign of the *intiha'* of the cycle to Gemini."[35] So there was significant interest in Persian astrology in measuring millennia and world years by zodiac signs, and by movement along the ecliptic, but these techniques were limited by the same misunderstanding of precession that plagued later European astrologers.

The Persian Precessional Year

Persians also made efforts to accommodate Ptolemy's precessional rate of 1° every 100 years, and its resulting world year of 36,000 years, into their millennial system. In the Persian *zij* of *Shams-i Munajjim* we find: "...according to the claim of the people of Fars [Pars, Persia] it [the beginning of the world year] was from that time when the conjunction of the planets occurred at the first of Aries until the year of the Flood a hundred and eighty thousand solar years passed. According to their claim the days of the world are three hundred and sixty thousand years, and the astrologers [*ashab-i ahkam*] put the beginning of the *tasyirat* and *intiha'at* and *fardarat* then."[36]

This Persian world year of 360,000 solar years was equal to 10 complete circuits of the Ptolemy's precessional cycle, and in this system, the Great Deluge occurred exactly at the halfway point.

The Fish and the Virgin

The Persians and their Magi were as fascinated by the possibilities of precession as anyone, and they contrived creative ways of working it into their chronologies. They had plenty of company in these efforts, as many of their contemporaries strove to incorporate precession in some meaningful way into their worldview and soteriology. They tiptoed all around the idea of the Age of Pisces, but it's doubtful that their state of knowledge would have led them to such a conclusion. On reflection, perhaps the only place where precession goes completely missing is in the astronomy—especially that crucial period between Hipparchus and Ptolemy—and why that is remains open to question.

Certainly Matthew's Magi would have been equally interested in precession, and probably would have discussed it with their Christian associates. It is entirely possible, even probable, that someone, somewhere, could have been sufficiently inspired by the approaching shift of the Vernal Equinox into the constellation Pisces to conceive of it as the harbinger of a "new age." These speculations could have eventually focused on Pisces as a symbol for the savior, or the guiding spirit of the age. The presence of both the virgin and the fish together in certain literature from the early Christian era does seem to indicate that at least someone saw Christ and his holy mother symbolized in the two signs, Virgo and Pisces, which were just then taking up their posts at the equinoxes. But there are no texts that clearly spell this out for us, so we are dealing here with speculation, not evidence, all the while raising very good questions about some important symbolism of the early Christian Church. I hope to explore this more fully in another book, where these questions can receive the kind of detailed analysis they deserve.

For the time being, any assumptions regarding the Magi's belief in the astrological Age of Pisces are a lot more complex than most imagine, and I, for one, would not be so quick to say that the Magi would have preferred the Pisces triple conjunction of 7 BCE on that basis.

Chapter 10
The Magi's Messiah

Zoroaster's Star in Early Christian Documents

Within the body of early Christian literature, it is not hard to find evidence of the belief that Zoroaster predicted both the Star of the Magi and the birth of Christ. In some of the earliest communities of believers, many perceived the Persian religion as a prophetic precursor of their own. Consider this passage from the apocryphal *Arabic Gospel of the Savior's Infancy*, a Syriac document dating from approximately the fourth or fifth century CE. Chapter 7 reads: "And it came to pass, when the Lord Jesus was born at Bethlehem of Judea, in the time of King Herod, behold, magi came from the east to Jerusalem, as Zeraduscht had predicted; and there were with them gifts, gold and frankincense, and myrrh."

What did Zeraduscht (Zarathustra) predict? At this point, we can only imagine, but similar references are scattered throughout the early documents. For instance, the late-second-century church father, Clement of Alexandria, makes a very telling comment. In speaking of the Prodiceans, an early Christian sect, he says, "Of the secret books of this man [Zoroaster], those who follow the heresy of Prodicus boast to be in possession."[1] Many sects throughout the ancient world claimed to be in possession of the secret books of Zoroaster, but here is evidence of a group of *Christians*, however heretical, boasting of this knowledge.

In the regions where the Persians had traditionally held sway—where their religion was more indelibly imprinted into the cultural landscape, and therefore harder to erase—an appreciation of the role of the Persian religion in the birth of Christianity, as well as Zoroaster's connection to the Magi and the Star of Bethlehem, persisted well into the Middle Ages.

In 1700 CE, Oxford scholar Thomas Hyde wrote a groundbreaking text on Persian religion entitled *Historia Religionis Veterum Persarum Eorumque Magorum*. In Chapter 3, he quoted the *Historia Dynastiarum* of Abulfaragius, a 13th-century Arab-Christian historian, for the following story, in which Zoroaster instructs his followers regarding the star that would herald the virgin birth of their coming savior: "'You, my sons,' exclaimed the seer, 'will perceive its rising before any other nation. As soon, therefore, as you shall behold the star, follow it, whithersoever it shall lead you; and adore that mysterious child, offering your gifts to him, with profound humility.'"[2]

Both spurious and late, this passage indicates that these beliefs about Zoroaster and the Star of the Magi were still current in the 13th century. The Reverend S.K. Nweeya, who spent many years as a Christian minister in the Middle East, wrote in his 1904 book, *Persia: The Land of the Magi*, that the Assyrian, or Nestorian church, had always taught about Zoroaster's prophecy of the Star: "According to the Assyrian or Nestorian church fathers the holy prophet Zoroaster thus taught the Persians concerning the birth of Christ: When a fixed period has come and the time has been fulfilled a Savior will come to the world."[3]

In describing a then contemporary belief, Nweeya used much of the same phraseology that we find in the 13th-century writings of Abulfaragius. Clearly, some Christians have always known of the connection between Zoroastrian prophecies and the birth of Christ. So how did we in the West manage to forget?

There is no one, easy answer, but the early Church did purposefully craft a unique and powerful identity for its new religion. As Burton Mack put it, "The fundamental persuasion is that Christianity appeared unexpectedly in human history, that it was (is) at core a brand new vision of human existence, and that, since this is so, only a sterling moment could account for its emergence at the beginning. The code word serving as a sign for the novelty that appeared is the term unique (meaning singular, incomparable, without analogue)."[4]

Their Christianity was revealed by God alone, and owed nothing to any culture or creed that had gone before, save one. The Christian Church proclaimed a singular authority for the select set of Judean texts we now call the Bible, and for the Judean temple cult that produced them, exalting the narrow, exclusive monotheism of the Judean priesthood into the highest theological virtue. By limiting the orthodox apprehension of Christian origins to this singular source, they also laid the groundwork for their own monolithic power base, contriving a lineage for the transmission of God's authority that led right into their own hands, while casting much of the genuine history of religious development in the ancient Near East onto the dust heap. We are all much the poorer for it.

They were the consummate historiographers, and their one truth of the one God, the highly contrived Judeo-Christian "salvation history," is a myth—a man-made, medieval, monolinear myth—and yet, it is a myth that still holds the Western mind in its thrall. It remains with us, unconscious and embedded, so that we continue to retell and even relive it, regardless of the consequences. All the while, there are better stories waiting to be told.

For instance, this one, which describes the birth of Christ, and the Star of the Magi, from a completely different perspective. It comes from an early third-century document entitled *Events Happening in Persia on the Birth of Christ*. The text is attributed to Sextus Julius Africanus, who bears the distinction of being the first Christian chronographer; a man devoted to establishing a Christian universal history of the ages to rival the ancient chronologies of the Pagan world. It opens with: "Christ first of all became known from Persia. For nothing escapes the learned jurists of that country, who investigate all things with the utmost care...for it is from the temples there, and the priests connected with them, that the name of Christ has been heard of."[5]

The document then relates the most amazing story about a temple in Persia, which the author claims was built by Cyrus himself. The king came to visit the temple one morning, seeking an interpretation of his dreams, when he was suddenly greeted by the priest with the news that Juno had conceived! Naturally, the king was confused, but the priest reassured him:

> ...the time for these things is at hand. For during the whole night, the images, both of gods and goddesses, continued beating the ground, saying to each other, Come, let us congratulate Juno. And they say to me, Prophet, come forward; congratulate Juno, for she has been embraced...and is no longer called Juno, but Urania. For the mighty Sol has embraced her. Then the goddesses say to the gods, making the matter plainer, *Pege* [meaning a fountain, spring, or stream] is she who is embraced;.... And the gods say,

That she is rightly called *Pege*, we admit. Her name, moreover, is *Myria*; for she bears in her womb, as in the deep, a vessel of a myriad talents' burden. And as to this title *Pege*, let it be understood thus: This stream of water sends forth the perennial stream of spirit—a stream containing but a single fish, taken with the hook of Divinity, and sustaining the whole world with its flesh as though it were in the sea.

The story continues as the roof opens and a bright star descends and stands above the pillar of *Pege*. A voice, presumably that of the star, is heard to say: "Sovereign *Pege*, the mighty Son has sent me...to do you service in parturition, designing blameless nuptials with you, O mother of the chief of all ranks of being, bride of the triune Deity. And the child begotten by extraordinary generation is called the *Beginning* and the *End....* To Myria is given the blessed lot of bearing Pege in Bethlehem, and of conceiving grace of grace.... With right do women dance, and say, Lady *Pege*, Spring-bearer, thou mother of the heavenly constellation...."

The king then calls his Magi together, loads them down with gifts, and off they go to Bethlehem, with the Star leading the way. This unique document sets the annunciation where I believe it more rightly belongs—in a Persian goddess temple. As was Anahita, this great virgin mother goddess, with her "extraordinary generation" and "blameless nuptials," is imaged as a stream or a spring of pure water that brings forth the Christ-fish. In the tradition of inclusive monotheism, the names and attributes of myriad goddesses are bound up in this one Great Mother, who is alternatively called Juno, Urania, Pege, and Myria, and who ultimately manifests her glory as a simple Jewish virgin. The story goes on to say that when the Magi first met Mary and her child in Bethlehem, they hailed her as: "Mother, mother, all the gods of the Persians have called thee blessed. Thy glory is great; for thou art exalted above all women of renown,...more queenly than all queens."

This may be the most complete example remaining of the tradition to which the author of Matthew refers, and we can count ourselves very lucky that this wee scrap escaped the orthodox censors for all these years, hidden among the works of so esteemed a chronographer as Sextus Julius Africanus. Whether Africanus actually wrote this himself is anybody's guess.

The astronomical and astrological allusions are obvious. Consider the imagery of the goddess, the mother of the heavenly constellation, who was

once but is no longer Juno, and who, after being embraced by Sol, becomes the spring or fountain wherein is begotten, by extraordinary generation, the fish whose flesh sustains the world, and so on. These are the
kind of allusions Percy Seymour referred to when he wrote: "...symbolism,
particularly *astrological* symbolism, was a universal feature of myth and
religion for the centuries before and following Christ's birth. While several groups argued and fought over their differences in religious belief, all
learned men knew about astrology, and astrological symbolism was often
used as a form of common language.... However, this *lingua franca* of symbolism was clearly the culmination of non-Christian and pre-Christian
ideas."[6]

This surely raises the question of whether the author of this story, by
combining the imagery of the fish and the virgin goddess, is making an
oblique reference to the precession of the equinoxes, or at least to the
constellations Pisces and Virgo and the impending arrival of the equinoxes
there. It would be helpful if he had just come out and said so, but such is
the nature of myth. Any attempt to read myth without acknowledging the
astronomical dimension is missing quite a bit, but I'm not sure that we can
definitively answer this question here.

What does emerge plainly from this literature is that many of the earliest Christians, Matthew among them, possessed a great awareness and
appreciation of the religious traditions of the Persians, and of their impact
on Judaism. These Christians perceived their own emerging religion as
fitting within the broader Persian framework, seeking not so much to break
from the Persian traditions of the past, but to fulfill them. They possessed
a surprisingly universal awareness of a God who manifested throughout
all humanity and all time, rather than just through one specific nation at
one time. This kind of inclusive monotheism persisted in Persian circles at
least until the time of Masha'allah, when Persian astrology afforded a similar
appreciation of Mohammed.

The orthodox impetus was exactly the opposite, and strove to limit
God's interest and intervention in human society exclusively to the Judea of
the Bible, and then to the Christian Church. They alone were chosen, and
everyone else was comparatively God-forsaken. Consequently, any references to Christian origins outside of Judea became anathema. Nowhere is
this drive more evident than in the response of early Christian apologists to
the problem presented by the presence of Matthew's Magi. In trying to
explain away the Persian influence on the first gospel, Christians created

entire alternative histories, in which biblical characters such as Balaam and Daniel instructed the Magi early on in Jewish monotheism. Among these medieval attempts to keep the Judeo-Christian "bloodline," and its presumed transmission of God's authority, pure and intact, we find this piece from Ambrose of Milan: "But who are these Magi unless those who, as a certain history teaches, derive from the stock of Balaam, by whom it was prophesied 'a star shall arise out of Jacob' [Num 24.17]? Therefore these are heirs not less of faith than of succession."[7]

Consider his words carefully. Ambrose was a powerful authority figure in the early Roman church, and his emphasis on "heirs" and "succession" is deliberate. The venerable Origen goes even deeper into the details of this "certain history":

> If Balaam's prophecies were included in the sacred books by Moses, how much more would they have been copied by those who were then living in Mesopotamia, among whom Balaam had a great reputation and who are known to have been disciples in his art. It is said that the race of Magi descends from him, and that their institution flourishes in eastern lands, and that they had copied among them all of Balaam's prophecies, including "A star shall arise out of Jacob." The Magi had these things written among themselves, and so when Jesus was born they recognized the star and understood that the prophecy was fulfilled.[8]

Here, all of history is forced through the narrow lens of the Bible, and no other race—neither the Persians, nor the Magi—has any relevance in and of itself. The Jewish books alone are absolute, and other traditions only have value in as much as they can be fit into the biblical framework. Thus, the line of authority stays intact.

If only it had stopped there, but this medieval mindset is still with us, permeating our Western attitudes towards history, and unconsciously imposing the orthodox delusion of pure, untainted lines of transmission that lead straight to "us," while obviously bypassing "them." As Walter Burkert so masterfully demonstrated in *The Orientalizing Revolution*, in the 18th and 19th century, European scholars grew increasingly enthralled with "an image of a pure, classical Greece in splendid isolation" and with "the concept of classical-national Greek identity as a self-contained and self-sufficient model of civilization," in glaring contrast to the uncivilized barbarians of Persia and the ancient Near East. He marveled that "even today it should be difficult to undertake unprejudiced discussion of connections between classical Greece and the East. But whoever tries will encounter entrenched positions, uneasiness, apology, if not resentment." So is it any wonder that we are at war with these people—still?

This need to see the Greeks as unique, pure, and singularly authoritative (or to believe the same of Judaism, and of Christianity, its one, true heir), no doubt stems from our own desire to see ourselves that way. In comparison, the inclusive monotheism that radiates through the astrology of Masha'allah—which emphasized the ultimate, underlying unity of all who claim to worship the one God; honoring the various contributions of Jews, Christians, Muslims, and Persians, while at the same time respecting their differences—seems infinitely more inspired.

Conclusions

So what was the Star of Bethlehem? I'm not entirely sure, and I'm not convinced that Matthew knew either. At least some of my reticence stems from a personal distaste for the rather high-handed tones other authors have adopted in staking their competing claims. I don't want to pretend that this is the last word on anything; it's more like the opening chapter in a new version of an old story that everyone thinks they already know. So it might be wiser to admit up front that even if we were lucky enough to stumble upon all the right answers, it would still be nigh on impossible to prove it, at least to everyone's satisfaction. Nothing short of unearthing the "Lost Gospel of the Magi" would do, and on the off chance that such a text did come to light, we could easily spend the next 100 years refuting the fundamentalists' claims that it was a clever forgery.

Why not raise the bar altogether? Instead of arguing about dates and times that we can't possibly know, much less prove, why not make the most out of what little we actually do know? That little goes a surprisingly long way.

The Problem With Matthew

The historicity of the account in the Gospel of Matthew is open to question, and I don't put a lot of faith into any astronomical arguments derived from it. I have yet to see any reliable evidence of Magian or Chaldean astrologers saddling up their camels and riding off across the desert chasing something in the sky. The story not only sounds fanciful, but it's also too far removed from any primary sources to be reliable, especially as astronomy. It does sound suspiciously similar to folklore—

the kind of folklore that arose among those who lacked the Magi's mathematical skills, but were nevertheless impressed by their "magic"; in other words, the general public. Now, as always, people don't need to understand the math. They just love to tell the stories.

Of course, I could be wrong about that. Still, the result of centuries of taking the text seriously is a mountain of conflicting conclusions, not only about the identity of the Star, but about the meaning of Matthew's choice of words.

Even if I am wrong about Matthew's astronomy, the fact remains that in introducing the Magi and their astrology, he was making a strong and calculated appeal to contemporary Judeans. He was appealing specifically to their respect for the messianic astrological traditions of the Persian religion, and to their undying hope that God would once again work through the Persians to save them from the hands of their enemies. Since Matthew's time, we have utterly lost that context in the West. At the same time, it has survived in certain Eastern traditions, especially in the former Persian territories, where it would have been a lot harder to ignore. In my opinion, that context is a lot more important than worrying about whether things happened exactly as Matthew said they did; especially since no one seems able to agree on exactly what it was he said in the first place.

I also have to wonder whether this story in Matthew, which was a rather late insertion into his Gospel, does not more accurately reflect the concerns and conditions prevailing among Jews and Persians in the period circa 75 to 90 CE, after the destruction of the temple. By then, they would have had plenty of time to reflect on the implications of the shift of the conjunctions into the fire signs, and to incorporate all the synchronous events—the birth of Christ, the rise of Rome, the fall of Jerusalem, and so on—into their ongoing astrological traditions.

In other words, I have my doubts as to whether any astrologers actually figured all of this out beforehand. In my experience, astrologers are often much better at reading meaning into the past than at making specific predictions about the future. Of course, I could be wrong about that too. Maybe Matthew's Magi were exceptionally good astrologers, or divinely inspired, for that matter. The bottom line is that accepting the historicity of the account in Matthew includes a tacit acknowledgement that his Magi possessed a degree of astrological skill and foresight that is often lacking in later practice. I honestly don't know whether they did or did not, but it is worth thinking about.

Although I'm not entirely convinced that any Magi traveled to Judea looking for the baby Jesus, I do believe that the Parthian Persian Magi would have been very excited about the astrological signs of the times, particularly the cycle of Saturn-Jupiter conjunctions as it played out against their astrological millennia. My reasons for believing this stem from what the existing textual evidence reveals about Persian religious astrology.

The Triple Conjunction in Pisces

Many believe that the triple Saturn-Jupiter conjunction in Pisces in 6–7 BCE was the Star of Bethlehem. That theory is not without its detractors, but of all the proposed solutions, it has generated the greatest amount of consensus. In all honesty, I originally began this work in support of the triple-conjunction theory. My research eventually led me in other directions, for the PCH (for Planetary Conjunction Hypothesis), as it was termed in the 1970s and as it is currently understood, does not accord with the little we do know about Persian messianic astrology. As references to the Persian astrology of the Magi are conspicuously lacking throughout the literature on the PCH, that is hardly surprising.

Perhaps the PCH is a case of coming close to the right answer, but for the wrong reasons. Certainly, of all the astronomical phenomena occurring in or around the time of the birth of Christ, the triple conjunction was a standout, attracting a lot of attention then, as now. However, Masha'allah and 'Umar don't mention it at all. They set their sights on the millennial shift of the conjunctions from the water into the fire signs, and on the first conjunction in Leo of that new millennium. They didn't seem to think that triple conjunctions were particularly important. So if the modern PCH is correct, then some explanation is needed as to why it did not survive into later Persian astrology.

Among those who support the PCH, many claim that it must have been especially important because it was in the constellation Pisces. After all, the Vernal Equinox was just about to "precess" out of Aries and cross that invisible border into Pisces. Percy Seymour's opinions on that were covered in the earlier chapter on Pisces and precession, but he is hardly alone in such a stance. For instance, Dr. Kucko von Stuckrad, drawing upon the earlier work of August Strobel, makes some fascinating claims for the triple conjunction of 7 BCE, which he euphemistically describes as a "great conjunction," occurring exactly on the Vernal Equinox.

In his article, "Jewish and Christian Astrology in Late Antiquity," von Stuckrad discusses the "great conjunction's" impact on King Herod the Great, who, by Josephus's account, suffered a bout of "persecution mania" in the years 6–7 BCE. Herod went off on a killing spree, disposing of his wife, sons, and any number of enemies, presumably in response to the planetary threat posed by this great conjunction. This "genuine great conjunction," which von Stuckrad repeatedly places exactly on the Vernal Equinox, was further stressed by the approach of the planet Mars. Its importance was such that it was eventually molded by the Gospel writers into the "Star of Bethlehem," to grant greater credence to the Christians' claims.

I'm sure that von Stuckrad is correct about Herod's interest in political astrology. His points regarding the general interest throughout the region in the Jupiter-Saturn conjunctions and their role in the rise and fall of rulers and dynasties are all quite valid. However, his astronomy is considerably off.

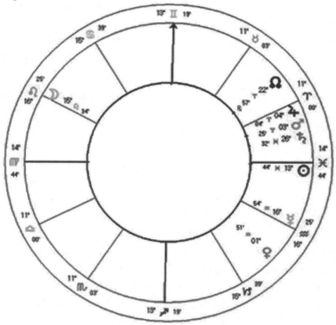

An astrological chart set for March 3, 6 BCE at 6 p.m. at Jerusalem, showing Jupiter setting together in the west after the sun (Sidereal Zodiac). Image created by Courtney Roberts using Esoteric Technologies' Solar Fire software.

The triple conjunction of 6–7 BCE did not occur exactly on the Vernal Equinox. It was some distance away. The first conjunction, ca. May 29, 7 BCE, took place at 21° of the tropical sign Pisces—9° away from the point of the Vernal Equinox. Then the conjunction went retrograde. The first retrograde conjunction took place ca. October 1, 7 BCE, at 17° of the sign Pisces, or 13° away from the Vernal Equinox. The third conjunction occurred ca. December 6, 7 BCE at 15° of the sign Pisces, or fully half a sign away from the Vernal Equinox.[1] This was not nearly as impressive as it is being made out to be.

The planet Mars caught up with Jupiter and Saturn the following spring, but the "great conjunction" had separated considerably by then. Mars did conjunct Jupiter near the Vernal Equinox ca. March 5, 6 BCE, but Saturn and Jupiter were already a good 8° apart. The three planets, Jupiter, Saturn, and Mars, although spread out over 8° and two constellations, did appear in the heliacal setting phase; in other words, setting in the western sky just after the sun. No doubt it made quite an impression. As von Stuckrad claims, it could have troubled Herod greatly, and triggered the usual messianic clamor, which among the Jews and Persians needed but little encouragement.

Even though this planetary alignment lacked the precision of a "genuine great conjunction on the vernal equinox," it did portend great things to come. Astute astronomers would have surmised that the next Saturn-Jupiter conjunction in Pisces would fall much closer to the actual vernal point. That's exactly what happened almost 60 years later, in 54 CE.

A Genuine Great Conjunction on the Vernal Equinox

In March of 54 CE, there was another Saturn-Jupiter conjunction in Pisces, but this one occurred right at the very end of Pisces, almost exactly on the point of the equinox, at 28°. We have already seen how Masha'allah calculated his history of the Saturn-Jupiter conjunctions by casting the "year-transfer" chart for the first day of spring, when the sun crossed the Vernal Equinox and entered the tropical sign Aries. Any Magian astrologer who calculated a "year-transfer" chart in 54 CE would have been immediately struck by the fact that on the Vernal Equinox, the sun, Jupiter, and Saturn were all tightly joined together, right on that crucial border between Pisces and Aries—the very threshold of the zodiac.

Further, for nearly a month, this "great conjunction on the Vernal Equinox" was in its heliacal rising phase, dominating the morning skies, rising at dawn before the sun. In Mesopotamian astronomy, the heliacal rising was considered one of the most important phases of any planetary cycle. The triple conjunction has no such pedigree.

This extraordinary omen of a New Age took place much nearer to the time when Matthew was actually composing his Gospel. Further, this particular Saturn-Jupiter conjunction in 54 CE would have been in force during the 20-year period that included the destruction of Jerusalem (66–70 CE), an event of unparalleled importance for all contemporary Christians and Jews. As the Parthian Magi commiserated with their Jewish and Christian allies about this, their ultimate loss to the Romans, these charts would have been pored over endlessly. By all accounts, it is only after this that the story of the Magi appears in the Gospel of Matthew.

If we can divorce the search for the Star from the questionable historicity of the account in the Gospel of Matthew, it widens our entire perspective, and gives time for this sweeping astrological tradition to grow and develop, as such traditions do. As long as we treat Matthew's story as history, we are stuck with the astronomical events of a relatively narrow time frame that, although no doubt troubling and impressive, were not retained in the Persian religious astrology that has come down to us.

We have already seen how, in that tradition (or what little remains of it), the first conjunction in the royal sign of Leo, as cited by 'Umar and Masha'allah, was highly indicative of the impending changes in world order. At the same time, it's entirely possible that the last conjunction at the end of Pisces, and that first conjunction at the beginning of Aries, would have been perceived in some quarters as the symbolic end of the old cycle, and the beginning of the new. This point was further emphasized by the realization that the conjunction cycle was also temporarily coinciding with the impending shift of the Vernal Equinox from Aries back into Pisces. That's what was going on in Matthew's time, during the early days of the Church.

Regardless of whether the Magi had the foresight to seek the baby Jesus, they would have been teaching and talking about the temper of the times, and expecting extraordinary things, because that's what Magian astrologers did. They were intellectual aristocrats, highly skilled in mathematics and astronomy. They calculated charts and vast chronological schemes, and discussed and debated them endlessly in their schools, temples, and courts.

Matthew's Magi were living in extraordinary times, and they knew it. The Saturn-Jupiter conjunctions were accompanying the Vernal Equinoxes across the threshold of the zodiac, inaugurating not only a new millennium, but a whole New Aeon under the signs of the Virgin and the Fish. It wasn't just some one-off conjunction. It was a process, and one whose full significance could only emerge upon reflection.

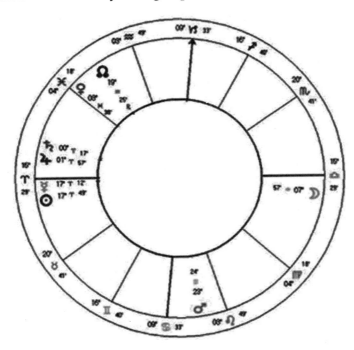

An astrological chart set for April 10, 54 CE at 5:37 a.m. in Jerusalem, showing Jupiter and Saturn in conjunction on the vernal point, and rising in the east before the sun (Tropical Zodiac). Image created by Courtney Roberts using Esoteric Technologies' Solar Fire software.

The Persians, the Jews, and the Triple Conjunction

Both August Strobel and von Stuckrad have made some impressive arguments regarding the Judeans' reliance on the Saturn-Jupiter cycle in general, and the triple conjunction in particular, in their efforts to liberate

Judea and establish messianic home rule. Unfortunately, the astronomy does not always support their arguments. I hate to criticize their work, which for the most part is excellent, but the calculations are puzzling, to say the least.

For instance, in bolstering his claims for the importance of the triple conjunction of 7 BCE, von Stuckrad asserts that, just as we would suspect, the next triple contact between Jupiter and Saturn in the year 134 CE raised "old questions anew," in the form of the ill-fated Bar Kokhba revolt. It is entirely possible that this blatantly messianic uprising (which actually began in 132 CE) led by the "Son of the Star," as Simon bar Kosiba styled himself, was timed to coincide with the Jupiter-Saturn conjunction in January, 134 CE—and so was the Roman response. Von Stuckrad makes that case very well, but this was definitely not a triple conjunction. Jupiter and Saturn only joined together one time on that pass, on approximately January 20, 134 CE, at approximately 21° of the tropical sign Sagittarius, coinciding with the Roman crackdown that eventually brought that bitter war to an end.

Von Stuckrad also claims that the Jewish Hasmonean ruler, Alexander Janneus, made much of the fact that he was born in the year of a "so-called great conjunction." Janneus was born in 126 BCE, which von Stuckrad claims was marked by a highly significant celestial event, a triple conjunction of Jupiter and Saturn in Pisces, caused by the planets' retrograde motion.

The term *great conjunction* does get thrown around quite loosely here. We have already seen that there was still considerable disagreement over the question of which conjunction was the "great conjunction" well into the ninth century and beyond, but by all accounts, the conjunction in 126 BCE doesn't even come close. Even von Stuckrad admits in a footnote that it wasn't a real triple conjunction, missing the mark by a degree or so, and yet he still claims, a few paragraphs on, that the year 126 BCE beheld "the last important conjunction" of Jupiter and Saturn, which "brought forth a Jewish kingdom that was to last for 27 years...."

I beg to differ here. The last genuine triple conjunction before 7 BCE occurred in 146–145 BCE, and coincided significantly with the sudden rise of the Parthian Persian Empire. The Parthian Arsacid dynasty traced its origins back to the time of the Jupiter-Saturn conjunction of 245 BCE, but in the years 147–141 BCE, under the daring leadership of Mithridates I, their kingdom suddenly burgeoned into an imposing empire.

Under the auspices of that triple conjunction, Mithridates took Media, then Babylon and all of Mesopotamia, even moving the Parthian capital to Seleucia—all at the expense of the Greek Seleucids. Suddenly, the Persians were back! The Seleucid losses to the Parthians seriously undermined their grip on Judea, facilitating the establishment of an independent Jewish state under the rule of Simon Maccabeus in 143–142 BCE. Now that was a proper triple conjunction!

The real genesis of the Hasmonean dynasty lies in the heroic revolt of the Maccabees, which was also distinctly timed to the Jupiter-Saturn cycle. When the Seleucid ruler Antiochus IV came to the throne in 176 BCE, he outraged all of Judea with his attempts at enforced Hellenization. He brazenly defiled the temple by erecting a statue of Zeus, which looked uncannily like himself. He outlawed the Sabbath and circumcision, and ordered the sacrifice of pigs, the admission of foreigners, and other shocking abominations.

One brave priest, Mattathias by name, when ordered by Greek officials to sacrifice to a Pagan god, murdered the Greeks instead. Mattathias fled to the hills a condemned man, only to return with "The Hammer." The priest and his son Judah were soon leading a full-scale rebellion. They would go down in history as the *Maccabees*, named for their hammer-like blows against the accursed Greeks—or so the legend goes.

After some initial setbacks, they experienced sudden and seemingly miraculous success, as their desperate guerrilla tactics defeated armies many times their size. By the end of the year 165 BCE, they fought their way into Jerusalem, and took back the temple, which they then cleansed and rededicated to its proper service. This event is still commemorated every year in the celebration of Hannukah, when Jewish families light the candles of the menorah in memory of the miraculous burning of the temple lamp.

Coincidentally, in the autumn of 165 BCE, there was a Saturn-Jupiter conjunction in the constellation Scorpio. It was joined by Mars in early September, disappeared into the rays of the sun in November, and by December, as the Maccabees were restoring the temple, it was in its heliacal rising phase, dominating the sky at dawn. Even though it took another 20-plus years of fighting to win a throne, this was the birth of the Hasmonean dynasty, under the auspices of the Jupiter-Saturn conjunction.

In all fairness, there is some disagreement on the date, and some would place the cleansing of the temple in December of 164 BCE. In defense of the earlier date, and the significance of Saturn, Jupiter, and the sun in the liberation of the temple, consider the original connection between the menorah (the very symbol of Hannukah) and the planets, as Josephus tells it: "Now the seven lamps signified the seven planets; for so many there were springing out of the candlestick."[2]

Philo Juddaeus had this to say about the menorah:

> ...that the sacred candlestick and the seven lights upon it are an imitation of the wandering of the seven planets through the heaven...in the same manner as the lights, so also does every one of the planets shed its rays. They therefore, being more brilliant, do transmit more brilliant beams to the earth, and brilliant beyond them all is he who is the centre one of the seven, the sun.... The Creator therefore, wishing that there should be a model upon earth among us of the seven-lighted sphere as it exists in heaven, explained this exquisite work to be made, namely, this candlestick.[3]

Let's be clear about one thing here: This is not evidence of Jewish astrology, per se, but of the Jewish use of Persian and Magian astrology. The Jews were not a particularly mathematical people and had no long history of observations. They got their astrology from the Babylonians and the Persians, and then used it against the Greeks and the Romans.

My contention is that the Persians, and particularly the Magi, had been using the cycle of Saturn-Jupiter conjunctions, and the shifts between the elements, since at least the fateful year of 522 BCE, when the (presumably) Magian coup d'état was launched. Although we may never know the full details of what really happened then, and who the real imposter was, one thing is certain: It all coincided with a magnificent triple conjunction of Saturn and Jupiter in the constellation of Libra, which was also a highly anomalous shift. The cycle had long been in the earth signs, and continued to be in the earth signs for another 60 years. This very temporary shift into Libra would certainly have made an impression, especially because, for the first time in history, all the astronomical elements necessary for understanding such a cycle—zodiac signs, planetary orbits, triplicities, and so on—were in use. Ironically, that conjunction occurred 500 years, or half a millennium, before the conjunction in Leo marking the birth of Christ.

Christianity: The Original New Age Religion

What remains blazingly apparent throughout all of this is that Matthew and his Christian, Jewish, and Persian contemporaries definitely believed they were living at both the end of the world and the beginning of a new era. This kind of thinking dominates all the earliest Christian literature, and it is only when we investigate the Persian astrology of the Magi that we find the chronological reckoning behind it all.

The Zoroastrian traditions of the Magi provide the entire underlying context: political, religious, historical, and astrological, where everything comes together and starts to make sense. Once we understand how the Persian Magi used astrology in their politics and religion, we understand why Matthew needed the Magi in his Gospel, and why this would have been so convincing to his Jewish contemporaries. If Matthew's Magi did not actually come as reported, he would have done well to invent them. The status of Jesus as both the king of the Jews and as a potential world savior was boosted immeasurably by their appearance, and by the implied coincidence of his birth with the Jupiter-Saturn conjunctions and the new millennium. It was that important to Matthew's contemporaries, to his fellow Jews, and all their brothers in arms against Rome that Christ's advent should fit into the sacred chronology that we find in Zurvan Zoroastrianism, and in the astrology and teachings of the Magi.

Even though these Persian traditions have been almost completely written out of mainstream, orthodox monotheism (which prefers to see itself as "revealed religion"), they continue to animate it underground, from within. The most obvious example of that is our continuing fascination with the story of the Star of Bethlehem.

Sometimes, getting the right answers comes down to asking the right questions. A question such as "What was the Star of Bethlehem?" has produced centuries of debate and very little consensus. On the other hand, this question: "Why would the authors (and editors) of the Christian Gospels choose Persian Magi and astrology to herald the coming of Jesus Christ?" raises much better answers—answers that ultimately expand our entire understanding of how the three great monotheisms and their messianic expectations evolved, bringing us all a lot closer together in the process. Whether fact or fiction, Matthew's Magi and their Star still shed a great light on the common religious heritage we all share—or at least, that we should share—and better late than never.

Chapter Notes

Introduction

1. Schaefer, "Review," 77.
2. Yamamoto and Burnett, *Abu Masar*, 573, n. 2.
3. Cohn, *Cosmos*, 231.
4. Arjomand, "Messianism," 107.
5. Blenkinsopp, *Ezra-Nehemiah*, 12. In his commentary on Ezra-Nehemiah, Blenkinsopp quotes Hans Heinrich Schraeder regarding the standard approach to postexilic Judaism in Christian scholarship.
6. Spong, "The God."
7. O'Dea, "Peace."
8. Paffenroth, "The Star," 449.

Chapter 1

1. Maas, "Genealogy."
2. Lancaster, *Aramaic Peshitta*, 5–7.
3. Jacquier, "Gospel."
4. The contentious debate over whether Aramaic or Greek was the original language of the Gospel of Matthew has yet to be resolved, but there is serious doubt that "Matthew" composed his gospel in Hebrew. Few in his target audience would have understood it. In his time, Hebrew was almost a dead language; mainly preserved in the temple cult in Jerusalem, not unlike the Latin of the (pre-Vatican II) Catholic Mass. It would have been equally impractical for Matthew to compose his gospel in Greek, for the same reason. The general assumption in the West has been that after the conquest of Alexander, subject peoples willingly took up the "universal" Greek language of the occupying forces. However, there is a growing body of evidence indicating

that Jewish and Persian nationals specifically resisted the language, as yet another form of rebellion against the hated Hellenists.

5. The Gospel of Matthew contains more allusions (more than 60) than any of the other Gospels to Old Testament passages that supposedly predict and foreshadow Christ.

6. One of the reasons we assume this Gospel was first used in this region is because the earliest extant quotations from it are found in the works of Ignatius, bishop of Antioch of Syria (110 CE); for instance, his epistle to the Smyrnaeans, 1:1. See Schaff, 2001.

7. Finklestein and Silberman, *David and Solomon*; and *The Bible Unearthed*, Ch. 5, "Memories of a Golden Age." See also Miller, "King David."

8. For more on the highly significant differences between Israel and Judea, and between El and Yahweh, see Barre, *History and Tradition*; and "El, god of Israel." See Also Smith, Mark S., *Origins*, and *Early History*.

9. Kitchen, "Physical Text." There is also a good article on the stele on the Wikipedia site: *http://en.wikipedia.org/wiki/Merneptah_Stele*.

10. Smith, Mark A., *Early History*: "It is at present impossible to establish, on the basis of archaeological information, distinctions between Israelites and Canaanites in the Iron I period." Of course, this raises the much larger question: What exactly was a Canaanite? The definitive answer has yet to emerge, but the debate receives a thorough analysis in Smith, 2001, 14–18.

11. Sayce, *Early Israel*, Part 1.

12. For more on the origins of Judah, see Smith, Mark, *Origins*, Chapter 7: "El, Yahweh, and the Original God of Isra-El and the Exodus," 135–148.

13. Giveon, *Les Bedouins*, 26–28, 74–77. In the temple of Amon in Soleb (Nubia) there is a topographical list from the time of Amenhotep III (1408–1372 BCE). The listed itself has been dated to 1386 B.C.E. In column IV.A2 is written *t3 ssw yhw3*, which means "Yahweh of the land of the Shasu."

14. Finklestein and Silberman, *Bible Unearthed*, 150.

15. Ibid., 144.

16. The Revolt of Israel also occurs in II Chronicles, Ch. 10.

17. Crossan, *Jesus*, 16–17.

18. Massih, "Meditations": "The Gospel...refers to three monetary units...not mentioned any other place in the New Testament...the 'two-drachma' (Matthew 17:24), the 'stater' (Matthew 17:27), and the 'talent' (Matthew 18:24),...the writer...was familiar with the different kinds of currencies and...was interested in identifying and defining their values...."

Chapter 2

1. The Persian emperor Cyrus the Great appears frequently in the Old Testament. His emancipation of the Jews and order to rebuild the temple:

2 Chronicles 36:22, 23; Ezra 1; 3:7; 4:3; 5:13,14; 6:3 "Prophecies" in Isaiah that are interpreted as referring to Cyrus: 13:17-22; 21:2; 41:2; 44:28; 45:1-4,13; 46:11 See also: Jahanian, Darius, "Zoroastrianism and Biblical Connections," at *http://www.iranian.ws/cyrus.htm.*

2. For more information on how the colony of Yehud fit into Persia's overall plans: Berquist, Jon. L, "Shifting," and Olmstead, *History*. For an in-depth assessment of how Yehud fit into the Persians' overall plans for Egypt and the region, see: Edelman, *Origins*. Edelman proposes that neither Cyrus nor Darius authorized the rebuilding of the temple, but that the entire enterprise was initiated under Artaxerxes I. See also Edelman, "Redating."

3. Finklestein and Silberman, *Bible Unearthed*, Part Three, "Judah and the Making of Biblical History." For an alternative viewpoint, see Davies, Philip, "Origin." Davies seeks the source of the fusing of Judah and Israel in the period of the Babylonian Exile, when the Jews who remained in the land conceivably would have moved their worship back to the site at Bethel.

4. Finklestein and Silberman, *Bible Unearthed*, Part Three, "Judah and the Making of Biblical History."

5. The finds at Ras Shamra have provided a wealth of information on Canaanite religion and deities. Some good sources for this material are: Cross, *Canaanite*; Handy, *Among the Host*; Smith, Mark S., *Origins*.

6. This distinction between El and Yahweh, with Yahweh as one god among the divine cabinet, or pantheon, still survives throughout the Old Testament, where it is often hidden in translation within the different names of God. For instance: Deuteronomy 32: 8–9; Psalm 82; I Kings 22.

7. Barre, "El, god of Israel."

8. II Samuel, Ch. 6.

9. The Wikipedia site has a good article on the documentary hypothesis at *http://en.wikipedia.org/wiki/Documentary_hypothesis* (accessed September 2007). Also see the Religious Tolerance Website at *http://www.religioustolerance.org/chr_tora1.htm* (accessed September 2007).

10. Finklestein and Silberman, *Bible Unearthed*.

11. Smith, Mark S., *Early History*, 17.

12. Henotheism, according to *The Shorter Oxford English Dictionary*, 1983, is "the belief in a single god without asserting that he is the only God: a stage of belief between polytheism and monotheism."

13. *www.avesta.org* is an excellent resource for Zoroastrian literature and history. So is The Circle of Ancient Iranian Studies site at *http://www.caissoas.com/CAIS/frontpage.htm* (accessed September 2007).

14. Edelman, *Triumph of Elohim*, 1996. Also, Trotter, *Reading Hosea*, 137; and Blenkinsopp, *Ezra-Nehemiah*, 75.

15. Budge, *Book of the Cave*, Introduction, 15–16.

16. Ibid, 192.
17. Ibid.
18. The KJV of II Esdras is available at *http://www.earlyjewishwritings.com/text/2esdras.html*. The Wikipedia site has a good article on II Esdras at *http://en.wikipedia.org/wiki/2_Esdras*.
19. Friedman, *Bible With Sources*; and *Who Wrote the Bible?*
20. Grabbe, *Judaic Religion*, 14.
21. Ezra, Ch. 7.
22. Berquist, Judaism, 63.
23. Ibid., 81.
24. Blenkinsopp, *Ezra-Nehemiah*, 76.
25. The 10 tribes remained a presence in Media-Adiabene until well into Roman times.
26. Finklestein and Silberman, *Bible Unearthed*, 305–308.
27. Trotter, "Reading Hosea," 79.
28. Berquist, *Judaism*, 80.
29. See the Samaritan Website: *http://www.the-samaritans.com/info.htm*. The Wikipedia site also has a worthwhile article on the Samaritans at *en.wikipedia.org/wiki/Samaritan*.
30. Shen, Peidong, et al., "Reconstruction of Patrilineages."
31. Ereira, "Talking About the Samaritans," at *http://www.mystae.com/reflections/messiah/samjudah/yahwist.html1*.

Chapter 3

1. Herodotus, *Histories*, 1.101, Godley translation.
2. Book I, Prologue, available at http://classicpersuasion.org/pw/Diogenes.
3. Plutarch, in an early essay, "On the Malignity of Herodotus."
4. Herodotus, *Histories,* 1.107.1–2, Godley translation.
5. Herodotus, *Histories*, 1.20, Rawlinson translation.
6. Herodotus, *Histories*, 3.63, Godley translation.
7. Ibid., 3.64.
8. Ibid., 7.43.
9. Siculus, *Diodorus of Sicily*, "Bibliotheca," 17.72.
10. Thais the courtesan and the burning of Persepolis became a very popular story, but this version is disputed by the account in Arrian's *Anabasis*, 3.18.11, which does not mention her.
11. Yonge, *Diogenes Laertius*, Books I and III.
12. Plato, *Epinomis*, 987 E.
13. Van der Waerden, *Science Awakening*, 89.

14. Ch. 33, Verse 14.
15. Cumont, *Mysteries of Mithra*, iii–iv. See also, Dhalla, *History*, 295–296.
16. Cumont, *Mysteries*, 10.
17. Eddy, S.K., 1961, 67.
18. Cumont, 1903, 11. See also Eddy, S.K., 1961, 68, n. 9. Eddy lists extensive primary sources for the Magi's locations.
19. Eddy, *King*, 1961, 65.
20. Letters: CCLVIII.
21. Olmstead, *History*, 17–19. An English version of the *Vivedat* is available online at *www.Avesta.org*.
22. Cumont, *Mysteries*, 9–11.
23. Iamblichus, *Life of Pythagoras*, 3–4.
24. Van der Waerden, *Science Awakening*, 94–97.
25. Boyce, Mary, 1979, 1.
26. Laertius, *Lives*, 1.2.
27. Boyce, *History*, 3, 190, 348.
28. Eddy, *King*, 67.

Chapter 4

1. Berquist, *Judaism*, 57.
2. Olmstead, *History*, 42.
3. Atkinson, "Legitimacy of Cambyses."
4. For complete texts, see Grayson, *Assyrian*; and Beaulieu, *Reign*. The Cyrus cylinder text is available online at: *http://www.cais-soas.com/CAIS/History/hakhamaneshian/Cyrus-the-great/cyrus_cylinder_complete.htm*. The Chronicles of Nabonidus text is online at: *http://www.livius.org/ct-cz/cyrus_I/babylon02.html*.
5. Bolin, "Temple of Yahweh," 139.
6. Thompson, Thomas, "Intellectual Matrix," 22.
7. Bolin, "Temple of Yahweh," 128.
8. Two translations of the Darius inscription at Behistun are available at: *http://www.livius.org/be-bm/behistun/behistun03.html* (accessed Sept. 2007).
9. Eddy, *King*, 47.
10. Frye, *Heritage of Persia*, 151.
11. Eddy, *King*, 47.
12. Souvay, "Isaias."
13. Josephus, *Works*, "Antiquities of the Jews," Book XI, Ch. 1, Vs. 2. Available online at: *http://www.ccel.org/j/josephus/works/ant-11.htm*.
14. Edelman, *Triumph of Elohim*, 21.

15. Ibid., 20. Edelman quotes from Sargon's account of the battle of Mussair from the translation in Cogan, *Imperialism*, 20.
16. Eddy, *King*, 48.
17. Edelman, *Triumph of Elohim*, 22.
18. Jaspers and Bullock, *Origin*, 1; and Armstrong, *Great Transformation*.
19. Holland, *Persian Fire*, xxv.
20. West, M.L., *East Face of Helicon*, 545.
21. Bellah, "What is Axial?"
22. Eddy, *King*, 65.
23. Blenkinsopp, *Ezra-Nehemiah*, 75.
24. Edelman, *Triumph of Elohim*, 22.
25. Olmstead, T., *History*, 304–305. Olmstead remarks that Ezra's book was significantly entitled *data,* just as was the Persian king's law.
26. Davis, *Readings*, 58–61.
27. Berquist, *Judaism*, 63–64.
28. Ibid., 64–65; and Grabbe, *Judaic Religion*, 14–16.
29. Micah, Ch. 4; or Isaiah, Ch. 53.
30. Neusner, *History*, 26–27.
31. Ibid.
32. Missler, "Who Were the Magi?"
33. Dhalla, *History*, 294.
34. Von Stuckrad, "Jewish," 28–32.

Chapter 5

1. Yonge, *Works of Philo Judaeus*, Book III.
2. Seymour, *Birth*, 77.
3. Kusukawa, "Astrology."
4. See Kepler, *Concerning*; Kitson, *History*; Koestler, *Watershed*; and Negus, *Kepler's Astrology*.
5. *Culture and Cosmos, A Journal of the History of Astrology and Cultural Astronomy*, vol. 7, no. 1, Spring-Summer 2004, entitled *Galileo's Astrology*, contains more of Kollerstrom's work and many other detailed articles on the subject. *http://www.cultureandcosmos.com/galileosastrology.htm*.
6. The Galileo Project at Rice University *http://galileo.rice.edu/index.html* is an excellent example of revisionist, *scientistic* history. In what appears to be an accurate, academic portrayal of the man and his times, the fact that Galileo practiced, believed in, and taught astrology throughout his entire career is never mentioned. The few references made to the practice of astrology by Galileo's contemporaries attempt to explain it *away*, rather than explain it.

7. Manuel, *Portrait*, 380.
8. Manuel, *Isaac Newton*, 5–6.
9. Ibid.
10. Dawkins, *Root*.
11. The following two texts are good sources on the role of astrology in Christian Europe: Smoller, *History*; and Zambelli, *Astrology*.
12. Roberts, C., "Christian Astrology."
13. Prima Pars: 115: Reply to Objection 3. The full text of the *Summa* in English translation can be found at: *http://www.newadvent.org/summa*.
14. Roberts and Donaldson, *Recognitions*.
15. Wedel, T., *Medieval Attitude*, 27–28.
16. Jacobi, "Astrology,"
17. North, *Fontana*, 41.
18. Ibid., 40.
19. 29th ahû tablet of *Enûma Anu Enlil*, obv. 59–61.
20. Text XIII, numbers. Reiner, E. *Babylonian Planetary Omens*. For more omen literature, see Thompson, R. Campbell, "Reports."
21. Cumont, *Astrology*.
22. Thompson, Gary D., "Influence." Thompson quotes from Van der Waerden's *Science Awakening II, the Birth of Astronomy* (1965) chapter on "Cosmic religion, astrology, and astronomy."
23. Cumont, *Astrology*, 18.
24. Ibid., 8.
25. Rochberg, *Heavenly Writing*, 8–9.
26. Ibid., 61.
27. North, *Fontana*, 40.
28. Cumont, *Astrology*, 16.
29. See note 22.
30. Cumont, *Astrology*, 17–18.
31. An English translation of the *Greater Bundahisn*, containing full explanations of the Zorastrian chronologies, can be found at *www.avesta.org*.
32. Von Stuckrad, "Jewish," 1.
33. Ness, *Written*, 141.
34. Roberts and Donaldson, *Recognitions*, Book 1, Ch. 32.
35. Dobin, *Astrological*.
36. Humm, Kanyamas, and Kocot, "Physignomic," Frag.1 Col. 2. Paraphrased by Katie Kanyamas.

37. Von Stuckrad, "Jewish," 8, n. 14. Von Stuckrad borrowed the term *emplotment* from Hayden White, who originally used it, along with *argument* and *ideological implication,* to describe three ways that academics attempt to impart to their treatises a pretence of explanation. cf. White, 1973.
38. Ibid., 4.

Chapter 6

1. Bulmer-Thomas, "Star," 367.
2. Ferrari d'Occhieppo, "Star," 519.
3. Bulmer-Thomas, "Star," 371.
4. Kidger, *Star*, 257–258.
5. Hughes, *Star*, 209.
6. Paffenroth, "Star," 455.
7. Ferrari d'Occhieppo, "Star," 517.
8. Mosley, John, "Common."
9. Humphreys, "Star," sec. 3.
10. Molnar, *Star*, 14.
11. Hughes, *Star*, 16–17.
12. Ibid., 216, 228.
13. Seymour, *Birth*, 145.
14. For more on Robert Schmidt and his work with Project Hindsight, see *http://www.projecthindsight.com/geninfo/about.html.*
15. For more on Dorian Gieseler Greenbaum, see *http://www.classicalastrology.org.*
16. Birdsall, Book Review, 391.
17. In the geocentric system used by most astrologers, Mercury is never more than 28° from the sun, so a Pisces, meaning someone born with the sun in Pisces, can only have Mercury in Aquarius, Pisces, or Aries, not Scorpio. Also, the full moon occurs when the sun and moon are diametrically opposed to each other from opposite signs of the zodiac. Consequently, if the sun is in Leo, the full moon is in Aquarius, or at least somewhere thereabouts. The moon in Taurus would be at the third quarter phase.
18. Molnar, *Star*, 32–33.
19. Ibid., 39.
20. Ibid., 28.

Chapter 7

1. Yamamoto and Burnett, *Abu Masar*, 585.
2. According to Jafarey, "Zoroastrian": "The Old Persian word *magu,* meaning a member of the priestly caste (Greek *magoi,* English *magus,* plural *magi*),

evolved into the subsequent Pahlavi *magopat, mowbad*; Persian *mobad, mobed.*"

3. Hooker, "Islam." See also: O'Leary, *How Greek Science*, Chapter XI.

4. The date is variously given as July 30 or 31, and the time is usually set in the afternoon, after 2 p.m. The most salient features of the chart are Jupiter rising in Sagittarius, trine the sun in Leo, and opposite Mars in Gemini in the seventh house. However, the date, time, and the zodiac used are all disputed. See: Revilla, "Horoscope of Baghdad"; Holden, *History*, 99–129; Allawi, "Some Evolutionary," 61–66.

5. Kennedy and Pingree, *Astrological*, v. This Arabic fragment of Ibn Hibinta's work can be found in Munich Cod. Arab. 852, ff 214v to 233v.

6. Kennedy, Edward S., "Ramifications," 23.

7. Ibid., 38.

8. Yamamoto and Burnett, *Abu Masar*, 585.

9. Ibid., 584.

10. Actually, that conjunction was still in the water signs (Scorpio), depending upon which zodiac you use. Masha'allah and his contemporaries probably used the positions from the *Zij al-Shah*, the Tables of the Shah, compiled during the reign of Khusrau I, corresponding to the "Sasanian" zero point in 564 CE of the Toledan and Khwarizmian tables. This was a sidereal zodiac, and it differed by about 4° from the tropical zodiac in the eighth century CE. So while the conjunction in 46 BCE was in Scorpio in the tropical zodiac, using Masha'allah's Persian zodiac, combined with some really awkward math, the conjunction arrives in the fire sign, Sagittarius. See: Revilla, "Horoscope of Baghdad"; and Holden, *History*.

11. See Revilla, "Horoscope of Muhammed." Also, Kennedy and Pingree, *Astrological*, 127.

12. Yamamoto and Burnett, *Abu Masar*, 581, n. 26 (quoted in Kennedy, Edward S., "Sasanian," 256, 329).

13. Ibid., 585–586.

14. Campion, *Great Year*.

15. See Smoller, *History*; and Zambelli, *Astrologi*.

16. Watts, "Science."

17. Bobrick, *Fated*, 4.

18. Kennedy and Pingree, *Astrological*, v.

19. Arjomand, *Messianism*, 12–15.

Chapter 8

1. Kennedy, Edward, "Ramifications," 37.

2. Ghadially, "Changes," 1; and Boyce, *Textual Sources*, 96–97.

3. See Zaehner, *Zurvan*, 409–416 for the text of *Ulema I Islam*.

4. West, E.W., *Bundahishn*; and Anklesaria, *Iranian*. Both are available at *www.avesta.org*.

5. Griffiths, *Plutarch's*, 193–195.

6. Zaehner, *Zurvan*, 97.

7. Yamamoto and Burnett, *Abu Masar*, 573 (n. 2). The authors refer to Kusyar ibn Lannan (mid-10th to mid-11th century), who distinguishes between Ptolemaic general astrology and that of "the Persians." This directly contradicts Molnar's claim that "...the Magi, although they came from the East, they practiced not archaic Babylonian astrology but a newer Hellenistic astrology."

8. Mills, L.H., *Sacred*. The Gathas/Yasnas are available at *www.avesta.org*.

9. Kennedy and Pingree, *Astrological*, 69–75. See also Boyce, *Textual Sources*, 20–21.

10. Yamamoto and Burnett, *Abu Masar*, 574.

11. Cumont, *Mysteries*, 63.

Chapter 9

1. Among Seymour's innovative works are *Cosmic Magnetism* (1986), *Astrology: The Evidence of Science* (1991), *The Scientific Basis of Astrology* (1997), and *The Scientific Proof of Astrology* (2004).

2. Neugebauer, "Alleged," 1–8. Schnabel (in 1923 and 1927) argued that the Babylonian astronomer Kidinnu discovered precession, but Neugebauer presumably put his arguments to rest.

3. Neugebauer, *History*, 5.

4. Toomer, *Ptolemy's*, 1.

5. Taub, "Hipparchus."

6. Neugebauer, *Exact Sciences*, 87.

7. Cumont, *Astrology*, 40.

8. Dicks, *Geographical*, 14.

9. Toomer, *Ptolemy's*, 207–224.

10. Ulansey, "Hipparchus's."

11. For the full text of Virgil's 4th Eclogue, see *http://classics.mit.edu/Virgil/eclogue.4.iv.html*. For an alternative translation, see *http://www.sacred-texts.com/cla/virgil/ecl/ecl04.htm*.

12. Swerdlow, "On the Cosmical Mysteries," 59.

13. Toomer, *Ptolemy's*, 322.

14. Ibid., 321–327.

15. Ibid., 327–328: "From this we find that the 1° rearward motion takes place in approximately 100 years, as Hipparchus too seems to have suspected,

according to the following quotation from his work, 'On the length of the year': 'For if the solstices and equinoxes were moving, from that cause, not less than 1/100 of a degree in advance (i.e., in the reverse order) of the signs, in the 300 years they should have moved not less than 3°.'"

16. North, *Richard of Wallingford*, 253.
17. North, *Stars*, 108.
18. Manuel, *Isaac Newton*, 67. In Book III of his *Principia* (Prop. xxix, Problem xx), Newton published both his theoretical explanations and his computations.
19. North, *Richard of Wallingford*, 265.
20. Grant, *Planets*, 498.
21. Swerdlow, "On the Cosmical Mysteries," 59.
22. Neugebauer, "Alleged," 7–8.
23. Grant, *Planets*, 315.
24. North, *Richard of Wallingford*, 238.
25. Grant, *Planets*, 315.
26. Ibid., 315–316.
27. North, *Richard of Wallingford*, III, 262.
28. Thorndike, *History*, V, 310–311.
29. North, *Stars*, 106.
30. Ibid., 108.
31. Ibid., 85; and Thorndike, *Sphere*, 387–388.
32. Examples of their work can be found at the Website of Dr. Shepherd Simpson at *http://www.geocities.com/astrologyages/searchingforanewage.htm.*
33. Kennedy, Edward S., "Ramifications," 26.
34. Ibid.
35. Kennedy and Pingree, *Astrological*, 48.
36. Kennedy, Edward S., "Ramifications," 24.

Chapter 10

1. Clement of Alexandria, *Stromata,* Bk. 1, Ch. 15.
2. Waite, *History*, 192 (Waite gives the English translation of the quote from Faber).
3. Nweeya, *Persia*, 102–103.
4. Smith, J.Z., in *Drudgery Divine*, 38–39, quotes from Mack, *Myth*.
5. Roberts and Donaldson, *Ante-Nicene Fathers*, Vol VI.
6. Seymour, *Birth*, 88–89.
7. Hegedus, "Magi," quotes from CSEL 32/4, p. 67–68.2.
8. Ibid., quotes *Homilien zum Hexateuch in Rufins Übersetzung*, ed. Baehrens (GCS), vol. 2, 118.14–22.

Conclusions

1. Calculations were done using Esoteric Technologies' Solar Fire software. Rates may vary.
2. Josephus, *Works*, "Wars of the Jews," Book V, Ch 5:5.
3. Yonge, *Works*, "Who Is the Heir of Divine Things?," XLV.

Bibliography

Allawi, Ibrahim. "Some Evolutionary and Cosmological Aspects to Early Islamic Town Planning." In *Theories and Principles of Design in the Architecture of Islamic Societies*, edited by Margaret Bentley Sevcenko. Cambridge, Mass.: Aga Khan Program for Islamic Architecture, 1988. *http://archnet.org/library/documents/one-document.tcl?document_id=3776* (accessed Sept. 2007).

Anklesaria, B.T., trans. *Iranian, or Greater Bundahishn*. Bombay, India: Rahnumae Mazdayasnan Sabha, 1956. *http://www.avesta.org/mp/grb.htm* (accessed Sept. 2007). Digital edition © 2002 by Joseph H. Peterson.

Arjomand, S.A. "Messianism, Millenialism and Revolution." *Imagining the End: Visions of Apocalypse from the Ancient Middle East to Modern America*, edited by Amanat and Bernhardsson. London: I.B. Tauris, 2002.

Armstrong, Karen. *The Great Transformation: The Beginning of our Religious Traditions*. New York: Knopf, 2006.

Arrian. *Anabasis*. In *The Anabasis of Alexander*, translated by E.J. Chinnock. London: George Bell & Sons, 1893. *http://websfor.org/alexander/arrian/intro.asp* (accessed Sept. 2007).

Atkinson, K.M.T. "The Legitimacy of Cambyses and Darius as Kings of Egypt." *Journal of the American Oriental Society* 76, no. 3 (July–September 1956): 167–177.

Barre, Lloyd. *History and Tradition in Early Israel*. Tucson, Ariz.: Fenestra Books, 2002.

———. "El, god of Israel: Yahweh, god of Judah." Biblical Heritage Center, at *http://www.biblicalheritage.org/God/el-goi.htm* (accessed Sept. 2007).

Barton, Tamsyn. *Ancient Astrology*. London: Routledge, 1994.

———. *Power and Knowledge: Astrology, Physiognomics, and Medicine under the Roman Empire*. Ann Arbor, Mich.: University of Michigan Press, 1994.

Beaulieu, Paul-Alain. *Reign of Nabonidus King of Babylon: 556–539 BC* (Yale Near Eastern Researches). New Haven, Conn.: Yale University Press, 1990.

Bellah, Robert N. "What is Axial about the Axial Age?" *European Journal of Sociology* 46, Issue 01 (April 2005): 69–89.

Ben Zvi, Ehud. "Inclusion in and Exclusion From Israel as Conveyed by the Use of the Term 'Israel' in Postmonarchic Biblical Texts." In *The Pitcher is Broken: Memorial Essays for Gosta W. Ahlstrom*, edited by S.W. Hollaway and L.K. Handy. Sheffield, England: JSOT Press, 1995, 95–100.

Berquist, Jon L. *Judaism in Persia's Shadow: A Social and Historical Approach.* Eugene, Ore.: Wipf and Stock Publishers, 1995.

———. "The Shifting Frontier: The Achaemenid Empire's Treatment of Western Colonies." *Journal of World Systems' Research* 1 (November 17, 1995).

Birdsall, J. Neville. Book Review of *The Star of Bethlehem: The Legacy of the Magi*, by Michael R. Molnar. *Journal for the History of Astronomy* 33, no. 113, part 4 (2002).

Blavatsky, Helena Petrovna. "The Esoteric Character of the Gospels." *Lúcifer* 1, no. 2 (1887): 96.

Blenkinsopp, J. *Ezra-Nehemiah: A Commentary.* Philadelphia: Westminster Press, 1988.

Bobrick, Benson. *The Fated Sky, Astrology in History.* New York: Simon and Schuster Paperbacks, 2005.

Bolin, Thomas. "The Temple of Yahweh at Elephantine and Persian Religious Policy." *The Triumph of Elohim: From Yahwisms to Judaisms.* Grand Rapids: Eerdmans, 1996, 127–144.

Boyce, M. *History of Zoroastrianism.* Vol. I: *The Early Period.* Leiden, Holland: Brill, 1996.

———. *Textual Sources for the Study of Zoroastrianism.* Manchester, England: Manchester University Press, 1984.

———. *Zoroastrians: Their Religious Beliefs and Practices.* London: Routledge and Kegan Paul, 1979.

Brown, David. *Mesopotamian Planetary Astronomy-Astrology.* Groningen, Netherlands: Styx Press, 2000.

Budge, E.A.W., trans. *The Book of the Cave of Treasures.* London: The Religious Tract Society, 1927.

———. *The Miracles of the Blessed Virgin Mary and the Life of Hanna (Saint Anne).* London: W. Griggs, 1900.

Bulmer-Thomas, Ian. "The Star of Bethlehem—A New Explanation: Stationary Point of a Planet." *Quarterly Journal of the Royal Astronomical Society* 33 (1992): 363–374.

Burkert, Walter. *The Orientalizing Revolution: Near Eastern Influence on Greek Culture in the Early Archaic Age.* Cambridge: Harvard University Press, 1998.

Campion, N. *The Great Year, Astrology, Millenarianism, and History in the Western Tradition*. London: Penguin/Arkana, 1994.

———. "The Concept of Destiny in Islamic Astrology and its Impact on Medieval European Thought." *ARAM (The Journal for Syro-Mesopotamian Culture)*, Vol. 1 no 2, Summer 1989, pp 281–289, at *http://www.nickcampion.com/nc/history/articles/islamic.htm* (accessed Sept. 2007).

Catullus. *The Carmina of Caius Valerius Catullus*. Translated by Richard Burton and Leonard Smithers. Project Gutenberg Ebook. *http://www.gutenberg.org/files/20732/20732-8.txt* (accessed Sept. 2007).

Clark, D.H., J.H. Parkinson, and F.R. Stephenson. "An Astronomical Reappraisal of the Star of Bethlehem: A Nova in 5 B.C." *Quarterly Journal of the Royal Astronomical Society* 18, no.4 (1977): 443–449.

Clement of Alexandria. *The Stomata, or Miscellanies*. In *The Ante-Nice Fathers*. Vol. II. Edited by Roberts and Donaldson. *http://www.sacred-texts.com/chr/ecf/002/0020292.htm* (accessed September 2007).

Cogan, M. *Imperialism and Religion: Assyria, Judah, and Israel in the Eighth and Seventh Centuries B.C.E.* SBLMS 19. Missoula, Mont: SBL and Scholars, 1974.

Cohn, Norman. *Cosmos, Chaos, and the World to Come*. New Haven, Conn.: Yale University Press, 2001.

Cross, Frank Moore. *Canaanite Myth and Hebrew Epic*. Cambridge, Mass.: Harvard University Press, 1997.

Crossan, J.D. *Jesus: A Revolutionary Biography*. San Francisco: Harper, 1994.

Cumont, Franz. *The Mysteries of Mithra*. Translated from the second revised French edition by Thomas J. McCormack. Chicago: Open Court, 1903. *http://www.sacred-texts.com/cla/mom/mom00.htm* (accessed Sept. 2007).

———. *Astrology and Religion Among the Greeks and Romans*. New York: Dover Publications, Inc., 1960. *http://www.sacred-texts.com/astro/argr/index.htm* (accessed Sept. 2007).

Davies, Philip. "The Origin of Biblical Israel." *The Journal of Hebrew Scriptures* 5, Article 17 (2005). *http://www.arts.ualberta.ca/JHS/abstracts-articles.html* (accessed April 2006).

Davis, William Stearns. *Readings in Ancient History: Illustrative Extracts from the Sources*. Vol. 2: *Greece and the East*. Boston: Allyn and Bacon, 1912.

Dawkins, Richard. *The God Delusion*. New York: Houghton Mifflin Co., 2006.

———. *The Root of All Evil*. London: BBC4, 2006.

De Clerq, G. *Anno Domini: The Origins of the Christian Era*. Turnhout, Belgium: Brepols, 2000.

De Santillana, G., and H. von Dechend. *Hamlet's Mill: An Essay on Myth and the Frame of Time*. Boston: Gambit, 1969.

Dever, William G. *What Did the Biblical Writers Know and When Did They Know it? What Archaeology Can Tell Us About the Reality of Ancient Israel.* Grand Rapids, Mich.: Eerdman's Publishing Co., 2002.

Dhalla, Maneckji. *History of Zoroastrianism.* New York: Oxford University Press, 1938.

Dicks, D.R. *The Geographical Fragments of Hipparchus.* London: University of London Press, 1960.

Dobin, Rabbi J.C. *The Astrological Secrets of the Hebrew Sages: To Rule Both Day and Night.* Rochester, Vt.: Inner Traditions, 1977.

Drum, Walter. "Magi." *The Catholic Encyclopedia* IX. New York: Robert Appleton Company, 1910. *http://www.newadvent.org/cathen/09527a.htm* (accessed Sept. 2007).

Duchesne-Guillemin, J. *Symbols and Values in Zoroastrianism: Their Survival and Renewal.* New York: Harper and Row, 1966.

Dupont-Sommer, A. "Deux documents horoscopiques esséniens découverts à Qoumrân, près de la mer Morte." *Comptes rendus de l'Académie des Inscriptions et des Belles-Lettres* (Séance du 25 juin, 1965): 239–253.

Eddy, Samuel K. *The King Is Dead: Studies in the Near Eastern Resistance to Hellenism, 334-31 B.C.* Lincoln, Nebr.: University of Nebraska Press, 1961.

Edelman, Diana V. *The Origins of the "Second" Temple: Persian Imperial Policy and the Rebuilding of Jerusalem.* London: Equinox Publishing, 2006.

———. "Redating the Building of the Second Temple." 2005. *http://www.bibleinterp.com/articles/Edelman_Redating_Second_Temple.htm* (accessed Sept. 2007).

Edelman, Diana V., ed. *The Triumph of Elohim: From Yahwisms to Judaisms.* Grand Rapids, Mich.: Eerdmans Publishing Co., 1996.

Ellis, P. *The Men and the Message of the Old Testament.* Collegeville, Minn.: The Liturgical Press, 1962.

Ereira, Alan. "Talking About the Samaritans." *http://www.mystae.com/reflections/messiah/samjudah/yahwist.html1* (accessed April 2006).

Ferrari d'Occhieppo, K. "The Star of Bethlehem (Correspondence)" *R.A.S. Quarterly Journal* 19 (March 1978): 519.

Finklestein, Israel, and Neil A. Silberman. *The Bible Unearthed.* New York: Touchstone/Simon and Schuster, 2001.

———. *David and Solomon: In Search of the Bible's Sacred Kings and the Roots of the Western Tradition.* New York: Free Press/Simon and Schuster, 2006.

Friedman, Richard. *The Bible With Sources Revealed.* San Francisco: Harper, 2003.

———. *Who Wrote the Bible?* Englewood Cliffs, N.J.: Prentice Hall, 1987.

Frye, Richard. *The Heritage of Persia: The Pre-Islamic History of One of the World's Great Civilizations.* New York: World Publishing Company, 1963.

Ghadially, Rashna. "Changes in Zarathushtra's Teachings During the Parthian and Sasanian Periods." 2000. *http://www.cais-soas.com/CAIS/Religions/iranian/Zarathushtrian/zarathushtras_teachings.htm* (accessed Sept. 2007).

Gilbert, A.G. *Magi: The Quest for a Secret Tradition.* London: Bloomsbury, 1996.

Gillispie, Charles Coulston, ed. "Hipparchus." *Dictionary of Scientific Biography.* Vol. XV, suppl I. New York: Scribner's, 1978.

Giveon, R. *Les Bedouins Shosou des Documents Egyptiens.* Leiden, Belgium: Brill, 1971.

Grabbe, Lester L. *Judaic Religion in the Second Temple Period: Belief and Practice from the Exile to Yavneh.* London: Routledge, 2000.

Grant, E. *Planets, Star, and Orbs: The Medieval Cosmos, 1200-1687.* Cambridge, Mass.: Cambridge University Press, 1996.

Grayson, Albert Kirk. *Assyrian and Babylonian Chronicles (Texts from Cuneiform Sources).* Winona Lake, Ind.: Eisenbrauns, 2000.

Greenfield, J.C., and M. Sokoloff. "Astrological and Related Omen Texts in Jewish Palestinian Aramaic." *Journal of Near Eastern Studies* 48, no. 3 (1989): 201–214.

Griffiths, J. Gwyn, trans. *Plutarch's De Iside et Osiride.* Cardiff, Wales: University of Wales Press, 1970.

Gutas, Dimitri. *Greek Thought, Arabic Culture.* London: Routledge, 1998.

Hand, Robert. *The Astrological Record of the Early Sages in Greek.* Berkeley Springs, W.Va.: The Golden Hind Press, 1995. *http://www.accessnewage.com/articles/astro/rhist3.htm* (accessed Sept. 2007).

Handy, Lowell K. *Among the Host of Heaven: The Syro-Palestinian Pantheon as Bureaucracy.* Winona Lake, Ind.: Eisenbrauns, 1994.

Hanson, K.C. "The Cyrus Cylinder." 1994. *http://www.kchanson.com/ANCDOCS/meso/cyrus.html#R* (accessed Sept. 2007).

Hegedus, Tim. "The Magi and the Star in the Gospel of Matthew and Early Christian Tradition." *Laval Théologique et Philosophique* 59, no. 1 (Février 2003). *http://www.erudit.org/revue/ltp/2003/v59/n1/000790ar.html* (accessed Sept. 2007).

Herodotus. *The Histories.* Translated by A.D. Godley. Cambridge, Mass.: Harvard University Press, 1920. *http://www.perseus.tufts.edu/cgi-bin/ptext?doc=Perseus%3Atext%3A1999.01.0126* (accessed Sept. 2007).

———. *The Histories.* Translated by George Rawlinson. *http://classics.mit.edu/Herodotus/history.html* (accessed Sept. 2007).

Holden, James H. *A History of Horoscopic Astrology.* Tempe, Ariz.: American Federation of Astrologers, 1996.

Holland, Tom. *Persian Fire.* London: Abacus, 2005.

Hooker, Richard. "The Persians: Mesopotamia." *World Civilizations: An Internet Classroom and Anthology.* Pullman: Washington State University Press, 1996. *http://www.wsu.edu/~dee/MESO/PERSIANS.HTM* (accessed Sept. 2007).

———. "Islam, The 'Abbasid Dynasty." *World Civilizations: An Internet Classroom and Anthology.* Pullman: Washington State University Press, 1996. *http://www.wsu.edu/~dee/ISLAM/ABASSID.HTM* (accessed Sept. 2007).

Hughes, David. *The Star of Bethlehem Mystery.* London: J.M. Dent & Sons Ltd., 1979. Also published: London: Corgi Books, 1981.

Humm, Alan, Katie Kanyamas, and Robin Kocot. "Physiognomic Horoscopes, 4QCryptic-4Q186, 4QPhysiogn=4Q561." 1988, at *http://ccat.sas.upenn.edu/~humm/Resources/StudTxts/4Q186!.html* (accessed Sept. 2007).

Humphreys, Colin. "The Star of Bethlehem." *Science and Christian Belief 5* (October 1995): 83–101. *http://www.asa3.org/ASA/topics/Astronomy-Cosmology/S&CB%2010-93Humphreys.html* (accessed Sept. 2007).

Hyde, Thomas. *Historia Religionis Veterum Persarum Eorumque Magorum.* Oxford, England: Unknown publisher, 1700.

Iamblichus. *Life of Pythagoras.* Translated by Thomas Taylor. Rochester, Ver.: Inner Traditions, 1986.

Irenæus, Saint. *Adversus Haereses. http://www.newadvent.org/fathers/0103.htm* (accessed Sept. 2007).

Jacobi, Max. "Astrology." *The Catholic Encyclopedia* II. New York: Robert Appleton Company, 1907. *http://www.newadvent.org/cathen/02018e.htm* (accessed Sept. 2007).

Jacquier, E. "Gospel of St. Matthew." *The Catholic Encyclopedia* II. New York: Robert Appleton Company, 1911. *http://www.newadvent.org/cathen/10057a.htm* (accessed Sept. 2007).

Jafarey, Ali A. "The Zoroastrian Priest In The Avesta." 1992. *http://www.zoroastrian.org/articles/Zoroastrian%20Priest%20in%20the%20Avesta.htm* (accessed Sept. 2007).

Jahanian, Darius. "Zoroastrianism and Biblical Connections." 1994. *http://www.iranian.ws/cyrus.htm* (accessed Sept. 2007).

Jaspers, Karl, and Michael Bullock, trans. *The Origin and Goal of History* (1st English Ed.). London: Routledge and Keegan Paul, 1953. Originally published as *Vom Ursprung und Ziel der Geschichte* (1st Ed.), by Karl Jaspers. Munich: Piper Verlag, 1949.

Josephus, Flavius. *The Works of Flavius Josephus.* Translated by William Whiston. Auburn, Ala. and Buffalo, N.Y.: John E. Beardsley, 1895. *http://www.ccel.org/j/josephus/works/ant-11.htm* (accessed Sept. 2007).

Kennedy, Edward S. *Astronomy and Astrology in the Medieval Islamic World.* Aldershot, U.K.: Ashgate Variorum, 1998.

———. "Ramifications of the World Year Concept in Islamic Astrology." *Proceedings of the Tenth International Congress of the History of Science.* Paris: Hermann, 1962, 23–43.

———. "The Sasanian Astronomical Handbook Zif-I Shah and the Astrological Doctrine of 'Transit' (Mamarr)." *Journal of the American Oriental Society* 78, no. 4 (October–December 1958): 246–262.

Kennedy, E.S., and D. Pingree. *The Astrological History of Masha'Allah.* Cambridge, Mass.: Harvard University Press, 1961.

Kepler, J. *Concerning the More Certain Fundamentals of Astrology.* Edmonds,Wash.: Sure Fire Press, 1988.

———. *Harmonies of the World.* Translated by C.G. Wallis, C.G. Annapolis, Md.: The St. John's Bookstore, 1939. *http://www.sacred-texts.com/astro/how/index.htm#contents* (accessed Sept. 2007).

Kidger, M. *The Star of Bethlehem: An Astronomer's View.* Princeton, N.J.: Princeton University Press, 1999.

Kitchen, Kenneth Anderson. "The Physical Text of Merneptah's Victory Hymn (The "Israel Stela")." *Journal of the Society for the Study of Egyptian Antiquities* 24 (1994): 71–76.

Kitson, A., Ed. *History and Astrology: Clio and Urania Confer.* London: Unwin, 1989.

Klausner, Joseph. *The Messianic Idea in Israel from its Beginning to the Completion of the Mishnah.* London: George Allen and Unwin Ltd., 1956.

Koestler, Arthur. *The Watershed: A Biography of Johannes Kepler.* New York: DoubleDay, 1960.

Kollerstom, Nick. "Galileo's Astrology." *Largo Campo di Filosofare Eurosymposium Galileo 2001.* Edited by Montesinos and Solis, pp. 421–432. At *http://www.skyscript.co.uk/galast.html* (accessed Sept. 2007).

Kuhn, T. *The Structure of Scientific Revolutions.* Chicago: Phoenix Books/The University of Chicago Press, 1962.

Kusukawa, Sachiko. "Astrology." *The Electronic History of Astronomy.* The Whipple Museum of the History of Science, 1999. *http://www.hps.cam.ac.uk/starry/astrology.html* (accessed Sept. 2007).

———. "Kepler and Astrology." *The Electronic History of Astronomy.* The Whipple Museum of the History of Science, 1999. *http://www.hps.cam.ac.uk/starry/keplerastrol.html* (accessed Sept. 2007).

Lancaster, Christopher. *Aramaic Peshitta Primacy for Dummies: A Quick Journey Through Every Book of the New Testament to Determine the Original Language—Greek or Aramaic?* 2005. *http://www.aramaicpeshitta.com/Peshitta_Dummies_FirstED.pdf* (accessed Sept. 2007).

Little, William, H.W. Fowler, and Jessie Coulson. *The Shorter Oxford English Dictionary.* London: Book Club Associates, Oxford University Press, 1983.

Maas, A.J. "Genealogy of Christ." *The Catholic Encyclopedia* VI. New York: Robert Appleton Company, 1909. *http://www.newadvent.org/cathen/ 06410a.htm* (accessed Sept. 2007).

Mack, Burton. *A Myth of Innocence: Mark and Christian Origins*. Philadelphia: Fortress Press, 1988.

Manilius. *Astronomica*. Cambridge, Mass.: Harvard University Press, 1977.

Manuel, F.E. *Isaac Newton Historian*. Cambridge, Mass.: Harvard University Press, 1963.

———. *A Portrait of Isaac Newton*. London: Frederick Muller Limited, 1980.

Martin, Dr. Earnest L. *The Birth of Christ Recalculated*. Pasadena, Calif.: Foundation for Biblical Research, 1980.

———. *The Star That Astonished the World*. Portland. Ore.: Assoc. for Scriptural Knowledge, 1991.

Massey, Gerald. *The Historical Jesus and Mythical Christ*. Springfield, Mass.: Star Publishing Co., 1886.

Massih, Abdul. "Meditations on the Gospel of Christ According to the Evangelist Matthew." Matten, Lebanon: Al-Hayat Al-Foudla, Mazra'at Yashou, 2001. *http://waters-of-life.org/Matthew1.htm* (accessed Sept. 2007).

Maternus, Fermicus. *Ancient Astrology: Theory and Practice—Matheseos Libri VIII*. Translated by Jean Rhys Bram. Park Ridge, N.J.: Noyes Press, 1975.

Miller, Laura. "King David was a Nebbish." *Salon.com*, 2001. *http:// dir.salon.com/story/books/feature/2001/02/07/solomon/index.html* (accessed Sept. 2007).

Mills, L.H., trans. *Sacred Books of the East*. 1898. *http://www.avesta.org/yasna/ y0to8s.htm* (accessed Sept. 2007).

Mills, L.M. *Our Own Religion in Ancient Persia*. Edinburgh, Scotland: Open Court Publishing, 1913.

Missler, Chuck. "Who Were the Magi?" 1999. *http://www.ldolphin.org/magi.html* (accessed Sept. 2007).

Molnar, Michael R. *The Star of Bethlehem: The Legacy of the Magi*. New Brunswick, N.J.: Rutgers University Press, 1999.

Momigliano, Arnaldo. *Alien Wisdom: The Limits of Hellenization*. Cambridge, Mass.: Cambridge University Press, 1975.

Morehouse, A.J. "The Christmas Star as a Supernova in Aquila." *Journal of the Royal Astronomical Society of Canada* 72, no.2 (1978): 65–68.

Mosley, John. "Common Errors in 'Star of Bethlehem' Planetarium Shows." *Planetarian* (third quarter 1981). *http://www.ips-planetarium.org/planetarian/ articles/common_errors_xmas.html* (accessed Sept. 2007).

Negus, Ken. *Kepler's Astrology: Excerpts*. Princeton, N.J.: Eucopia, 1987. *http:// cura.free.fr/docum/15kep-en.html* (accessed Sept. 2007).

Ness, L. *Written in the Stars: Ancient Zodiac Mosaics.* Warren Center, Pa.: Marco Polo Monographs, 1999.

Neugebauer, Otto. *A History of Ancient Mathematical Astronomy.* New York: Springer-Verlag, 1975.

———. *The Exact Sciences in Antiquity.* New York: Dover Publications, 1969.

———. "The Alleged Babylonian Discovery of the Precession of the Equinoxes." *Journal of the American Oriental Society* LXX (1950): 1–8.

———. "The History of Wretched Subjects." *Isis* 42 (June 1951).

Neusner, Jacob. *A History of the Jews in Babylonia* I. *The Parthian Period.* Chico, Calif.: Scholars Press, 1984.

Nock, Arthur Darby. "Paul and the Magus." In *The Beginnings of Christianity.* Pt. I: *The Acts of the Apostles*, edited by F.J. Jackson and K. Lake. London: Macmillan and Co., Ltd., 1933.

North, John. *The Fontana History of Astronomy and Cosmology.* London: Fontana Press, 1994.

———. *Stars, Minds and Fate.* London: The Hambledon Press, 1989.

———. *Richard of Wallingford.* Oxford: Clarendon Press, 1976.

Nweeya, Rev. S.K. *Persia: The Land of the Magi.* Indianapolis: Wood-Weaver, 1904.

O'Leary, DeLacy. *How Greek Science Passed to the Arabs.* London: Routledge and Kegan Paul, Ltd., 1949. *http://evans-experientialism.freewebspace.com/oleary05.htm* (accessed Sept. 2007).

O'Dea, James. "Peace: A New Center of Human Becoming." *Shift*: *At the Frontiers of Consciousness* 13 (February 2007). Petaluma, Calif.: Institute of Noetic Sciences.

Olmstead, A.T. *History of the Persian Empire.* Chicago: University of Chicago Press, 1948.

Paffenroth, Kim. "The Star of Bethlehem Casts Light on its Modern Interpreters." *R.A.S. Quarterly Journal* V, 34:4 (December 1993): 449–460.

Plato. *Epinomis: Plato in Twelve Volumes*, Vol. 9. Translated by W.R.M. Lamb. Cambridge, Mass.: Harvard University Press, 1925. *http//www.perseus.tufts.edu/cgi-bin/ptext?* (accessed September 2007).

Plutarch. *On the Malice of Herodotus.* Translated by A.J. Bowen. Oxford: Aris and Phillips, 1992.

———. *Life of Alexander.* Loeb Classical Library, Cambridge, Mass.: Harvard University Press, 1917. *http://penelope.uchicago.edu/Thayer/E/Roman/Texts/Plutarch/Lives/Alexander*/home.html* (accessed Sept. 2007).

Poppi, Antonino. "Galileo Faces the Inquisition: Tried by the Holy Office at Padua—For Astral Fatalism." *Culture and Cosmos, A Journal of the History of Astrology and Cultural Astronomy, Galileo's Astrology* 7, no.1 (2003).

Price, Massoume. "Translation Movements in Iran: Sassanian Era to Year 2000, Expansion, Preservation and Modernization." 2002. *http:// www.iranchamber.com/podium/literature/ 030206_translation_movement_iran.php* (accessed Sept. 2007).

Reiner, Erica. *Babylonian Planetary Omens II: Enuma Anu Enlil.* Malibu, Calif.: Undena Publications, 1981.

Revilla, Juan Antonio. "The Horoscope of Baghdad: Historical, Astronomical, and Astrological Notes." 2003. *http://www.expreso.co.cr/centaurs/posts/ mundane/baghdad.htm* (accessed April 2006).

———. "The Horoscope Of Muhammed, Historical and Astrological Notes." 2005. *http://www.expreso.co.cr/centaurs/posts/mundane/mahoma.html* (accessed Sept. 2007).

Roberts, Rev. Alexander, and James Donaldson, eds. *The Recognitions of Clement.* From *The Ante-Nicene Fathers*, Vol. VIII. Grand Rapids, Mich.: Eerdmans Publishing Co., 1995.

———. *Ante-Nicene Fathers.* Vol. VI, *Gregory Thaumaturgus, Dionysius the Great, Julius Africanus, Anatolius and Minor Writers, Methodius, Arnobius.* Grand Rapids, Mich.: Eerdmans Publishing Co., 1995. *http://www.ccel.org/ ccel/schaff/anf06.toc.html* (accessed Sept. 2007).

Roberts, C. "Christian Astrology, the Dark Ages, and the Celtic Church." C.U.R.A. University Centre for Astrological Research. 2003. *http:// cura.free.fr/xxx/29robts.html* (accessed Sept. 2007).

Roberts, P.W. *Journey of the Magi: Travels In Search of the Birth of Jesus.* London, Tauris Parke, 2006.

Rochberg, Francesca. *The Heavenly Writing: Divination, Horoscopy, and Astronomy in Mesopotamian Culture.* Cambridge, Mass.: Cambridge University Press, 2004.

———. *Babylonian Horoscopes.* Philadelphia: Transactions of the American Philosophical Society, 1998.

———. *Aspects of Babylonian Celestial Divination: The Lunar Eclipse Tablets of Enuma Anu Enlil.* Horn, Austria: Verlag Ferdinand Berger and Sohne, 1988.

Rogers, Robert William. *Cuneiform Parallels to the Old Testament.* New York: Eaton and Mains, 1912.

Sachs, Abraham J., and Hermann Hunger. *Astronomical Diaries and Related Texts from Babylonia.* Vols. I–III. Vienna: Verlag Der Osterreichischen Akademie der Wissenschaften, 1988.

Saliba, George. *A History of Arabic Astronomy: Planetary Theories During the Golden Age of Islam.* New York: New York University Press, 1994.

Sancisi-Weerdenburg, Heleen, Amelie Kuhrt, and Margaret Cool Root. *Achaemenid History.* Vol. VI, *Asia Minor and Egypt: Old Cultures in a New Empire.* Proceedings of Groningen 1988 Achaemenid History Workshop, 1991.

———. *Achaemenid History*. Vol. VIII, *Continuity and Change*. Proceedings of the Last Achaemenid History Workshop. Leiden, Belgium: Nederlands Instintituut Voor Het Nablie Oosten, 1994.

Sarton, G. "Chaldean Astronomy of the Last Three Centuries, B.C." *Journal of the American Oriental Society* 75, no. 3 (July–September 1955).

Sayce, Archibald. *Early Israel and the Surrounding Nations*. London: Service and Paton, 1899. *http://www.fullbooks.com/Early-Israel-and-the-Surrounding-Nations1.html* (accessed Sept. 2007).

Schaff, Philip. *Eusebius Pamphilius: Church History, Life of Constantine, Oration in Praise of Constantine*. New York: Christian Literature Publishing Company, 1890. *http://www.ccel.org/ccel/schaff/npnf201.txt* (accessed Sept. 2007).

———. *The Principle Works of St. Jerome*. New York: Christian Literature Publishing Company, 1892. *http://www.ccel.org/ccel/schaff/npnf206.txt* (accessed Sept. 2007).

———. *The Apostolic Fathers with Justin Martyr and Irenaeus*. Grand Rapids, Mich.: Eerdmans Publishing Co., 2001. *http://www.ccel.org/ccel/schaff/anf01.txt* (accessed Sept. 2007).

Schaefer, Bradley E. "Review: The Star of Bethlehem." *Sky & Telescope*, December 1999.

Schmidt, Francis. "Ancient Jewish Astrology: An Attempt to Interpret 4QCryptic (4Q186)." In *Biblical Perspectives: Early Use and Interpretation of the Bible in Light of the Dead Sea Scrolls. Proceedings of the First International Symposium of the Orion Center for the Study of the Dead Sea Scrolls and Associated Literature*, edited by Michael E. Stone and Esther G. Chazon. 12–14 May 1996. *http://web.archive.org/web/20030413212520/orion.mscc.huji.ac.il/orion/symposiums/1st/papers/Schmidt96.html* (accessed Sept. 2007).

Seymour, Percy. *The Birth of Christ: Exploding the Myth*. London: Virgin, 1999.

Shaked, Shaul. *From Zoroastrian Iran to Islam*. Aldershot, England: Variorum, 1995.

Shen, Peidong, Tal Lavi, Toomas Kivisild, Vivian Chou, Deniz Sengun, Dov Gefel, Issac Shpirer, Eilon Woolf, Jossi Hillel, Marcus W. Feldman, and Peter J. Oefner. "Reconstruction of Patrilineages and Matrilineages of Samaritans and Other Israeli Populations from Y-Chromosome and Mitochondrial DNA Sequence Variation." *Human Mutation* 24 (2004): 248–260. Wiley-Liss, Inc. *http://evolutsioon.ut.ee/publications/Shen2004.pdf* (accessed Sept. 2007).

Siculus, Diodorus. *Diodorus of Sicily in Twelve Volumes with an English Translation by C.H. Oldfather*. Vols. 4–8. Cambridge, Mass.: Harvard University Press, 1989. *http://www.perseus.tufts.edu* (accessed Sept. 2007).

Silvers, R., ed. *Hidden Histories of Science*. London: Granta Books, 1995.

Slotkin, J.S. "On a Possible Lack of Incest Regulations in Old Iran." American Anthropologist 49, no.4, part I (October–December 1947): 612–617.

Smith, J.Z. *Drudgery Divine: On the Comparison of Early Christianities and the Religions of Late Antiquity*. Chicago: University of Chicago Press, 1990.

Smith, Mark S. *The Origins of Biblical Monotheism: Israel's Polytheistic Background and the Ugaritic Tests*. Oxford: Oxford University Press, 2001.

———. *The Early History of God, Yahweh and the Other Deities in Ancient Israel*. Grand Rapids, Mich: Eerdmans Publishing Co., 2002.

Smoller, L.A. *History, Prophecy, and the Stars*. Princeton, N.J.: Princeton University Press, 1994.

Souvay, Charles. "Isaias." *The Catholic Encyclopedia* VII. New York: Robert Appleton Company, 1910. *http://www.newadvent.org/cathen/08179b.htm* (accessed Sept. 2007).

Spong, John Shelby. "The God Beyond Theism." *The Bishop's Voice: the Voice of the Episcopal Diocese of Newark*, October 1999. *http://www.dioceseofnewark.org/vox31099.html* (accessed Sept. 2007).

Starcky, J. "Un texte messianique araméen de la grotte 4 de Qumrân." *Mémorial du Cinquantenaire 1914-1964*. L'École des Langues Orientales Anciennes de l'Institut Catholique de Paris, 1964, 51–66.

Strabo. *Geography*. Translated by Horace Leonard Jones. The Loeb Classical Library. Cambridge, Mass: Harvard University Press, 1917. *http://penelope.uchicago.edu/Thayer/E/Roman/Texts/Strabo/home.html* (accessed Sept. 2007)

Swerdlow, Noel. "On the Cosmical Mysteries of Mithras." *Classical Philology* 86.1 (January 1991): 59.

Sykes, Percy. *A History of Persia*. Vol. I–II. London: Routledge and Kegan Paul, 1969.

Talmon, S. "Biblical Traditions in Samaritan History." In *The Samaritans*, edited by E. Stern and H. Eshel. Jerusalem: Yad Ben-Zvi Press, 2002.

Taub, L. "Hipparchus and Astrology." 1999. *http://www.hps.cam.ac.uk/starry/hippastrol.html* (accessed Sept. 2007).

Tester, J. *A History of Western Astrology*. Woodbridge, England: The Boydell Press, 1987.

Thompson, Gary D. "The Influence of Religion and Astronomy on the Development of Astrology." 2004. *http://www.members.optusnet.com.au/~gtosiris/page9h.html* (accessed Sept. 2007).

Thompson, R. Campbell. "The Reports of the Magicians and Astrologers of Nineveh and Babylon." *Assyrian and Babylonian Literature: Selected Transactions*, by Anonymous, 451–460. New York: D. Appleton & Co., 1904. *http://www.fordham.edu/halsall/ancient/bablylonian-astrology.html* (accessed Sept. 2007).

Thompson, Thomas L. "The Intellectual Matrix of Early Biblical Narrative: Inclusive Monotheism in Persian Period Palestine." In *The Triumph of Elohim: From Yahwisms to Judaisms*, by Diana Vikander Edelman, 107–126. Grand Rapids, Mich.: Eerdmans Publishing Co., 1996.

Thorndike, Lynn. *A History of Magic and Experimental Science.* Vol. V–VI. New York: Columbia University Press, 1941.

———. *The Sphere of Sacrobosco and Its Commentators.* Chicago: The University of Chicago Press, 1949.

Toomer, G.J. *Ptolemy's Almagest.* Princeton, N.J.: Princeton University Press, 1998.

Trotter, James M. *Reading Hosea in Achaemenid Yehud.* Published by the *Journal for the Study of the Old Testament.* Supplement Series 328. London: Sheffield Academic Press, 2001.

Ulansey, David. *The Origins of the Mithraic Mysteries, Cosmology and Salvation in the Ancient World.* New York: Oxford University Press, 1989.

———. "Hipparchus's Understanding of the Precession." From the German translation of *The Origins of the Mithraic Mysteries, Cosmology and Salvation in the Ancient World. http://www.well.com/user/davidu/appendix4.html* (accessed Sept. 2007).

Van der Waerden, B.L. *Science Awakening.* New York: John Wiley and Sons, 1963.

Vermes, Geza. *The Complete Dead Sea Scrolls In English.* New York: Allen Lane, The Penguin Press, 1997.

von Stuckrad, K. "Jewish and Christian Astrology in Late Antiquity: A New Approach." *Numen* 47, no.1 (2002).

Waite, Charles B. *History of the Christian Religion.* Chicago: C.V. Waite and Co., 1908.

Watts, P.M. "Science, Religion, and Columbus's Enterprise of the Indies." *American Historical Review* 90, no. 1(February 1985): 73–102. *http://muweb.millersville.edu/ ~ columbus/data/art/WATTS03.ART* (accessed Sept. 2007).

Wedel, T. *The Medieval Attitude Toward Astrology Particularly in England.* New Haven, Conn.: Yale University Press, 1920.

Weiss, Rick, and Gregory Grieve. "Illuminating the Half-life of Tradition: Legitimation, Agency and Counter-Hegemonies." In *Historicizing Tradition*, edited by Gregory Grieve and Steven Engler. Berlin, Germany: Walter de Gruyter, 2005.

West, E.W. *The Bundahishn: Sacred Books of the East.* Vol. 5. Oxford: Oxford University Press, 1897. *http://www.avesta.org/mp/bundahis.html* (accessed Sept. 2007).

West, M.L. *The East Face of Helicon.* New York: Oxford University Press, 1999.

White, H. *Metahistory: The Historical Imagination in Nineteenth-Century Europe.* Baltimore, Md.: The Johns Hopkins University Press, 1973.

Williams, Frank, trans. *The Panarion of Epiphanius of Salamis.* Book I (Sects 1-46). Leiden, Begium: E.J. Brill, 1987.

Yamamoto, Keiji, and Charles Burnett. *Abu Masar on Historical Astrology: The Book of Religions and Dynasties (On the Great Conjunctions).* Leiden, Belgium: Brill, 2000.

Yonge, C.D., trans. *The Works of Philo Judaeus.* London: Henry G. Bohn, 1855. *http://www.earlychristianwritings.com/yonge/book17.html* (accessed Sept. 2007).

———. *Diogenes Laertius, Lives and Opinions of Eminent Philosophers.* London, England: George Bell & Sons, 1895. *http://classicpersuasion.org/pw/diogenes/* (accessed Sept. 2007).

Zaehner, R.C. *Zurvan: A Zoroastrian Dilemma.* Oxford: The Clarendon Press, 1955.

———. *The Teachings of the Magi.* London: Sheldon Press, 1956.

Zafran, E. "Saturn and the Jews." *Journal of the Warburg and Courtauld Institutes* 42 (1979): 16–27.

Zambelli, P., ed. *"Astrologi Hallucinati" Stars and the End of the World in Luther's Time.* Berlin, Germany: Walter de Gruyter, 1986.

Bibles

New American Bible. Washington, D.C.: Confraternity of Christian Doctrine, Inc., 1991.

Revised Standard Version. New York: Division of Christian Education of the National Council of the Churches of Christ in the USA, 1946, 1952, 1971.

The Authorized King James Version. Oxford, England: Oxford University Press, 1611.

The Holy Scriptures According to The Masoretic Text. Philadelphia: The Jewish Publication Society of America, 1917, 1945.

The New English Bible. Oxford: Oxford University Press, 1970.

The New International Version. Grand Rapids, Mich.: Zondervans, International Bible Society, 1973, 1978, 1984.

The New Testament in the Original Greek, by B.F. Westcott and F.J.A. Hort. London: Macmillan, 1881.

Index

About the Author

Courtney Roberts, MA, is a writer, teacher, and consultant, originally from Miami, Florida. Her work reflects a unique perspective: a real passion for the "big picture," combining cosmology, religious studies, and history with a lifetime of observing the dynamic interaction of man and the cosmos.

Courtney is a graduate of the revolutionary masters program in cultural astronomy and astrology at Bath Spa University in England, where she studied with leaders in the field such as Dr. Nick Campion, Dr. Patrick Curry, and Dr. Michael York. There, she developed her specialization in the role of astrology in religion, particularly Persian Zoroastrianism and Western monotheism. An avid traveler and world citizen, she has a fascination with Celtic culture—the language, music, and history—which has kept her overseas for years, living in Ireland and Britain, while her Buddhist studies led to extended residence in Asia. She currently maintains a busy schedule, lecturing and teaching to audiences of every persuasion on both sides of the Atlantic.

Courtney has more than 25 years of experience in astrology: in consulting, teaching, publishing, research, and organizational work. She is a former president of the Astrological Research Guild and founding president of the Central Florida Chapter of the NCGR (National Council of Geocosmic Research), and her work has been featured regularly in astrological publications such as *The Mountain Astrologer* and StarIQ.com. She is also a world-renowned sports astrologer, whose Real-Time methods represent a major breakthrough in event analysis, and her extensive sports data collections are published by Astrolabe, Inc., in the Astrodatabank, and in Cosmic Patterns's Kepler Program.